# THE BATTLE
# FOR BRITAIN

"Demonstrating the difference that conceptual nuance and historical specificity make in reading present crises, this important book outlines past contested conjunctural formations that continue to haunt and hamstring our beliefs and practices today. Clarke insightfully critiques simplistic explanations of how we got here – and of who 'we' even are in the first place."
**John L. Jackson, Jr., author of**
***Real Black: Adventures in Racial Sincerity***

"Brilliantly shows how conjunctural analysis can make sense of contemporary British politics. A wonderfully accomplished work."
**Davina Cooper, King's College London**

"John Clarke has done it again. With wit, verve and intellectual rigour, he provides a highly original account of Brexit and the wider cultural and political battles reshaping the UK. Masterfully using conjunctural analysis to shine new light on current crises, conflicts and complexities, *The Battle for Britain* makes essential reading for scholars and activists who are working to counter reactionary politics and for those committed to thinking politics otherwise."
**Jeff Maskovsky, City University of New York**

# THE BATTLE FOR BRITAIN

## Crises, Conflicts and the Conjuncture

John Clarke

BRISTOL
UNIVERSITY
PRESS

First published in Great Britain in 2023 by

Bristol University Press
University of Bristol
1–9 Old Park Hill
Bristol
BS2 8BB
UK
t: +44 (0)117 374 6645
e: bup-info@bristol.ac.uk

Details of international sales and distribution partners are available at bristoluniversitypress.co.uk

British Library Cataloguing in Publication Data
A catalogue record for this book is available from the British Library

ISBN 978-1-5292-2766-6 hardcover
ISBN 978-1-5292-2768-0 paperback
ISBN 978-1-5292-2770-3 ePdf
ISBN 978-1-5292-2769-7 ePub

Cover design: Andrew Corbett
Front cover image: Pixabay/LunarSeaArt
Bristol University Press use environmentally responsible print partners.
Printed and bound in Great Britain by CPI Group (UK) Ltd, Croydon, CR0 4YY

# Contents

# Acknowledgements

Books tend to take a long time to come together and involve a lot of people in their making – and this one is no exception. It began as a short and bad-tempered intervention during what was supposed to be a short paper about expertise at an Interpretive Policy Analysis conference in Hull in June 2016. I am very grateful to the panel organisers – Paul Stubbs and Mislav Žitko – for allowing me to deviate from the planned presentation to express my frustrations about both the events surrounding the Brexit vote and the emerging explanations for it. It became a brief but impassioned plea for a more conjunctural approach. This argument was picked up by Kathrin Braun and became an article co-authored with Janet Newman in *Critical Policy Studies* (Clarke and Newman, 2017). As Brexit's fame grew, invitations to speak and write increased. This book builds on much talking and writing and I am grateful to the following:

- Jamie Peck, Marion Werner, Rebecca Lave and Brett Christophers for the chance to imagine a dialogue with Doreen Massey (Clarke, 2018);
- Paul and Mislav for persisting with the question of expertise and putting together a special issue of *Innovation* in which a collaborative argument with Janet Newman for thinking conjuncturally about expertise, knowledge and power appeared (Newman and Clarke, 2018);
- Jeremy Gilbert for the invitation to contribute to the special issue of *New Formations* on 'This Conjuncture' (Clarke, 2019);
- Eleni Andreouli, David Kaposi and Paul Stenner for organising the Brexit workshops at the Open University and accepting the piece that Janet Newman and I wrote for the subsequent special issue of the *Journal of Community and Applied Social Psychology* (Clarke and Newman, 2019);
- Eric Maigret and Laurent Martin for the invitation to the Chateau de Cerisy-la-Salle to take part in a colloquium on *Culture Studies beyond Identity Politics* and the resulting publication (Clarke, 2020d);
- Don Nonini and Ida Susser for their invitation to think about the turbulent politics of scale and the ensuing publication, even though I missed the workshop itself (Clarke, 2020b);

- Sophie Bjork-James and Jeff Maskovsky for their invitation to take part in the 'angry politics' workshops in Nashville and New York and to write for the resulting book (Clarke, 2020e);
- Humboldt University's Centre for British Studies for their invitation to participate in a Brexit workshop and write about some of the issues afterwards (Clarke, 2020c);
- Sally Davison and the editorial collective at *Soundings* for the invitation to write about the new Johnson government (Clarke, 2020a);
- Ilker Corut and Joost Jongerden for their invitation to think and write about nations and nationalisms in the context of Brexit (Clarke, 2021a);
- Ted Striphas and John Erni for organising a special issue of *Cultural Studies* on COVID-19 and for accepting (and improving) my contribution (Clarke, 2021b);
- Moritz Ege and Johannes Springer for the invitation to their anti-elitism workshop in Göttingen and inclusion in the subsequent publication (Clarke, forthcoming a); and
- Catherine Kellogg, Lois Harder and Steve Patten for the invitation to contribute to a *Festschrift* for Janine Brodie on her retirement from the University of Alberta (Clarke, forthcoming b).

Many conversations – too many to remember, much less name – have contributed to the development of the ideas and arguments in the book. But I am grateful to Jeanette Edwards, Kirsten Forkert and Colin Lorne – indeed, to everyone who tried to help me think and think better. Particular thanks to Jackie Stacey and Megan Wood for sharing their workings following a recent Cultural Studies conference. They made a difference!

I owe big debts of thanks to the many people who have read and responded to drafts of the book at different points: Davina Cooper, Kirsten Forkert, Larry Grossberg, Gill Hart, John L. Jackson, Jr, Tony Jefferson, Gail Lewis, Tania Li, Jeff Maskovsky, Janet Newman, Giulia Pelillo-Hestermeyer, Gil Rodman, Paul Stubbs and Fiona Williams. Special thanks to Larry, Tony, Jeff and Fiona for detailed annotations of the whole first draft, and to Larry and Tania for doing the same for the second draft. Their generosity and thoughtfulness have made the book better than I could have.

In May 2022, I was fortunate to have a series of conversations with Larry Grossberg, Jeff Maskovsky, Gil Rodman and Gill Hart which raised and resolved a series of puzzles for me in typically thoughtful and creative ways. In the same month, Chapter 2 was given a thorough working over by members of the Temporalities reading group (Tanja Andic, Leyla Safta-Zecheria, Paul Stubbs and Joe Thurgate in a lengthy Zoom meeting). In June 2022, a draft of the book went to the Press and was fortunate enough to arrive with Morag McDermont as reader/reviewer. She delivered a generous, thoughtful and productive commentary that was sensitive to my intentions and fierce in its insistence that I could do better. I have tried.

Although he never got to read any of it, the book is also shaped by a conversation with my late brother Alan that took place in 2019. We talked about the challenge of how to write in a state of fury while being calmly analytical. I am not sure we solved the problem, but our conversation has certainly been in my head during this process. Writing remains a rather strange form of therapy.

And finally, Janet Newman has read every word, many of them several times, without screaming. She has made it better and made me feel better about it. More than that, she is still willing to talk to me after all these words.

I owe a debt of gratitude to the Leverhulme Trust for awarding me an Emeritus Fellowship intended to support the book's dialogic development, enabling me to meet and talk with some of the first draft readers and rehearse some of the ideas publicly. It turned out not quite what was planned in pre-pandemic days but proved very helpful and was much appreciated, nonetheless. Thanks especially to Anna Grundy for patient and thoughtful grant management.

Two other networks have helped to keep me sane, and even thinking, during the pandemic times. So, thanks to my friends in the Temporalities group (Tanja Andic, Čarna Brković, Kevin Kenjar, Katarina Kušić, Noemi Lendvai-Bainton, Leyla Safta-Zecheria, Paul Stubbs and Joe Thurgate) for sanity preservation, constantly expansive conversations and vital reflections on the 'trouble with normal'. Thanks also to the Policy Ontologies group imagined and assembled by Rachael Dobson for timely reminders about why – and how – policy matters.

I am grateful to Caroline Clarke for rescuing Chapter 3 after a potentially disastrous computer malfunction. And then my thanks are due to the people of Bristol University Press for making it come together, especially Anna Richardson and my friend/editor Emily Watt who coped graciously with my frustrations. Thanks to Rachel Carter for the careful and sensitive copy-editing. And thanks to Kelly Winter for gracefully negotiating me through the complexities of the proofs. Thanks also to three of the four reviewers of the original proposal who made helpful and productive suggestions about how the book might develop. As my mother might have observed: the less said about the fourth, the better.

# Introduction: The Battle for Britain and Conjunctural Thinking

'And our mission is to deliver Brexit on the 31st of October for the purpose of uniting and re-energising our great United Kingdom and making this country the greatest place on earth … Our children and grandchildren will be living longer, happier, healthier, wealthier lives.'

Boris Johnson, 25 July 2019

I started work on this book in 2018, driven by multiple frustrations. Since then, the UK has had four Prime Ministers, left the European Union (with some details still to be sorted out), experienced a sterling crisis, entered a period of unprecedented economic hardship, joined in a global pandemic and was – fleetingly – described as "the best country in the world to be a black person" (Kemi Badenoch, MP). There have been various stories told about this political and social turbulence and its alarming acceleration in mid-2022. Some centre on the fractious fortunes of the Conservative Party. Others have pointed to the dislocations of Brexit, following the referendum over whether to remain in the EU (2016). A different story identifies the global financial crisis of 2008 (and its after-effects, including austerity politics) as the point of entry. Meanwhile, other accounts have traced the origins of our present troubles to the liberalisation of global trade, inaugurated by the Reagan–Thatcher alliance in 1979–1980 and often described as the beginning of 'neoliberal globalisation'. In this book, I explore how all of these moments – and more – came together and were condensed in our current conflicts. Rather than focusing on one story, I suggest that it is vital to examine the ways in which these stories are entangled both with each other and with still longer histories to make these different moments possible.

I examine how these different moments are connected with, and contribute to, a wider 'Battle for Britain', one that is distinctively marked by the rise of political-cultural movements committed to British/English nationalism. I stress *political-cultural* since these conflicts extend well beyond what is conventionally understood as politics – into arguments about who 'we' are (the nation, the people), about 'our history' (and how to memorialise or protect it), about how Britain might be 'Great' again. This battle – or, more accurately, this series of battles – is animated by the ways in which politics, culture and power are inextricably entangled in the struggles over how the way forward might be constructed – in the light of the proliferating crises, contradictions and conflicts.

What I offer here is an approach through *conjunctural analysis* – an approach central to one version of Cultural Studies that has been important to my own work over a long period and has become a focus of renewed interest in recent years (for example, the double special issue of *New Formations*, published in 2019). My starting point is to treat a conjuncture as a distinctive configuration of time and space: it is a *spatio-temporal* phenomenon. Conjunctures have distinctive trajectories driven by the multiple social relations and dynamics that are compressed and condensed within their specific temporal and spatial frame. By *condensed*, I mean to convey the sense of being squeezed together under pressure so that they entangle and interfere with one another. Such dynamics drive a further multiplicity: the proliferation of crises, tensions, antagonisms and conflicts which give the specific conjuncture its distinctive character and trajectory. I will come back to this approach in more detail but think there is some value in grounding this starting point in my own encounter with conjunctural analysis.

## A mugging gone wrong? Coming to conjunctural analysis

In 1973, I was a postgraduate student at the Centre for Contemporary Cultural Studies at the University of Birmingham and part of a working group on youth subcultures (whose work eventually became *Resistance Through Rituals* (Hall and Jefferson, 1976)). In 1973, three young men from the Handsworth area of Birmingham were given exceptionally long sentences for a robbery that was described in court (and in much of the media coverage) as "a mugging gone wrong". The young men were known to another student at the Centre – Chas Critcher – who also worked at an advice centre in Handsworth. He suggested that we might do something to help the campaign against the sentences, utilising our limited expertise about criminal justice, the media and the treatment of crime and deviance. We collaborated to produce a short, cyclostyled, pamphlet – entitled *20 Years* – for the Paul, Jimmy and Musty Support Committee.

This triggered a much larger – and longer – programme of collaborative work that began from the Handsworth events and contextualised them in multiple ways, from the history of the term 'mugging' to the networks of definition that connected police, politicians, courts and the mass media. The analysis then expanded to a wider framing – the social, economic and political-cultural history of Britain and its descent into crises of different kinds. That hyphen between political and cultural will be a recurring feature of the book: Cultural Studies has stressed the importance of an analytic framing that sees politics and culture as always entangled, rather than as separate fields. The two terms are connected through their mobilisations – and contestations – of power, enmeshed in relations of domination and subordination, marginalisation and exclusion and more.

Our historical approach was framed as a conjunctural analysis – a term borrowed from readings of the early translations of selections from Antonio Gramsci's *Prison Notebooks* (Gramsci, 1971). Two themes particularly engaged us: first, Gramsci's distinction between the organic and the conjunctural and, second, his attention to how dominant social groups rule by exercising 'leadership' or 'hegemony' – constructing forms of consent, rather than just dominating by force or coercion. Arguments still rage about these words (see, for example, the discussions in Koivisto and Lahtinen (2012) on conjuncture, and Worth (2015) on hegemony). But what became known locally as the 'Mugging group' borrowed and bent them to a distinctive purpose in what eventually became *Policing the Crisis: Mugging, the State and Law and Order* (Stuart Hall, Chas Critcher, Tony Jefferson, John Clarke and Brian Roberts, 2013 (first published in 1978)). For us, the particular conjuncture was constituted by the trajectory of the post-war settlement: the political-cultural consensus solidified around a combination of managed capitalism, full male employment, expanded consumption and a welfare state – and the ways in which it came apart.

The central chapters of the book (Hall et al, 2013) trace the fortunes of that settlement, as the consent of subordinate or subaltern groups eroded into proliferating forms of dissent and conflict. We drew out how consent was fractured and undermined in the face of different crises and the tightening hold exercised by the state over social fractures and dissent of various kinds, from rebellious youth to industrial militancy. In the process, a political-cultural consensus centred on a sort of social democratic capitalism gave way to increasingly repressive measures and their legitimation through projections of a 'law and order' crisis. We pointed to the rise of what we called *authoritarian populism* – a political-cultural strategy that became the foundation for Thatcherism (and a concept that was central to Stuart Hall's subsequent work on Thatcherism (Hall, 1979, 1988)). Authoritarian populism combined an attempt to recreate consent from a narrower social base: the 'right thinking', socially anxious, culturally traditionalist, sections of the middle and working classes summoned as the 'people' against their enemies: militants, extremists, criminals of all kinds but especially young black men, engaged in mugging. This last point is important because one crucial theme of the book concerned how these condensed crises became *racialised* and, as we will see, questions of 'race' are rarely far away from political-cultural conflicts in the UK.

## *Policing the Crisis* **and its legacy**

*Policing the Crisis* underpins this book in many ways, providing its orientation, its way of problematising the present, and many of its conceptual and analytical starting points. The book was much discussed and debated (for example, Jessop et al, 1984 and Hall's reply, 1985; Sumner, 1981). It continues to be a significant point of reference within Cultural Studies and beyond (for example, Hart, 2019) and, 35 years on, a second edition of the book was produced in 2013.

In this book, I am once again concerned with how culture, politics and power are entangled. It is oriented to questions of how (multiple) relations of domination and subordination are reproduced, legitimated and challenged. It explores the question of consent and asks whether the accumulation of challenges to political authority are bringing us – again – in sight of a 'crisis of authority' and a related 'crisis of the state':

> It is with the posing of this problem – the 'problem of authority' – that our analysis can no longer remain at the level of analysing ideologies of crime. ... The 'problem of authority' directs us to a different level of analysis, a different terrain of social organisation: as Gramsci put it: 'A "crisis of authority" is spoken of: this is precisely the crisis of hegemony, or general crisis of the State.' (Hall et al, 2013: 175)

In what follows, I explore how crises in the UK continue to be suffused with questions of 'race' and consider the recurring temptations of using the state coercively to divide 'the people' from their 'enemies' – and to discipline those enemies. The state is a crucial site for the construction and solidification of authority, leadership and hegemony. In relation to the state, *Policing the Crisis* drew heavily on Gramsci:

> Through the state, a particular combination of class fractions – an 'historical bloc' – was able to propagate itself throughout society – bringing about not only a unison of economic and political aims, but also intellectual and moral unity, posing all the questions around which the struggle rages, not on a corporate but on a 'universal' plane, and thus creating the hegemony of a fundamental social group over a series of subordinate groups. (Hall et al, 2013: 201)

This book will also pursue the puzzles of how historical blocs are put together and come to present themselves as embodying 'the people' and promise a way forward from our present troubles to the 'sunlit uplands' (a Winston Churchill phrase, much borrowed by Boris Johnson and his Brexit fellow travellers). Doing so demands paying attention to some of the changing conditions (and conceptualisations) in which such issues are now posed. This includes thinking again about the state, beginning from Gramsci's suggestive observation that 'the life of the state can be conceived as a series of unstable equilibria' (1971: 182). This compelling image of the formation of settlements (moments of equilibrium), and the dynamics through which they become unsettled or destabilised, always feels to me like a productive starting point for thinking about present troubles.

One other thread from my Cultural Studies past also runs throughout this book. This is Raymond Williams' distinction between 'epochal' and 'authentic historical' types of analysis (1977). His concern about the tendency of epochal analysis to over-reach into the analysis of concrete historical moments has provided me with a foundation for resisting the temptation to define the present as an Epoch or an Age of something or other (neoliberalism, globalisation, populism, nationalism, rage, and so on) which represents a distinctive break from the Past. He distinguished between 'epochal analysis' in which a cultural system has 'determinate dominant features' (such as feudal culture or bourgeois culture) and 'authentic historical analysis' in which it is necessary to examine 'the complex interrelationships between movements and tendencies both within and beyond a specific effective dominance (Williams, 1977: 121). That is, there are two different types of analysis that should not be conflated. I think that Williams' 'authentic historical analysis' is close to the idea of conjunctural analysis, not least because of the way he insists that 'authentic historical analysis' requires us to think beyond the 'dominant' to examine the other movements and tendencies in play:

> We have certainly to speak of the 'dominant' and the 'effective', and in these senses of the hegemonic. But we find that we have also to speak, and indeed with further differentiation of each, of the 'residual' and the 'emergent', which in any real historical process, and at any moment in the process, are significant both in themselves and in what they reveal of the characteristics of the 'dominant'. (1977: 121–122)

For me, this has always been a critical point of analytical leverage. Williams reminds us that dominant formations are always accompanied by others, particularly the *residual* (what he described as the persistence of questions that cannot be answered in the terms of the dominant) and the *emergent*, which he identified as the rise of new questions and new demands that were, however, always at risk of being absorbed – or incorporated – into the dominant. In the present, we might distinguish, for example, between 'residual' attachments to welfarism (and, indeed, statism) in the face of the destruction of the public realm and 'emergent' movements concerned with the climate catastrophe, or the claim that Black Lives Matter in the face of racist policing and penal policies (in the US and elsewhere). This triangulation of the political-cultural field (dominant-residual-emergent) forms a useful device for thinking about the heterogeneity of the conjuncture and escaping the temptation to focus on the dominant formation alone (see most discussions of neoliberalism, for example). Characteristically, Williams makes the framework even more demanding by suggesting that analysis should also 'recognize the complex interrelationships *between* movements and tendencies' (my emphasis). That is, the dominant is itself a contested formation as it is composed of different elements and tendencies and different forces contend to lead it and give it shape and direction. At the same time, that dominant formation is always engaged in the political-cultural work of subordination: aiming to actively residualise the residual ('this is just old-fashioned thinking') while trying to either marginalise or incorporate the emergent.

I keep returning to Williams because he offers a suggestive way of framing the discordant and unsettled relationships between different social forces and their political-cultural struggles. The conjuncture, then, forms the landscape for thinking about 'the complex interrelationships between movements and tendencies' and the political-cultural work of assembling – or *articulating* – different social groups into political blocs. This political work aims to construct and sustain forms of social authority, leadership or even hegemony.

These inheritances provide some of the orientations for the book. But I hope it will become clear that the book is not simply a reworking of the work of the 1970s, either empirically or analytically. The conjuncture is different, and emergent intellectual resources both problematise some of the formulations of *Policing the Crisis* and provide new – and productive – ways of assessing what is going on. Some of these concern questions about what Gramsci delicately calls 'social groups' (fundamental and otherwise). These are typically decoded as social classes but in what follows I will deliberately – *wilfully*, perhaps – exploit the ambiguity created by Gramsci's phrasing to ask what social groups might be in play in contemporary struggles over hegemony – not least because of the continuing salience of arguments about 'race' and racialised divisions in this conjuncture.

This last point highlights the complicated and often tendentious relationship between Cultural Studies (especially in its Birmingham variant) and varieties of Marxism. Birmingham Cultural Studies was profoundly shaped by Marxism, especially by borrowings from Althusser and Gramsci in the early 1970s, but also via Marxist historiography (including recurring connections and arguments with E.P. Thompson) and literary theory (Raymond Williams). Indeed, questions of the role of culture in class domination and resistance dominated the 1970s (for me, at least). But this was always a rather strained relationship, with more orthodox Marxist critics challenging both our apparent tendency to become preoccupied with 'superstructural froth' and our failure to deal adequately and fully with Marxist political economy (see, for example, the critique of authoritarian populism and *Policing the Crisis* by Jessop et al (1984); and Donaldson (2008), on 'post-Marxist' uses of Gramsci). In return, we tended to resist what we saw as economistic, functionalist and reductive versions of Marxist analysis that paid little attention to things ranging from the complexities of state formation to the significance of cultural forms and practices as sites of political struggle. By the end of the 1970s, Cultural Studies was being stretched to think about social relations beyond class – especially by feminist approaches to gender and social reproduction (for example, *Women Take Issue* (Women's Studies Group, 1976)) and by work on racialised divisions and their centrality to the British, as well as global, architectures of domination (*The Empire Strikes Back* (CCCS, 1982)).

Yet *Policing the Crisis* is hardly a straightforward starting point for this book. First, it was a profoundly collaborative effort of thinking and writing, and I have argued elsewhere that conjunctural analysis was not an approach that could be easily undertaken by a single researcher: 'No one scholar can grasp the multiplicity of forces, pressures, tendencies, tensions, antagonisms and contradictions that make up a conjuncture' (Clarke, 2017: 84). I continue to believe this: as a result, this book is a necessarily *thin* version of a conjunctural analysis, not least in the context of the pandemic which dislocated my plans for collaborative working. Despite my gratitude to the people drawn into conversations and comments on drafts, it cannot get anywhere near what a fully collaborative process might have delivered.

Second, this book is profoundly *argumentative*: it takes issue with a range of approaches, analyses and arguments in order to establish the case for a conjunctural analysis. This sometimes takes the form of pointing to misjudgements; for example, the tendency to ignore the role middle-class voters played in the vote for Brexit in favour of simplifying – if not tabloid-like – contrasts between the liberal/cosmopolitan middle classes and the nationalist working class (sometimes as heroes, sometimes as villains). But my arguments and interpretations more often take the form of what someone (thankyou, Bob) once described as my *contrarian* or 'yes, but' style of thinking: yes, that matters, but it's not the only thing … we need to understand how it co-exists and interacts with X, Y and Z. Conjunctural analysis places a premium on thinking about multiplicities and how heterogeneous processes, forces, possibilities come together in contradictory, often uncomfortable, ways to make certain things possible. A more generous way of framing this process is that it bears the marks of what David Scott has called Stuart Hall's style of 'clarifying' through conversation:

> Clarification is a way of approaching thinking – and learning – that aims to make us more aware of what we are thinking or doing. … That is to say, clarification involves endlessly saying the *next* thing, never the

last thing. Clarification therefore does not presume the possibility of resolution; on the contrary, there is no presumption of closure, only successive provisional resting points along the way where we gather our thoughts for further dialogic probing. (Scott, 2017: 16, italics in original)

So, quite a lot of the book is devoted to saying 'yes, but' and to teasing out the important ways in which different dynamics are complexly entangled in the conjuncture. At a recent Cultural Studies conference (https://blogs. brighton.ac.uk/cmnh/2022/08/26/whats-happening-to-culture-studies-online-event-14-16-september-2022/), I was among those castigated for an excessive – and nostalgic – attachment to 'complexity' when the present moment demanded a more streamlined clarity or simplicity of analysis. I am old enough to think that this has *always* been the argument (at least since the mid-1970s): the current crisis – whatever it may be – demands a clear and timely response. I am not convinced on both empirical and analytic grounds (clarity that is wrong is not helpful). Wendy Brown once argued for the necessary 'untimeliness' of critical thinking and I think she is correct to insist *both* that 'critical theory cannot let itself be bound by political exigency' and that critique must 'affirm life, affirm value and, above all affirm possibilities in the present and the future' (Brown, 2005: 15). I hope this book contributes to that ambition, in however small a way.

## Structure of the book

*Chapter 1 – Nations, Nationalisms and the Conjuncture*

Brexit exemplified the ways in which the national question became central to contemporary political movements; yet it needs to be revisited in the space between 'methodological nationalism' and 'methodological globalism'. My exploration of the spatial aspects of the spatio-temporal formation of the conjuncture starts from conceiving places as the nodes of multiple spatial relationships (following Doreen Massey). Concretely, this is developed through an examination of the transnational relationships that dominate the formation of Britain (exemplified in the *figures* of America, Empire and Europe). These are difficult, ambivalent and contested relationships as the recent struggles over Europe indicate. At the same time, the unstable formation of the 'United Kingdom' has become increasingly unsettled by Brexit and its aftermath. Internal and external relationships have been recast by the rise of a distinctive variant of English Nationalism.

*Chapter 2 – Turbulent Times: The Making of the Present*

Just as the place of the conjuncture is complicated, so is the challenge of telling its time. Conjunctures are formed in the intersection of different temporalities and are shaped by their different rhythms. The chapter begins and ends with the *longue durée* of the environmental catastrophe – and its rapidly quickening pace. The chapter also argues for attention to the long and unfinished trajectory of the post-colonial and its interweaving with the profoundly contested field of the social. Here differences, divisions and inequalities of different sorts have been denaturalised and made politically contestable – and resisted by 'restorationist' strategies. A quicker rhythm is evident in the temporality of the successive transformations of the 'UK economy' from failed Fordism to failed neoliberalisation and into the stagnations of rentier capitalism. Finally, political time is marked by the shifting attempts to manage these fields, their intersections and their accumulating crises, in which Brexit forms a distinctive rupture. Political time, however, also involves the articulation of nostalgias of different kinds, from Empire to Fordist relations of work and welfare.

## Chapter 3 – Accounting for Brexit

Brexit is a distinctive – if long drawn out – moment in this conjuncture. For some, it marks a turning point as a new configuration of forces, identities and possibilities is established (captured in Sobolewska and Ford's image of Britain as 'Brexitland' (2020a)). For others, it resembles an unfinished transition, an 'interregnum' that is marked (in a much-quoted phrase from Gramsci) by the 'variety of morbid symptoms' that arise 'when the old is dying and the new cannot be born'. This chapter critically examines three ways in which Brexit has been accounted for:

- as a variant of a wider contemporary shift towards populist politics;
- as a revolt against neoliberal globalisation;
- and as the revenge of the 'left behind'.

Each provides reasons for thinking conjuncturally, especially about social antagonisms, social forces and their political-cultural articulation and mobilisation. The chapter draws attention to the symbolic struggles and their mediations through both social media and the 'tabloidisation' of the Brexit conflict. Ideas of the 'left behind', however, link popular, mediatised and academic arguments in important ways and provided one route to the 'rediscovery of class' in the moment of Brexit.

## Chapter 4 – Thinking Relationally: Class and Its Others

The moment of Brexit heralded a renewed interest in the working class as an oppositional force. This chapter argues that there are both empirical and conceptual problems at stake in this rediscovery of the working class. Empirically, it neglects the powerful role played by sections of the middle classes (the 'suburbs and shires') in bringing Brexit about. Conceptually, it raises difficult questions about how to think of a working class in deindustrialised, de-collectivised and de-socialised settings. More importantly, perhaps, the pursuit of this working class has too readily *imagined* it as a white working class (in the UK and elsewhere, notably the US). The chapter asks when the working class became 'white' and how this identity became politically mobilised. The chapter concludes with an argument for a more expansively relational understanding of social forces – as complexly classed, raced, gendered and embodied – as a precondition for thinking about the dynamics of political mobilisation and demobilisation.

## Chapter 5 – Building Blocs: Towards a Politics of Articulation

Developing the previous chapter's understanding of social forces, this chapter draws on Hall's concept of *articulation* to argue for a view of political mobilisation as accomplished through selective and contingent articulations. Rather than claims about decisive shifts in the political-cultural landscape, the chapter suggests that contemporary populisms and nationalisms have involved a distinctive practice of 'vernacular ventriloquism' as they imagine and project distinctions between the 'people' and their 'enemies'. The Leave campaigns for Brexit developed a distinctive British populism (entwined with English nationalism) that assembled a particular bloc for the referendum, articulating many forms of loss, grievance and frustration. Stabilising this bloc has proved challenging: its coherence was challenged by the Corbyn-led Labour Party in the 2017 general election which voiced different popular anxieties and desires. It was, however, reassembled in the 'Boris bloc' of 2019, although, by 2022, this was coming apart, partly because of its internal contradictions and partly because of the proliferating crises that the Conservative government had to confront.

## Chapter 6 – An Accumulation of Crises

The continued accumulation of crises suggests that the Brexit moment has not given rise to a stabilised social and political-cultural equilibrium. Rather the pace of accumulation has increased as long-running crises acquire increasing urgency (the climate catastrophe) and encounter deepening ones (the intensification of inequality), while the challenge of making the spatial, scalar and sovereignty imaginaries of Brexit *materialise* has proved difficult, both internationally and domestically. New crises kept arriving, from the pandemic to international conflicts, and from economic instabilities to the many forms taken by the deepening climate catastrophe. Meanwhile, finding ways of sustaining and subsidising capital, at least since 2008, has expended public resources on private wealth (through taxation, subsidy and contracting out, for example). This accumulation of crises has been shadowed by a rise of 'counter movements' challenging dominant political norms and narratives.

## Chapter 7 – 'The Best Country in the World': Race, Culture, History

Many of these accumulating crises were exacerbated by the pandemic. COVID-19 exposed the hollowed-out nature of the British state and was followed by failures of the favoured models of subcontracting. Although successful vaccination programmes averted some of the crisis (and partly rescued the government's reputation), other troubles became apparent. Central among these was the concentration of risks of infection and death among racialised minorities. The visibility of such inequalities coincided dramatically with the killing of George Floyd (not least in the global resonance of the phrase "I can't breathe") in the midst of a series of ongoing challenges to racialised inequalities (attacks on the *Windrush* generation, racist policing, and more). The government attempted to deflect, delay and displace these challenges, not least into the register of 'culture wars'. The idea of culture wars poses important questions about the relationships between culture and politics, in which different intersections of politics, power and culture are mobilised – and contested. As I have already suggested, the (shifting) relationships between politics and culture are vital to understanding this conjuncture.

## Chapter 8 – Holding It Together? The Coercive Turn and the Crises of Party and Bloc

However, the strategy of recasting challenges into what were called culture wars was only one element of a much larger repertoire. The Johnson government (like others) sought to 'retool the state', aiming to shrink democratic capacities and to enlarge policing powers. State centralisation, anti-democratic strategies, deepening authoritarianism and a narrowing conception of 'the people' dominated – and return us to the problematic of 'policing the crisis'. This chapter explores the ways in which the condensed crises and proliferating disaffection and dissent created instabilities that profoundly unsettled both the Conservative government (and Party) and the dominant bloc.

## Chapter 9 – Unstable Equilibria: The Life of the State

In this chapter, I argue that the current crisis of the UK state has three distinctive, although interconnected, aspects. First, there has been a *crisis of capacity* involving the state's ability to manage social, political, environmental and economic disorders. Second, a *crisis of legitimacy* has condensed varieties of anti-state scepticism alongside a deepening popular mistrust of politics and politicians. Third, this is linked to a *crisis of authority* in which the dominant bloc has found it harder to command popular support for its projects, policies and promises. Reflecting on the changing UK state formation and the problems it has encountered, I pose the question of what it means to 'perform like a state' in the light of its worsening performance problems.

## Chapter 10 – The Battle for Britain – and Beyond

The concluding chapter reflects on some of the organising themes of the book and its approach to conjunctural analysis. It explores the relevance of particular ideas taken from Gramsci that have been used to address the present moment: the conjuncture, interregnum and counter-hegemonic possibilities. I consider some of the ways in which the current field of the political is being shrunk and rendered inhospitable. In response, I explore lines of thinking opened out by geographers in terms of 'countertopographies' and topological 'power-geometries'. The chapter concludes by considering how the practices of reimagining, repairing and rearticulating might be ways of approaching the challenge of creating other futures.

# Nations, Nationalisms and the Conjuncture

The Battle for Britain has taken place on the political-cultural terrain of the nation as contending narratives about its past, present and future have tried to claim the nation for themselves. These contentions crystallised around Brexit, a moment which exemplified one dramatic trend – the revival of nationalism – and posed one profound analytical problem: how do we locate this nationalist revival in spatial terms? Do we attend to the varieties of nationalism in play, looking at their distinctive formations and trajectories? Or do we look beyond the national examples to a more global account of this phenomenon: is this an era of nationalism structured by international or global realignments? Although most academic – and media – attention has been focused on populism, I share Valluvan's view of this as a period of '*nationalist* populism' (2019: 11; emphasis in original). Such nationalist populisms have proliferated, connecting the British experience to many elsewheres: Trump's desire to make America Great again, Bolsanaro's rise to power in Brazil, Modi's Hindu nationalism in India, Orbán's *Fidesz* governments in Hungary, the Law and Justice Party in Poland, not to mention the rise of nationalist-populist movements, if not governments, across Europe, from the AfD in Germany to the *Rassemblement National* in France. Across these many settings, nationalism, populism, racism, authoritarianism and more have been bundled together – or, more accurately, articulated – in specific national forms. It remains important that Trumpism is not Orbánism which is not Brexit, even though they (and other instances) are connected in multiple material and symbolic ways. The chapter will argue that the challenge is to think about nations and nationalisms *transnationally* and *conjuncturally*. This forms the focus of the first section of the chapter.

This approach makes it possible to situate Brexit – and the wider Battle for Britain – within these larger transnational conjunctural dynamics of the national question rather than solely in terms of the UK's relationship to the EU (or some abstract 'global capitalism'). How the UK as nation and nation-state came to occupy this place is the focus of the second section. I suggest that processes of imagining the nation – and its Others – point to the triangulations of the UK within shifting transnational relations that centre on the *spatial imaginaries* of 'Empire', 'America' and 'Europe'. There I pause for a moment to think about the shape shifting formation that is the European Union before turning to the multiple nations of the increasingly 'disunited Kingdom' and the different nationalisms that are associated with them, including those that helped to shape Brexit. Although the chapter focuses on the spatial framing of the conjuncture, these features also have a distinctive temporal character. Conjunctures are *spatio-temporal* formations, so while this chapter foregrounds spatial dimensions and dynamics, it tries to keep in view the temporal dynamics that are the focus of the following chapter.

## Nations in question: between methodological nationalism and methodological globalism

The proliferation of nationalist-populist political movements suggests that many people still look to nation-states to provide support and create the conditions of well-being, even as these movements frequently translate those desires into nationalist/nativist framings: promising welfare and jobs for 'our people'. In this sense, it is hardly surprising that many recent political movements – including the campaigns for Brexit – have centred on the nation and the nation-state, promising to rescue *both* the nation-as-people and the nation-as-state. These promises to restore the nation work through a combination of two themes: the repatriation of 'sovereignty' and the rescue of the 'way of life' associated with the people. This double restoration underpins the demand to 'make X great again'.

How then do we understand these developments as connected without collapsing them into mere cases of a general trend or overemphasising their uniqueness as national events? The authors of *Policing the Crisis* described the concatenation of crises that the book examined as beginning from 'a crisis of and for British capitalism' (Hall et al, 2013: 310). This way of locating the crises as 'British' was not because we did not know that Britain was a post-colonial nation (and suffused by questions of 'race' as a consequence). Rather, at that time it seemed to make sense to think in terms of 'British capitalism', a British social formation, a British state and British politics and parties. Now, however, the taken-for-grantedness of this national framing has been unsettled. As Christophers has recently argued, it makes little sense to talk of 'British capitalism' or of 'national economies' in general. He notes that '[a]s globalization has proceeded, economies like the UK's have become increasingly entangled with economic structures and dynamics at larger scales … [and] as UK capital has expanded its own spatial footprint, the integrity of the UK economy has been dissolved from the inside out' (2020: 10–11).

There has been a growing interest in thinking more carefully about the spatial dimensions and dynamics of conjunctures, especially among geographers (see, inter alia, Peck, 2017; Hart, 2020; Leitner and Sheppard, 2020). Leitner and Sheppard argue that spatial questions have been relatively neglected in conjunctural approaches which have been historically focused and have tended to treat space and place as taken-for-granted categories – what they call (following Brenner, 2004) 'methodological territorialism'. They argue instead for a 'spatialised conjunctural analysis' which 'stretches explanatory frameworks not just backwards in time, but also outwards in space (identifying how local events are shaped by distant processes), and upwards and downwards in terms of geographical scale (whereby events at a particular scale may be shaped by both higher and lower scale processes)' (2020: 495). Although I agree about the shift to thinking more carefully in both spatial and scalar terms, there is a different risk at stake in this move. In such framings, attention can shift too easily to the global scale, foregrounding the processes and effects of globalisation. There is, then, a risk that specific places become the *scalar* diminutives of the global (the local instances of global processes). Similarly, they risk being reduced to the 'particulars' which can be set against the 'general' *levels* of conceptual framing in Leitner and Sheppard's concern with the dialectic between the 'general and the particular' (2020: 492). Carla Freeman's dissection of the gendered relationship between the global and local in the study of globalisation (2001) highlights some of the problems at stake in the conflation of scalar thinking and conceptual hierarchies where both 'local' and 'particular' tend to become the minor – and feminised – part of the pairings.

In an important recent intervention about the challenges of thinking conjuncturally, Gillian Hart refuses a 'global' orientation 'that treats neoliberalism as cause and right-wing nationalism/populism as effect', while equally rejecting the study of 'pre-given national "cases" as separate and independent of one another' (Hart, 2020: 234). Much conventional social science has been framed by the assumptions of *methodological nationalism* – treating things as taking place within the confines of the territorial frame of the nation. More recently, the fascination with globalisation has driven a *methodological globalism* in which spatial variations are flattened or subsumed into global processes. Finding a way between these poles of 'methodological nationalism' and 'methodological globalism' (Clarke et al, 2015: 19) is a particular challenge for conjunctural analysis, given that most such work has tended to take a national territorial framing for granted.

In examining the present conjuncture, it is equally important to avoid a simple – and simplifying – distinction between a 'national' past and a 'global' present. 'British capitalism' was never an entirely closed national system (understood as the opposite of an open, globalising economy). The long colonial history ensured it was deeply embedded in an earlier global economic and political system, whose effects persisted long after the formal period of decolonisation. It is this sense of *shifting* global orders (rather than a shift from the national to the global in any simple terms) that underpins Gillian Hart's project. She argues:

> The scaffolding is provided by a set of key global conjunctural moments, which I define as major turning points when interconnected forces at multiple levels and spatial scales in different regions of the world have come together to create new conditions with worldwide implications and reverberations – bearing in mind an understanding of conjuncture not just as a period of time, but an accumulation of contradictions. (2020: 235)

Hart identifies the first of these conjunctures as the Cold War Era, beginning in the late 1940s, characterised by 'projects of accumulation and hegemony, with the latter understood not as consent but as a contested process' (2020: 235) that connect the different trajectories of South Africa, India and the US. She goes on to argue that the ways in which these projects fell apart created the conditions which exploited the articulation of a neoliberal counter-revolution linked to a variety of exclusionary nationalisms and populist politics. These came to dominate the second conjuncture (from the late 1970s to the present).

This is a hugely ambitious framing but one that rightly insists that complex forms of connectedness – economic, political, cultural – constitute relations between different places (regions, nations, localities) that cannot be understood as separate container-spaces, nor collapsed into a 'global' world. Although Hart's focal points of attention (South Africa, India, the US) are not the same as mine in this book, the dimensions and dynamics that she sets out are formative for a world in which 'Britain' is, in significant ways, constituted through its relations with other places: from the end of Empire to its position in the Cold War era blocs (formally through NATO, less visibly through other varieties of political and cultural anti-communism). Equally, its shifting relations through the period of decolonisation to the search for a 'global role', and its indebted – economically, politically, culturally, militarily – relationship to the US, mark a shifting field of relations in which the UK developed. This was paralleled by the flows of migration from Empire to the UK that remade the 'British' population, unsettled cultural norms and were repeatedly met by racist immigration policies and controls aiming to preserve a 'way of life' and prevent it from being 'swamped' (in Thatcher's phrase). Finally, across these crisis-ridden and unstable conjunctures, the UK negotiated its uneasy insertion into the emerging global capitalism through its entry into the European Union – belatedly, and not without constant anxiety and scepticism.

This view raises the question of what has driven the nation and nationalism to their central place in contemporary political mobilisations. In this conjuncture – one shaped by the destabilisation of the old 'settlements' and the unleashing of the dynamics of neoliberal globalisation – crises of both the nation-form (Balibar, 1991) and the nation-state have come to the fore. No longer 'fit for purpose', the nation-state had to be 're-tooled', made 'lean and mean', entrepreneurial and efficient, and turned into a 'competition state' (Cerny, 1997) which could ensure that the nation was 'open for business'. Jessop (2000) describes this transition as involving the crisis of 'the national spatio-temporal fix': the forms of social regulation that provided the conditions for the earlier regime of capital accumulation (described by Jessop as Atlantic Fordism). But, as I have already tried to indicate, the relations that flow in and across these social formations are both more heterogeneous and contradictory than can be grasped solely from the standpoint of capital accumulation. An alternative view of this crisis of the nation-form and the nation-state is offered by Akhil Gupta, whose exploration of the post-colonial allows him to reveal the *contingency* of the connection between nation and state in 'this curiously hyphenated entity, the nation-state' (1998: 316). Gupta treats the destabilisation of that hyphenation of nation and state – as a central dynamic of the late 20th century, pointing to the ways in which it reveals the contingently constructed coupling of nation and state, such that they can be more easily recognised (and contested, both analytically and politically) as separate.

Shifting the frame to foreground colonialism and decolonisation changes what is at stake in thinking about nations, states and their articulations. We might then be able to think about the double dynamics in which the tendencies of both the post-colonial moment and the neoliberal globalisation of capital are entangled and have destabilising effects on both the nation and the state. Arguments about the rescaling of government, governance and the state; the proliferation of forms of anti-statism and the contemporary resurgence of nationalism swirl around that unsettled hyphen and the problem of how to reconstruct both its elements – and the form of their connection. This provides one route to understanding how Brexit (and its contemporary resonances in other places such as the US, Hungary and France) came to centre on that impossible object of desire – the nation. This imagined nation was invoked throughout the Brexit campaign and in its aftermath. For example, in 2016 Theresa May, the new Prime Minister and leader of the Conservative Party, addressed the Conservative Party Conference and extolled the Britain-to-come:

> 'A truly Global Britain is possible, and it is in sight. And it should be no surprise that it is. Because we are the fifth biggest economy in the world. Since 2010 we have grown faster than any economy in the

G7. And we attract a fifth of all foreign investment in the EU. We are the biggest foreign investor in the United States. We have more Nobel Laureates than any country outside America. We have the best intelligence services in the world, a military that can project its power around the globe, and friendships, partnerships and alliances in every continent. We have the greatest soft power in the world, we sit in exactly the right time zone for global trade, and our language is the language of the world.' (Theresa May speech to Conservative Party Conference, 2 October 2016)

Brexit enabled the renewal of imperial fantasies – a Britain engaging with the world as a sovereign power could both lead and benefit from a new phase of Free Trade. These fantasies promised resolutions to the challenges of the post-colonial (after all, we have 'friends' all over the world) and to the problem of how to insert the UK into a global economy (in the lead, of course).

Space and place were central to how the conjuncture was formed and took shape. The nation-form and the nation-state had been destabilised and, in Gramscian terms, efforts were made to create new equilibria – although these continually remained unstable. At the same time, what has emerged is not a denationalised 'global world' but one in which places have been reworked, brought into new relationships with each other and into new scalar configurations. So, the UK is not simply part of global capitalism (whether this is understood as financialised capitalism, knowledge capitalism, platform capitalism or surveillance capitalism – to name but four recent categorisations: Thrift, 2005; Lapavitsas, 2013; Zuboff, 2019; Gilbert and Williams, 2022). Rather it is part of those circuits and relationships while having – like other places – distinctive national features and dynamics. So, for example, Christophers' work on rentier capitalism (2020) treats it as both a general form of capital accumulation (with a global reach) and taking a distinctive dominant role in the UK economy (sustained by a particular set of political and cultural conditions). There are other ways in which space, place and the unsettled nation-form are central to the conjuncture – and the UK's distinctive trajectory within it.

## Triangulating Britain: the transnational dynamics of the national question

Doreen Massey's conception of space points to the dynamics that form – and transform – places as 'nodes' in fields of relationships. Writing about the mutual constitution of the local and the global, she argued that places 'are criss-crossings in the wider power-geometries which constitute both themselves and "the global"' (2005: 11; see also Massey, 1994). Within the field of relationships that have produced and sustained the UK, there are three particularly significant axes: relations with 'America', 'Empire' and 'Europe'. They simultaneously involve significant material flows and relationships and are the focus of potent spatial imaginaries – that is, they are projections of ideas and affects about people, places and politics. As a result, I call them America (rather than the United States) Empire (rather than the Commonwealth) and Europe (rather than the European Union). The material dynamics include networks along which people, capital, goods, power, political and cultural influences and more have flowed. At the same time, the spatial imaginaries of these places and their relationship to the UK have proved potent animators of British political-cultural life, carrying powerful emotional charges, not least in their capacity to combine attraction and repulsion in unsettlingly ambivalent ways. Massey pointed to the importance of such emotional charges in the formation of spatial identities: 'The politics associated with the rethinking of spatial identities have been, and continue to be, equally emotionally fraught and liable to touch deep feelings and desires not always immediately associated with "the political". Rethinking a politics of place, or nation, is an emotionally charged issue' (Massey, 2005: 6).

'America' (as the US) has, for instance, exerted a powerful attraction, often expressed in images of the 'special relationship', beloved of UK politicians. More generally, it has long represented a distinctively glossy route to 'modernity', enacted through shared linguistic and popular cultural repertoires. Yet America has also been a focus of repulsion (often expressed in an assumption of British cultural superiority). It has been a focus of anxiety: for example, about the US as the home of violence, especially racialised violence (it was, for example, the source of the 'mugging' imagery of the 1970s; Hall et al, 2013). America also offered a set of images about the dead ends of modernity, expressed, for example, in the dystopias of both 'mass culture' and 'consumer culture'. Such imaginaries, and their affective dynamics, run alongside, and are entwined in unsettling ways with, more material relationships. After 1945 the UK found itself occupying a position of structural subordination to the US. It became economically dependent (after the Marshall plan) and tied into US–UK flows of capital and consumer goods, most recently in the dominance of US-based new technology platforms (from Facebook to Amazon). This economic subordination was paralleled by a military subordination, organised in part through NATO and more directly visible in the UK's 'independent' nuclear deterrent (based on missiles bought or leased from the US). The UK's willingness to join in George W. Bush's war in Iraq in pursuit of the supposed 'weapons of mass destruction' came to symbolise this subordination. Meanwhile, British popular culture was dominated by US production (despite occasional, but much celebrated, 'British invasions'). Nonetheless, the US was reinvented in the moment of Brexit as a potent symbol of the UK's future as an independent trading nation, and favourable trade deals with an 'old ally' were much anticipated, although the replacement of Trump by Biden in 2020 dampened those dreams.

The second pole of these relationships – 'Empire' – remains a potent image of what was at stake when Britain was indeed 'Great Britain', embodying conceptions of global reach and images of power and rule, wrapped in narratives of a 'civilising mission'. Yet, at the same time, Empire has been a recurrent site of anxiety about loss: about what happens when Empire 'comes home', about who can claim to be 'British' and – increasingly – about how to understand, teach and memorialise 'our history'. Such emotional turbulence is interwoven with a complex material history, ranging from the profits from colonialism that undergirded British industrial and social development to the formation of taste and national culture (not least our attachment to tea and sugar). Decolonisation proved a traumatic transition for British politics and culture alike (and a violent experience for the colonised). The loss of global power was dramatised in the entangled transnational relations at the point of the Suez crisis (1956) when President Eisenhower threatened economic sanctions on both France and Britain if they did not withdraw the forces they had sent to Egypt as a response to President Nasser's nationalisation of the Suez Canal. That moment marked a symbolic recalibration of the UK's 'global standing' and demonstrated its subordination to the US in global power calculations (a reminder that the axes intersect in complex ways).

To borrow Stoler's phrase (2006), Britain has continued to be 'haunted by Empire', struggling to come to terms with the forms of political and cultural 'loss' that manifested themselves in the intense dynamics of what Paul Gilroy (2005) calls 'postcolonial melancholia'. Meanwhile, the 'internalization of colonialism' (Turner, 2018), via people migrating to the UK from former colonies and settling, transformed the population, culture and politics of the UK, not least in the recurrent obsession with 'managing immigration' and governing what became known as 'race relations'. While 'Empire' generated a constant stream of anxiety about the presence of 'these people' (understood as people 'out of place'), the UK continually revived and recycled narratives of Empire as national triumph; when 'we' ruled the world and 'civilised' our Others, back when we were a great trading nation. As Wemyss (2009) shows, the mercantilist framing of the colonial past as a set of *trading* relationships was crucial in discounting questions of slavery, colonial exploitation and the invention of a racialised global cartography, fixing peoples and places in global hierarchies.

Nonetheless, given its significance as the focal point for Brexit, the most recently visible axis of relationships along which the UK has been shaped is 'Europe' – a word that manages to refer to both the continent of Europe and the specific institutional arrangement that is the European Union. Europe as a continent has been the focus of a long history of competition (especially in the long period of European colonialism), conflict (wars and invasions stretching back to Julius Caesar's arrival/invasion in 55 BC) and cooperation (economic, political and military). The UK's relationship with Europe-as-EU has been equally structured by a profound sense of ambivalence. The founding of the European Economic Community was viewed with a sense of distance by the UK's political leaders, underpinned by a belief that the combination of Empire (in the new form of the Commonwealth) and America would be more than adequate to ensure Britain's trading interests. This sense of distance did not survive for long as the British economy began to falter, leading to applications to join the European Economic Community (EEC) in 1963 and 1967 (both vetoed by President De Gaulle). Membership was finally negotiated by the Heath government in 1972 and was confirmed by a referendum held by the Wilson government in 1975. The relationship was never an easy one, strained by continental anxieties about the UK's 'Anglo-Saxon' version of capitalism and by British 'Euroscepticism' from both Right and Left.

These material relationships were central to a particular period of British economic development (or, more accurately, *uneven* development: Macleod and Jones, 2018). Nevertheless, 'Europe' was a focus of profound, and increasingly fraught, ambivalence. In one register, it symbolised peaceful coexistence, an engagement with a (more sophisticated) 'continental' style and the possibilities of adventure (from holidays to new food and drink possibilities). Europe also offered alternative conceptions of modernity to transatlantic excess: German managed capitalism, French sophistication, Scandinavian cool. Yet Europe was always also our Other, whether in the form of old enemies (France and Germany), as the possessors of a suspicious sophistication (the other implication of 'continental' style), or – ultimately – as a super-power, embodied in 'Brussels bureaucrats' and their enterprise-strangling red tape.

In an important article, Stratton has argued that campaigns for Brexit mobilised a cluster of themes – invasion, immigration and the Second World War – that emphasised the risks and dangers of the UK's proximity to Europe. These ideas draw on a well-established and naturalised set of distinctions between native and foreign/invasive species (see Barua, 2021). Stratton points to the sliding representations of Britain-at-risk that are folded into versions of 'our island story':

> A characteristic of the English cultural imaginary is to think of England as a sovereign island. This subsumes Wales and Scotland, ignores Northern Ireland, and does not recognise the multiple islands that constitute what is really an archipelago. This way of thinking was

pervasive among those campaigning for Leave in the referendum. (Stratton, 2019: 4)

I will return to the complex alignments of England, Britain and the UK shortly, but first I want to consider a little further what it means to be 'on the edge of Europe'.

## On the edge? The EU and its peripheries

Against overly institutionalist or politicised analyses of the EU, I think it is more productive to think in terms of what Loftsdóttir, Smith and Hipfl (2018) call 'messy Europe'. They argue that '[d]ebates about Europe's predicament and future often mobilize or touch upon reified conceptions of "Europe," imagined as a fixed location inhabited by certain kinds of people ... we approach Europe differently, as a contested space and fluid construction with plural histories' (2018: 2). This emphasis on a contested and fluid space highlights a key aspect of the EU: its 'shape shifting' formation. The EU has had many incarnations (and shapes) since its first appearance in the guise of the European Coal and Steel Community in 1951. Since then, it has reworked its institutional form, its policy competencies and its geographical reach until its pre-Brexit 27-member peak as the European Union. Within the EU, there have been many different Europes, most obviously in the form of the eurozone (those countries using the euro as currency) and the Schengen zone (enabling free movement of people across national borders within the zone). Perhaps less obvious, but no less significant, has been the EU's capacity to manipulate, move and stretch its borders, increasingly outsourcing border controls and the management of migration to countries in the 'European Neighbourhood': non-EU countries around the Mediterranean region (see, for example, Walters, 2004; Bialasiewicz, 2012; Karadağ, 2019).

This externalising dynamic has produced a very particular version of what Balibar (2003) called the 'Euro-Mediterranean ensemble', embodying what some have identified as the EU's neocolonial character both within and beyond its borders (Langan, 2018; Mikelis, 2016). This Euro-Mediterranean space forms one of the EU's many peripheries, not merely through the conjunction of migration and securitisation, but also because of the European core's recurring doubts and anxieties about its 'Mediterranean' members: the so-called PIGS (Portugal, Italy, Greece and Spain), often characterised as 'less-developed' economies and societies. Roberto Dianotto's *Europe in Theory* (2007) explores them as Europe's 'internalised Other', expressed in contrasts between the 'real' Europe and its wayward Southern 'cousins', with the differences often racialised. This distinction deepened during the Eurozone crisis that followed the 2007–08 financial crash. Although most attention was focused on the possibility of Greek debt default (or even 'Grexit'), all the 'PIGS' were viewed as vulnerable (and indeed became the PIIGS as anxieties grew about Ireland).

The PIGS mark one of the EU's peripheries but it has others. There is an Eastern periphery, where former Soviet bloc countries have developed new (and differentiated) trajectories in relation to global and regional formations (compare the Czech Republic and Hungary, for example), but have all struggled to stabilise new national arrangements where the promise of European 'integration' uncomfortably encounters both the neoliberalisation of their economies and the reinvention of the nation. As Hungary experimented with what Fidesz called 'illiberal democracy' and Poland suspended or abolished aspects of democratic rights and the rule of law, this terrain became a focus for European 'anxieties' about the future of liberal democratic forms and processes.

Other European spaces have also become the focus of the strained dynamics of 'integration'. The region named for governmental/developmental purposes as 'South Eastern Europe' centred on the former Republic of Yugoslavia, sometimes known as the Balkans or Western Balkans (and the politics of naming matter here as elsewhere: Kolstø, 2016). Blagojević (2009) identifies the region as a distinctive 'semi-periphery' which has been the focus of many projects aimed at economic, political and social 'reform' – intended to make its countries fit to take their place in a 'modern Europe'. She argues that the region experiences a profoundly contradictory process of modernisation as a 'semi-other' (that is simultaneously viewed as like, and not like, the 'West'). It is both required to 'adjust' to the core (and its norms) and speed up the work of modernisation, yet the core constantly judges its reforms as too slow and/or merely formal. In this dynamic, the places of the semi-periphery are constantly vulnerable to instruction on how to become 'European', innovation (learning to become 'modern') and experimentation ('try this, it will be good for you'), while always being held responsible for the failures of these initiatives (just not European enough).

The UK has historically occupied a rather different sort of peripheral relation to the EU, often perceived as 'in but not of' Europe. Its early efforts to join what was then the EEC were viewed with some suspicion and rebuffed accordingly. The suspicion centred on the UK's perceived closeness to the US and its likely role as the carrier of the disease of 'Anglo-Saxon' capitalism (Bresser-Pereira, 2012). This version of capitalism was felt to be too lightly regulated, too focused on 'shareholder value' and, viewed from an emerging European consensus on a 'social dimension', was thought to be too anti-social. British membership involved the UK becoming subject to forms of economic regulation from the EU, although as Hyman indicates, the UK was also a powerful force in diluting some aspects of EU regulation, particularly those affecting labour (such as the Working Time Directive).

He suggests the UK drove a sort of 'convergence' especially in terms of the UK's impact on the 'social model': 'Thus we can discern a form of double movement. The processes of British industrial relations have in significant measure been Europeanised, despite often strenuous resistance by both Conservative and Labour governments. But the European social model has become in key respects increasingly Anglo-Saxon' (Hyman, 2008: 27).

This argument reshapes some of the debates about the EU as fundamentally neoliberal (a significant view from the Left in the UK and across Europe) in significant ways. Politically, the EU has occupied a sort of contradictory – and contested – space, attempting to manage Europe's insertion into globalisation while maintaining a social dimension. That social inclination has been recurrently diminished, and rendered subordinate to economic imperatives, particularly after the financial crisis. The UK's peripheral – and often antagonistic – position within the EU was celebrated (and rationalised) in then Prime Minister David Cameron's attempt to renegotiate the UK's relationship to the EU:

> 'I know that the United Kingdom is sometimes seen as an argumentative and rather strong-minded member of the family of European nations.
>
> And it's true that our geography has shaped our psychology.
>
> We have the character of an island nation – independent, forthright, passionate in defence of our sovereignty.
>
> We can no more change this British sensibility than we can drain the English Channel.
>
> And because of this sensibility, we come to the European Union with a frame of mind that is more practical than emotional.
>
> For us, the European Union is a means to an end – prosperity, stability, the anchor of freedom and democracy both within Europe and beyond her shores – not an end in itself.' (Cameron, 2013; see the analysis in Wodak, 2016)

That passionate 'defence of our sovereignty' became one of the key themes in the 2016 Referendum, although not in Cameron's hands. Instead, the Leave campaigns summoned up the spirit of an 'island nation' to great effect. But which nation, exactly?

## Brexit, nations and nationalisms

Three years after Cameron's speech, both his attempted renegotiations with the EU and his referendum gamble had failed: the UK voted to leave the EU by 52 per cent to 48 per cent. This tally conceals significant variations across the different nations which make up the United Kingdom (of Great Britain and Northern Ireland). In England, the vote was 53 per cent for

Leave and 47 per cent for Remain; and the returns were similar in Wales. Northern Ireland voted 56 per cent to Remain and 44 per cent to Leave, while Scotland voted 62 per cent to Remain and 38 per cent to Leave (Electoral Commission, 2016). These variations, their preconditions and their consequences all point to important questions about the relationship between nations and nationalisms within the assemblage of the United Kingdom.

At its simplest, England is the largest (in terms of territory and population) of the four main elements of the UK. More significantly, it acts as the core of the UK, working to draw the elements together under Westminster/London/English rule. There is, it should be noted, no straightforward equivalence between Westminster, London and England as significant differences and sources of tensions exist within those framings (Cochrane, 2020). However, this English dominance has been described by some scholars as the organising principle of a dynamic of 'internal colonialism' (Hechter, 1975) through which the 'Celtic nations' – Ireland, Scotland, Wales – became subjected to forms of English rule. The concept of internal colonialism also illuminates the double dynamic of internal and external colonialism that was essential to the making of 'Great Britain' as a global power. Those different colonial dynamics have historically intertwined, implicating the four nations in the imperial project in distinctive ways (see, for example, Devine (2006) and MacKenzie and Devine (2011) on Scotland and Empire).

Feelings of being subordinated – in economic, political and cultural terms – to that Westminster-London-English nexus fuelled a variety of nationalisms that have, from time to time, disrupted the projection of a happily United Kingdom. Echoes of the processes and experiences of subordination have persisted in political-cultural memory. The Highland clearances and the Irish famine continue to be markers of the brutality of English rule, while the economic power of English dominion, especially in relation to land and property, has been a frequent theme of popular conflicts, from arson attacks on English-owned second homes in Wales in the 1980s to the persistence of quasi-feudal estates in Scotland. During the 'Troubles' in the North of Ireland from the 1960s to the 1990s, the British army (as well as the civilian police) were identified by Nationalist political movements as an 'occupying army'. Most recently, the President of Ireland, writing as the centenary of the 1922 Partition of Ireland between the Republic and the North approached, called on the British to acknowledge the history of British imperialism:

> From the perspective of the British imperialist mind of its time, attitudes to the Irish for example, were never, and could never be, about a people who were equal, had a different culture, or could be trusted in a civilised discourse of equals. From the perspective of the Irish, who had their own ancient language, social and legal systems

and a rich monastic contribution to the world, this view had to be resisted. (Higgins, 2021)

The architecture of internal colonialism has had a variety of consequences but its role in the proliferation of nationalisms is significant. Irish nationalism took different forms through the 20th century, from the struggle for 'Home Rule' in the early 20th century to the pursuit of a 'united Ireland' in later decades. Scottish and Welsh nationalism also took various forms, coming to crystallise in political movements (and parties) in the late 20th century – Plaid Cymru in Wales and the Scottish National Party (SNP) in Scotland. The late 1990s saw significant constitutional changes in response to the internal strains and tensions of the United Kingdom – with devolution to new national assemblies in Belfast, Cardiff and Edinburgh (with different powers and principles, such as 'power sharing' between Unionist and Nationalist parties in the Stormont-devolved government in the North).

Until recently, least attention had been given to *English* nationalism among the varieties of nationalism in play across the UK. In some respects, this is not particularly surprising, given that Irish, Scottish and Welsh nationalisms were understood as *insurgent* nationalisms which had emerged from contexts of perceived subordination to English domination. That lack of attention also reflected the ways in which England – and Englishness – had formed the taken-for-granted centre of Britain/the UK/Britishness. Even now, the distinction between Britishness and Englishness – and between British nationalism and English nationalism – remains blurred, with Brexit sometimes being referred to as a result of British nationalism, sometimes as a result of English nationalism. Despite a long history, English nationalism emerged as a more visible and audible political-cultural formation articulated around the strained and conflicted relationships with the EU. Kenny (2014) argues that the recent rise of English nationalism focused on the EU because the UK's membership was coterminous with the effects – and experience – of globalisation and deindustrialisation. Wellings (2010) argues that, in this period, English nationalism had come to be embodied in a range of political forms – including the United Kingdom Independence Party (UKIP) and the English Defence League (EDL). These targeted the EU and resisted the threat of any deeper European integration, while articulating anti-migrant feelings, attacking both weak immigration control and EU freedom of movement policies, particularly after EU's enlargement eastwards.

Kenny situates this militantly anti-EU version of English nationalism alongside two other variants. One had emerged from, and drew on, a long-established rural imaginary – conceiving of England as the site of a calm cultural and political conservatism that was associated with a style (or at least self-image) of pragmatic social and political adaptation. This bucolic imaginary provided a fecund resource for the Conservative Party's self-representations, perhaps most famously/notoriously in the vision sketched by former Conservative Prime Minister John Major (with its characteristic elision of England and Britain):

'Fifty years on from now, Britain will still be the country of long shadows on county grounds, warm beer, invincible green suburbs, dog lovers and pools fillers and, as George Orwell said, "Old maids bicycling to holy communion through the morning mist" and, if we get our way, Shakespeare will still be read even in school.' (Major, 1993)

It should be noted, though, that the rural had also been attached to other political-cultural framings and projects, from the demands of the Diggers and the Levellers, through the anti-enclosure movements to mass trespass to demand access to the countryside. More recently, counter-cultural and environmental movements have articulated competing visions of the countryside (for a richer view of this complexity, see Ware (2022)).

Elements of political and cultural liberalism form 'the third broad pattern of national sentiment which has become embedded within contemporary English culture' (Kenny, 2014: 125). This variant has been the focus of recurring innovation, anxiety and argument for the Left in Britain, centred on the question: to what extent is it possible to imagine a non-reactionary Englishness as part of the struggle for progressive values? This question has been the focus of creative cultural work such as the singer Billy Bragg's constant striving to articulate a new England or Jeremy Dellar's reworkings of English political and cultural moments from Peterloo to rave culture. It has been a recurring theme in political writing and journalism, from Nairn's exploration of the 'Break-Up of Britain' (1977) to the efforts by the *Guardian* journalist John Harris to find ways to talk about Englishness differently (2019). This liberal or progressive strand has echoes of Simon Featherstone's (2008) examination of the changing – and contested – versions of Englishness that animated popular culture during the transition from Imperial power to a post-colonial nation. Featherstone argues that, in the tangled threads of English narratives, there may yet be a possibility of crafting a new – and more open – sense of Englishness: 'through its engagements with the most difficult and most productive consequences of its imperial history and expressions of its regional tradition and modernity. It is in those networks of difference and diversity that England and its Englishness can best be understood and developed' (2008: 182).

Featherstone's sense of the possibility of developing a more progressive Englishness has been reinforced by a number of developments, notably the longer histories of anti-colonialism and anti-racism, the emergence of a post-colonial 'culture of conviviality' (Gilroy, 2005) and the development of forms of 'everyday multiculture' (for example, Wilson, 2011; Neal et al,

2018; see also Valluvan, 2019: 202–207). Featherstone's interest in these possibilities carries echoes of Patrick Wright's call for a proliferation of alternative, diverse democratic and republican histories as a counter to the 'aggressively mournful fantasies of the old Imperial nation' (1985: 255).

Here, though, I am going to concentrate on the first – and dominant – strand in Kenny's triad of Englishness, not least because it was the one that dominated the moment of Brexit and inflected the decision to leave the EU in decisive ways. It has also remained at the centre of political-cultural conflicts since the referendum, not least in the recent Conservative attempts to foment 'culture wars' in 2020–22 (and the commitment to preserve 'our history') – a development that I will return to in later chapters. This Europhobic strand of Englishness drew on and articulated a range of sentiments, including loss, rage, shame and anxiety (see, inter alia, Aughey, 2010; Closs Stephens, 2019; Clarke, 2019). This strand makes visible the emotional register that is interwoven with the political-cultural framing that defines and denounces the 'threats to Englishness'. This potent affective-political-cultural combination has occupied the space between the Conservative Party (with its long, and increasingly virulent, history of Euroscepticism) and the shifting fringes of the Right, from UKIP to the EDL (and their predecessors such as the National Front and British National Party). The electoral successes of UKIP, which peaked at 13 per cent of the general election vote in 2015 and 28 per cent of the vote in the 2014 European elections, are widely viewed as having shaped the rightward shift of the Conservative Party in general, and David Cameron's decision to promise an EU referendum in particular. Several writers have explored the impact of this sense of Englishness in the referendum (as well as its relationship to other dynamics, such as imperial nostalgia, for example, Dorling and Tomlinson, 2019; Fitzgerald et al, 2020). In his examination of 'Brexit and the politics of pain', Fintan O'Toole discussed what he sees as a sense of victimhood and self-pity – projecting a once-proud imperial nation humiliated, dominated and oppressed by the European 'super-power' in which 'a sense of superiority and a sense of grievance' are potently combined (2018: 3).

This dominant version of English nationalism emerged in the 1950s, taking shape in the immediate post-colonial moment. Virdee and McGeever have argued that this version of English nationalism was articulated through a 'deep-rooted nostalgia for the British Imperial project' (2018: 1809). One of its most potent ventriloquists was Enoch Powell, former Conservative and Ulster Unionist Party (UUP) politician, who, Wellings argues, 'had a lasting impact on the emergence of contemporary English nationalism through his deployment of race and xenophobia. ... Powell sought to articulate a new vision of England based on race and eventually resistance to European integration' (2012: 103). The 2016 referendum provided a particularly productive terrain for the mobilisation of this English nationalism and its celebration of a lost 'way of life'. Throughout it, the Leave campaigns conflated conceptions of nation as *place* ('this scepter'd isle'), as *people* ('freedom loving') and as *polity* (the 'Mother of Parliaments'). Their promise of 'taking back control' articulated overlapping images of what might be restored by leaving the EU, condensed in the imagery of 'sovereignty'. Wellings argues that nationalism – and English nationalism in particular – worked through 'the legitimization of a particular location of sovereignty, be that sovereignty vested in the people or the state or both' (2012: 37). It was precisely that doubling – and blurring – of the *location* of 'sovereignty' that came to be a matter of contention once sovereignty was being reclaimed after the referendum: did it reside in Parliament, the government, or was it simply the 'Will of the People' (Gordon, 2016)?

Sovereignty mattered. It mattered for the mobilisation of the Leave vote, not least in the promise of collective agency ('take back control'). It also mattered for the political and governmental tangles that emerged as successive governments attempted to make 'Brexit mean Brexit' in practice. Extricating the UK from the EU involved translating potent *imaginaries* – of space, scale and sovereignty – into institutional arrangements, relations and practices (Clarke, 2020b). Indeed, making 'Brexit' happen involved troubles of many different kinds: political, governmental, constitutional, social and cultural, including the further fracturing of the UK. I will return to these troubles in later chapters.

## *Taking place: the spaces of the conjuncture*

Let me return to a question that I posed earlier in the chapter in relation to *Policing the Crisis*: *where* are the current crises taking place? Much current social and political analysis remains transfixed by the imagined geography of nations and nation-states with the result that crises – and conjunctures – are recurrently treated as national events, confined to the time-space of a particular place. The usual escape route from the straitjacket of this conceptual and methodological nationalism has been via an equally unsatisfactory methodological globalism, shifting scales but avoiding the rethinking of place and space. For me, as for many others, Doreen Massey's work has provided an illuminating way to think about the relational production of place. Her conception of space and place offers the chance to make conjunctural analysis simultaneously richer and more demanding. In an interview with Andrew Stevens, Massey gave this elegantly compressed statement of her relational understanding:

'For me, places are articulations of "natural" and social relations, relations that are not fully contained within the place itself. So, first, places are not closed or bounded – which, politically, lays the ground for critiques of exclusivity. Second, places are not "given" – they are always in open-ended process. They are in that sense "events". Third, they and their identity will always be contested (we could almost talk about local-level struggles for hegemony).' (Massey, nd)

This conception of places as articulations of multiple relations makes it possible to think about where the conjuncture takes place in ways that escape the national versus global binary. Instead, we can think of the conjuncture as articulating multiple spatial relations, such that politics come to play out on a terrain that *combines and condenses* multiple places and scales. We can consider the local (the deindustrialised city), the national (the more or less United Kingdom), the regional (the EU) and the global, while recognising that all of these are folded into one another. Massey's use of articulation echoes Stuart Hall and points to the possibility of thinking multiple places (and scales) *together*, rather than as separate entities (whether separated by borders or mechanically nested in scalar hierarchies). And, just as it did for Hall, 'articulation' points up the possibility of change: engaging the dynamics of dis-articulation and rearticulation rather than dealing with permanently fixed entities.

What may be distinctive about *this* conjuncture is the way it foregrounds one of those spatial formations – the nation – as both the focus and setting of political-cultural contestation. The idea of the nation emerged as a focal point for conflict and mobilisations, not least in the proliferation of imaginings of the 'way forward' that demand the restoration of the nation – making X great again. So, both 'Brexit' and the larger Battle for Britain have taken place on *nationalised* terrain. They were enacted through the strained and contradictory apparatuses of a nation-state and were articulated through potent national and nationalist imaginaries. Yet they were hardly 'national' in their causes, conditions or consequences, even as they promised the restoration of a liberated and sovereign nation. This nation was produced as a divided, unequal and contradictory place through complex dynamics which connected – and disrupted – many spaces and scales.

These multiple, overlaid and intersecting dynamics were condensed in lived experiences of dislocation, dispossession and despair that came to be articulated in a variety of forms of political 'disaffection' (Gilbert, 2015). Again, these were not uniquely British – the sense of dislocation and disaffection was widely shared – but they took distinctive national forms. Similarly, the forms of political articulation that brought them to voice as grievances, as a sense of loss or as anti-migrant anger, took specific national shapes and gave voice to distinct and divisive nationalisms. So I want to suggest that, far from the nation being the natural location for these experiences, or nationalism being the normal political response, the nation has been given distinctive salience and significance *conjuncturally*. That is, there was something distinctive about the ways in which the contradictions, forces and dynamics were *articulated* in and around the nation and nation-state. Valluvan points to this specificity when he argues that we are seeing 'the nationalist *overdetermination* particular to the present historical conjuncture' (2019: 15) or, in my terms, contemporary forms of nationalism may be best understood as conjuncturally specific formations, rather than viewing nationalism as a generic political orientation.

This chapter has explored one dimension of thinking conjuncturally. In treating conjunctures as distinct configurations of 'time-space', I hope to have clarified some of the current spatial dimension while keeping time and the dynamics of change in view. Questions of time – and temporality – become the focus of the following chapter (with spatial relations moving into the background). A pointer towards this shift of focus is provided by Goswami's argument that 'we need to think about the ways in which crisis implies, and this is a phrase from Lefebvre (2013), a "conflictual explosion of times". There is a multiplicity and contradictory logic to the temporalities that converge in a "crisis moment"' (2020: 271).

2

# Turbulent Times: The Making
# of the Present

As I argued in the previous chapter, conjunctural analysis is a spatio-temporal approach, exploring the particular configurations of time and place that make up a conjuncture. Somewhat artificially, I focused on the spatial dynamics and dimensions in the last chapter. Here I turn to the challenge of thinking about time. We can catch a glimpse of its complexity by considering the different stories that have been told about Brexit and the Battle for Britain. These narratives operate with different senses of time: some tell us about long histories (of decline or a fall from greatness); others offer fast-paced accounts of quickly moving events (stories of political calculation and manoeuvring). More rarely are these different senses of time brought together – as *multiple temporalities* (different orderings and experiences of time) that co-exist and interact. Felski, for example, has argued that time

> is a concept of enormous complexity, including questions of measurement, rhythm, synchronization, sequence, tempo and intensity. It spans the personal and the public, work and leisure, the instantaneous and the eternal, intimate relations and global structures, everyday life and conditions of extremity. It exists at many different levels and is experienced in radically divergent ways. (2000: 16–17)

Just as Chapter 1 argued that the space of the conjuncture is no simple matter (demanding thinking the nation transnationally), so this chapter will explore the multiple orderings and senses of time that are in play in the conjuncture. Thinking about temporalities, rather than time/times, is a way of trying to treat time as enmeshed in social, political-cultural and economic relations and processes and conflicts. Indeed, I will suggest, it is the intersections and entanglements of these different temporalities – the ways that they come to be *condensed* in the present – that gives the conjuncture its distinctive character. As a result, this chapter is organised around the notion of different temporalities. It will explore the different orderings of time that are associated with particular fields of relationships which have distinctive dynamics of crisis, contestations and (temporary) resolutions. These temporalities are, however, not entirely separate: each provides some of the conditions for the others and is affected in turn by their dynamics. They both enable and interfere with one another. They ensure that the 'now' of a particular conjuncture is always multifaceted, condensing different temporalities and their dynamics and intersections. Temporality matters in another way in the conjuncture, too. It is the focus of political-cultural conflicts as different projects struggle to 'tell the time', to construct persuasive and mobilising narratives, to tell the right version of 'our history', to control the present and to lay claim to the future.

Of course, this book, and this chapter, are not innocent in such matters: they are also ways of 'telling the time'. My attention to different temporalities, my presentation of them and the stories I want to tell about them are implicated in the political-cultural conflicts over time. With that in mind, the chapter begins from the time of the 'Anthropocene' – the way of naming climate change as a human product. The Anthropocene frames the present moment in complex ways – materially and symbolically. From there, the chapter moves to the long history of Empire and the shorter history of decolonisation. These both shape the present conjuncture and have become the focus of struggles over 'our history'. I link the conflicts over race, racialised inequalities and racism to the wider unsettling of the field of the social in the post-war conjuncture – and underline their ongoing significance for the current one.

The chapter then considers the social as a field of 'neoliberal governance' in the current conjuncture: the focus of efforts to create the right sort of people (and to discipline those who failed to 'do the right thing'). I connect this to an examination of the economic trajectory of this conjuncture, centred on the failures and frustrations of the neoliberal dream, and exploring the consolidation of rentier capitalism in the UK. From there, the chapter moves to consider the quickening rhythms of national politics as efforts have been made to manage, contain and exploit the accumulating crises, contradictions and conflicts of the present. The chapter concludes with some more general reflections on the significance of multiple temporalities for thinking conjuncturally.

## Encountering the Anthropocene

When I was first drafting this chapter in 2021, the UK was set to host COP26 (the UN Climate Change Conference) in the face of deepening fears about the climate catastrophe. The UK's hosting of COP26 felt like a perverse coincidence, given the state's nonchalant approach to climate policy and the deep involvement of UK-based finance capital in the fossil fuel industry. The period described as the Anthropocene marks the geological time frame within which human activity has had a significant effect on the planet's climate and ecosystems. For some, this dates from around 8000 BC while others highlight its intensifying effects in the last two centuries:

> We already live in the Anthropocene, so let us get used to this ugly word and the reality that it names. It is our epoch and our condition. This geological epoch is the product of the last few hundred years of history. The Anthropocene is the sign of our power, but also of our impotence. It is an Earth whose atmosphere has been damaged by the 1,500 billion tonnes of carbon dioxide we have spilled by burning coal and other fossil fuels. It is the impoverishment and artificializing of Earth's living tissue, permeated by a host of new synthetic chemical molecules that will even affect our descendants. It is a warmer world with a higher risk of catastrophes, a reduced ice cover, higher sea-levels and a climate out of control. (Bonneuil and Fressoz, 2016: 4)

The 'last few hundred years' identified by Bonneuil and Fressoz points to a more familiar epochal framing: this is the era of capitalism. Indeed, for some commentators, this framing demands a different way of naming the period: the Capitalocene (for example, Moore, 2016). In this view, capital consumes nature, wantonly, carelessly, in its pursuit of constant growth and has driven the planet to the point of collapse. This points to a more specific dynamic and agency (in contrast to the Anthropocene's generalised man/ humanity) focused on the accumulative and exploitative logics of capitalism. It also makes more visible the speeding-up of environmental devastation that has accompanied capitalism's global expansion. There are other ways of naming this epoch, for example, the Plantationocene (Davis et al, 2019) or the Chthulucene (Haraway, 2015): each focuses on different relationships and dynamics between the social and the material. All these framings point to crucial conditions of the conjuncture, even as they operate over much longer time scales. These conditions are active in the conjuncture in particular forms and combinations, not least in how the future of the planet has emerged as a focal point, with a new pace and intensity that demands attention and mobilises new forces.

## Haunted by Empire

The concept of the Plantationocene points to another significant *longue durée* temporality (Braudel, 1958; Braudel and Wallerstein, 2009) that shapes the conjuncture: that of colonialism and the 'unfinished business' of decolonisation. As Deborah Thomas (2019) has argued, it was colonialism, specifically in the form of slavery, that implanted the 'plantation logic' at the heart of European capitalism and its version of globalisation. Despite attempts to make slavery disappear through a 'mercantilist' framing of British imperial history (recycled in Brexiteering claims about Britain as a global trading nation), this logic still echoes into the present. It underpins relations between Britain and its former colonies, sometimes in the recurrent enthusiasm for *repatriation* (sending people of colour 'back to where they came from') or the persistent arguments for *reparations* (to repay the debts of slavery). It is brought to the fore by movements challenging the celebratory memorialisation of the country's colonial past in statues and naming practices, exemplified in Edward Colston's place in Bristol (Beebeejaun, 2021). It circulates through the elaborately racialised categorisation of places, names, body types, cultural competences and languages that run through official and popular discourses and practices in this society (see Fortier (2021) on citizenship's articulation with such formations).

Decolonisation has taken different trajectories in the places connected by that global system: settler-slave societies, such as the US or Brazil, are different in terms of what Omi and Winant (1986) call their 'racial formation' from the old colonial metropoles in Europe or their colonies in the global South. Consequently, specific places in these fields of relations have different trajectories through anti-colonial struggles to the emergent forms of decolonisation. I am not going to try to tell that long and violent story here, but do want to highlight several issues. First, both the business of slavery and the formal abolition of slavery provided a significant financial foundation for the development of industrial capitalism in Britain. Notably, the prices paid by the British government to 'emancipate' the slaves enabled their owners to invest both in lavish lifestyles and in new economic activity (Hall et al, 2016; Hall, 2020). In such ways, 'British capitalism' was always what Cedric Robinson (1983) called 'racial capitalism'. Second, racially subordinated labour never stopped being 'cheap labour' across the whole arc of colonisation and decolonisation: whether in slavery, indentured labour (the preferred system for replacing slaves), or as migrant labour in the period that followed the Second World War (Williams, 2021). This links to a third point about the articulation of those colonial relations through metropolitan states and their organisation of social reproduction. Bhambra (2022) has shown how a view of the British state as profoundly structured by colonial relations can enable a new understanding of the relations between colonies, state forms, systems of citizenship and the economic and social relations of welfare. She argues that 'the territorial boundaries of the British state, as well as its organisational structure, have never been congruent with what many see as the imagined nation and, at times, the imaginary of the *nation*-state has also extended include territories beyond the island or islands' (2022: 5). Her work, along with a growing number of others (for example, Shilliam,

2018; Williams, 2021), points to the importance of examining the shifting articulations of nation, nationality and nationalism.

As Hart (2019) argues, the moment of decolonisation marks the emergence of the first of the post-war conjunctures, conditioned by the variety of national and transnational struggles against colonialism. In the UK, this moment manifested itself as the beginning of sustained migration from the colonies to the 'motherland', symbolised in the arrival of the HMT *Empire Windrush* in 1948 (although this was not the first such ship to arrive from the Caribbean). This was also the year of the British Nationality Act which constructed forms of citizenship for people from the Commonwealth at a point when a series of former colonies were contemplating independence. The Act provided a way of symbolising the Commonwealth as a significant and valuable collectivity, even though – like many 'families' – the emergent Commonwealth was characterised by a series of divisions, stresses and strains (see Hansen, 2000). One of those sites of strain was the anxiety about the arrival in the UK of people from the 'New' Commonwealth (predominantly people of colour from the Indian sub-continent, former African colonies and the Caribbean). People from the 'New' Commonwealth were viewed as *essentially* different – and rather less desirable – from those arriving from the 'Old' Commonwealth, who were predominantly white people from settler-colonial societies such as Australia, Canada and New Zealand. This distinction – and variations on the theme – recurred throughout the regular rewriting of immigration and citizenship law over the next 60 years in ways that built on the anxieties about 'aliens' first formalised in the Aliens Act of 1905 (Fortier, 2021).

That resulting commitment to changing the conditions and character of citizenship and migration bears the marks of both Britain's obsession with 'race' and Britain's location in a shifting transnational field of mobility. A series of Acts from the 1960s onwards revealed the persistent concern with who was entitled to be a British citizen: notably, the Commonwealth Immigration Acts of 1962 and 1968, the Immigration Act of 1971, the Immigration, Asylum and Nationality Act of 2006 and the Immigration and Asylum Act of 2014. These issues underline a key part of Gilroy's argument about the condition of 'postcolonial melancholia' in which the UK is enfolded. He argues:

> Britain's inability to mourn its loss of empire and accommodate the empire's consequences developed slowly. Its unfolding revealed an extensively fragmented national collective that has not been able to meet the elemental challenge represented by the social, cultural and political transition with which the presence of postcolonial and other sanctuary seeking people has been unwittingly bound up. Instead, racist violence provides an easy means to 'purify' and rehomogenize

the nation. As one might anticipate, postimperial and postcolonial melancholia characteristically intercut this violence and the shame-faced tides of self-scrutiny and self-loathing that follow among decent folk, with outbursts of manic euphoria. (2005: 102)

The continuing drive to control immigration is never free of this shadow; while one effect of the shifting landscape of migration (in which different types and trajectories of migration are combined) is the creation of a strangely multifaceted image of the Migrant. This kaleidoscopic image shifts: from the Romanian agricultural worker to the Filipina nurse; from the Jamaican Yardie to the Muslim terrorist; from the Polish plumber to the exploitative 'health tourist'. But this imagery is always a 'rogues gallery', marked by difference of some kind or another (bodies, cultures, languages) which ensures that they are linked by not being 'really British'. This mix of shifting images and persistent foundations in the meaning system of British post-colonial racism was captured by Gary Younge just after the Brexit referendum: 'For decades, the issue of race (the colour of people) and immigration (the movement of people) have been neatly interwoven, as though they are one and the same thing – as though "British" people are not also black and black people are not British' (2016). This long trajectory of the post-colonial period has kept racialised differences in a central role in the British social formation and has given rise to a distinctive political-cultural effect, ensuring that its crises are often saturated with matters of 'race': from the endless question of immigration through the threat of street crime to riots in English cities or the current focus on 'our' history.

This effect crystallised distinctively in the assault on the 'Windrush generation' (Gentleman, 2019; Goodfellow, 2019). The government's commitment to driving out 'illegal' migrants involved the creation of a 'hostile environment' by then Home Secretary, Theresa May. The policy trapped long-settled Caribbean migrants and their families. Brexit was in part animated by this history – another reworking of what Lewis calls the 'now you see it, now you don't' character of British racism (2000: chapter 2). 'Race' continued as an organising principle of British society: the ongoing conflicts over racialised policing (stop and search; the use of weapons against black people; deaths in police custody and more), the inequalities of vulnerability to COVID-19; the demands to 'decolonise' British culture; and the global effects of the murder of George Floyd. I will return to these more recent interruptions and eruptions around 'race' in later chapters, but it is important to note the temporality imposed by the unfinished business of decolonisation across different conjunctures. It brings a distinct rhythm: reappearing to reframe particular moments, enfolding them in the collective psychodrama of melancholia and its oscillations between regret and rage. It intersects and is potently entangled with other temporalities in the making of this conjuncture, most evidently in the shifting formations of the social. It also underlines just how densely space and time are condensed together in the making of conjunctures.

## The unsettled social

Discussions of *social* history have all too often followed on from the 'big' histories of political and economic change, marking the social as the epiphenomenal froth on the surface of the deep movements of history. For many reasons, that seems an inappropriate response to the field of the social, in which social relations, identities, difference and connections are mapped, contested and subjected to constant efforts to regulate, govern and manage them. The social is, in short, the domain in which lives are lived in an unstable mix of material and imagined forms. Catherine Hall has explored how the making of social differences was central to the colonial project: 'Marking differences was a way of classifying, of categorising, of constructing boundaries for the body politic and the body social' (2002: 17). In the post-war period, the arrival of migrants from the 'New Commonwealth' generated a novel focus of governmental anxiety and intervention: the field of 'race relations' (embodied in the Race Relations Acts of 1965 and 1968: see Khan, 2015). That governmental anxiety was addressed to two different dynamics: white hostility towards, and discrimination against, these 'incomers', and black people's collective organisation to demand the rights owed to them as British citizens and subjects. Progress towards the latter has been slow and regularly overturned (as evidenced by the 'Windrush generation' scandal), while the former has passed through different phases, but has never subsided.

It is possible to see this emergence of 'race' as the focus for one of several social movements in the 1950s and 1960s that began to challenge the *social ordering* of British society. An anti-racist politics emerged that was committed to refuting the inherited imperial orthodoxy on race as a civilisational and biological hierarchy. It was followed by other movements, connected, although not necessarily united, by a deconstructionist politics, seeking to undo a *naturalised* normative order and its matrix of subordinations, exclusions and oppressions. The emergence of second wave feminism challenged patriarchy as a system founded on myths of male superiority and dominance; gay and lesbian movements contested the biological and psychological conceptions of perversion and deviance that underpinned social, economic, legal and political exclusions and subordinations. Subsequently, the movements of disabled people mounted parallel challenges to the myths of 'handicap' and 'incapacity' that had legitimated policies and practices ranging from incarceration to sterilisation. While each of these is a distinctive struggle with its own history, they are connected by this commitment to unlock *naturalising* justifications for subordination. Particularly visible in the field of citizenship, these movements often articulated demands for full membership in the society, refusing the conditions of 'second-class' citizenship in all its guises. Denaturalising these differences (and the varieties of inequality in which they were enacted) was the condition for being able to imagine – and enact – these relationships differently (see, for example, Clarke, 2004; Isin, 2008). Gail Lewis has argued that:

> social differences are formed in the dynamic interplay between domination and the struggle against it; between the attempt to establish the boundaries of the normal and attempts to dislodge and/or expand those boundaries; between the attempts to limit the criteria of access to resources (including those of welfare) and the struggle to breach or replace those criteria. (2003: 98)

These social movements challenged normative social ordering across a wide range of institutional domains: economic (struggles for employed equalities); legal (for forms of recognition as legal subjects); political (against forms of exclusion); and cultural (over forms of representation). They have been frequently dismissed (from the Left and Right) as merely 'identity politics' but they contributed in potent ways to what *Policing the Crisis* (Hall et al, 2013) called the 'crisis of social authority' that emerged during the 1970s in the UK. They continued in the current conjuncture, not least as the focus of efforts to roll back their victories or attempts to incorporate them into dominant formations (individualised and framed by a conception of 'diversity'). Such movements have also been revived and renewed as focal points of struggle – and have been joined by other counter movements (from the environment to trans politics). The forms and focal points certainly differ somewhat across the two periods – as does the character of the dominant response. And each has its own contested history, in which narratives of progress, incorporation and erasure collide (for example, MacLeavy et al (2021) on 'feminist futurity'). But movements contending the social have forged a key temporality, animating the conjuncture and connecting different domains within it.

## A neoliberal social?

Many accounts of neoliberalism have stressed its combination of anti-welfarism and anti-statism and its attempted replacement of the 'dependent' welfare subject by an independent and entrepreneurial individual (for example, Petersen et al, 1999). However, this emphasis on its individualising dynamic misses something important about the strategies that emerged in the new conjuncture for reforming the social. In the UK, this individualising dynamic is often referenced to the Thatcher dictum that 'there is no such thing as society'. But it is important to remember that this claim concluded: 'there are only individual men and women *and their families*' (my emphasis). This coupling of individualism and familialism formed a central site of articulations between neoliberalism and moral conservatism in both Thatcherism and Reaganism. It was a potent resource for reasserting 'traditional authority' and for refusing claims for social transformation (for example, in Thatcherite attacks on the 'pretend families' of gay and lesbian households).

However, the persistence of social movements into the 1980s and 1990s regularly interrupted the efforts of such restorationist politics and policies. At different points, concessions were made (in equal opportunities legislation, for example) while by the mid-1990s other social forms, such as 'community', were being emphasised as both subjects and sites of governing. Crucially, the idea(l) of community was central to Tony Blair's understanding of 'social-ism' as opposed to socialism (drawing on Christian and communitarian conceptions: see Worrad-Andrews, 2015). As Rose has argued, community became a central connective point for politics and governing strategies:

> Community constitutes a new spatialization of government: the territory for political programmes, both at the micro-level and the macro-level, for government through community. ... And in the name of community, a whole variety of groups and forces make their demands, wage their campaigns, stand up for their rights and enact their resistances. (1999: 135–136)

Governing through community was central to the period of New Labour rule (Cochrane, 2007). It seemed equally important for the Conservative–Liberal Democratic coalition that came to power in 2010, one of whose early themes was the 'Big Society' (Clarke, 2011; Somerville, 2011).

*The social*, then, has been a recurrently contested and reimagined field of relations, distinctions and differences. It might be treated as the object of either a specific class compromise (for example, Donzelot, 1984) or a specific form of governmentality (Rose, 1999). However, I think it is more productive to think of it as a field that is subject to shifting and conflicting 'mappings' in which its composition and configuration are represented, practised and lived in different ways. The outcomes of such contentions become embedded in government policies and practices, ranging from the law (community policing) to welfare (community care) and from urban policy (community planning) to economic planning (the Tory Party's recent commitment to 'levelling up'). Such institutionalisations are the traces left by 'social conquests' (Bourdieu, 1999: 33), registering the compromises emerging from political conflicts. At times, they involve accommodation or attempted incorporation (institutionalisations of equality and diversity, for example); at others, they involve the repression of specific struggles.

Thatcherite authoritarian populism was mainly directed towards repression – across the complete field of social struggles from industrial militancy to gay liberation. The expansion and intensification of policing were followed (in the 1990s) by a rapid expansion of the prison population as the UK developed its capacities as a carceral state. But repression was also always in the service of a moral order that valued 'tradition', 'authority' and 'discipline'. This led to what Theresa May was later to call the image problem of the Conservative Party: 'There's a lot we need to do in this party of ours. Our base is too narrow and so, occasionally, are our sympathies. You know what some people call us – the Nasty Party' (speech to Conservative Party Conference, October 2002). For a while, David Cameron toyed with 'humanising' the party before the English urban riots of 2011 persuaded him that before he could build the 'Big Society', he had to confront the 'broken society'. He identified this breakage as the result of *moral*, rather than economic or social, conditions – the sort of 'demoralisation' that conservative critics have identified as the result of dependency-inducing statism and welfarism (Murray, 1984).

The social has remained unsettled. Incorporative strategies proved profoundly contradictory, both frustrating their supposed beneficiaries with a lack of progress (for example, equal pay legislation) and producing a sense of grievance among groups who felt that their rights (or privileges) were being undermined by 'politically correct' initiatives. As I will argue in Chapter 5, these felt grievances were important in the assembling of the 'Brexit bloc'. At the same time, there have also been emergent challenges that have further unsettled the social, around migration and citizenship, environmental challenges, gender and sexuality, such that restorationist politics have remained contested. As hinted at above, such struggles intersect with the domain of the economy in significant ways but have their own distinctive temporality across the long post-war period, interrupting and intersecting with other fields.

## Failures and frustrations: the turbulent trajectory of neoliberal dreams

Deeply interwoven with the dynamics of decolonisation and the struggles to transform the social after the Second World War is the strange temporality of 'British capitalism' (a rather misleading naming, as I noted in the previous chapter). This might be best framed as a long series of accelerating crises, centred on a persistent dynamic of frustration and failure, from the attenuated and stumbling version of 'Fordism' (Jessop, 2014) elaborated in the 1950s and 1960s to the recurrently broken promises of neoliberal transformation.

Even allowing for the contradictory character of capitalism in general, the British version of Fordism was particularly flawed and uneven. The post-war period saw the British economy recurrently described as the 'sick man of Europe': experiencing low economic growth, low investment and low productivity. UK governments sought diverse solutions to this relative decline – from the promise of Harold Wilson's 'white heat of technology' in 1963 to attempts to join the European Economic Community (EEC), twice rebuffed by President de Gaulle (see the account in Anderson, 2021b). *Policing the Crisis* traced the accumulating contradictions and crises of British capitalism in the 1960s and 1970s, arguing that all capitalist economies undertook a process of reconstruction in the post-war period and that:

> Britain attempted such a deep transformation, too – on the basis, we suggest, of an extremely weak and vulnerable industrial and economic base. ... Its success was extremely limited and short-lived. Britain, in these late capitalist terms, remains unevenly developed, permanently stuck in 'the transition'. The effects of this stalemate position, this uncompleted transition, have been experienced at every level of society in the period since. (Hall et al, 2013: 310–311)

Atlantic Fordism required a distinctive form of what Jessop (1990) calls 'societalization': the conditions that would ensure its social reproduction. In the UK, this cannot be understood as just the expanded welfare state but also involved the complex articulation of desired formations of family, work and nation (Williams, 1989). This version of the social foregrounded the full male employment that promised the 'family wage' necessary to maintain the patriarchal nuclear family, imagined as white despite the growing significance of black and Asian labour, in both industrial production and the expanding welfare state. Being 'stuck in the transition' was experienced at every level: its strains were manifested in the growing challenges to racial subordination, to the confines of the family, and even to the promised consumerist future as the counter-culture took shape through its critiques of the fantasies of 'progress'. All of this, as *Policing the Crisis* detailed at length, intersected with the deepening of industrial militancy over wages, working conditions, control in the workplace and equal pay.

As we know now, it was Thatcherism – with its idiosyncratic mixture of neoliberalism and authoritarian populism – that seized the time. It promised solutions to the whole range of Britain's problems: from trade union power to 'alien cultures'; from street crime to an exhausted economy; from public spending to the thwarted desire to exercise choice (on this last point, see Judith Williamson's (1986) important and prefigurative argument about 'Consuming Passions' and the desire to exercise control). The 1979 election victory did not mark the arrival of neoliberalism in the UK but certainly moved its ideas to the centre of both political rhetoric and government policy-making. In the following decades, the assaults on trade unionism combined with the privatisation of public goods (from North Sea oil and gas to council houses) and the deregulation of financial capital to 'liberate' Britain's entrepreneurial spirit. Shifting the 'tax burden' freed capital from some of its state-imposed 'shackles' and created greater disposable income, at least for those still in employment after the first waves of deindustrialisation in the 1980s (as unemployment rocketed and the basis for calculating the unemployment figures was changed to conceal the full costs of 'liberalisation'). Public services were ransacked as potential sources for capital accumulation (through contracting out and privatisation) and where they were not likely to be profitable were subject to the discipline of mechanisms intended to mimic markets (see, inter alia, Clarke and Newman, 1997).

Despite the celebration of Thatcherism as one of the success stories of neoliberalisation, the UK experienced a contradictory and profoundly *uneven* form of development – with the effects of the 'shock therapy' of deindustrialisation and deunionisation still visible across the social and political landscape (marking the point at which those now called the 'left behind' were thrown from the speeding train – privatised, of course – of neoliberal progress). Tax cuts and more readily accessible credit masked the slide towards stalled (and then declining) wages – as did the shift towards a 'dual earner family' model of household income. A crucial dynamic in this period was the rapid deepening of both income and wealth inequalities, driven by a complex combination of changing taxation to indirect forms rather than progressive taxes on wealth and income, the rise of unemployment, under-employment and precarious employment combined with those stalled or declining wage levels. At the same time, the 'British' economy was inserted into new transnational networks and flows (Edgerton, 2019). This was most evident in the articulation of finance and the rise of London as a 'world city' (Massey, 2007). It also shaped the attraction of inward investment into other services and industry (most dramatically in the residues of steel-making and the automobile industry – tied into both international capital and international model design). And, despite Thatcher's rhetorical concern about being 'swamped' by 'alien cultures', the UK continued to find expanding uses for migrant labour in the increasingly privatised social care sector, health care, hospitality and agriculture.

The trajectory of neoliberalisation in the UK was punctuated by regular crises – economic, fiscal, political – that typically hinged on the failure of the promises of unbroken growth and plenty to materialise. These culminated in the global financial crisis of 2007–08 and the (apparent) necessity of bailing out financial institutions. The response to the financial crisis (in the UK as elsewhere) was driven by the familiar promise to restore growth – the projected natural condition of 'business as usual'. This growth-centric conception of capitalism is inextricably tied to its destructive effects on people and the planet. It requires the sustained extraction of resources from a depleted environment, sustained extraction of labour power and sustained extraction of profit from hyper-consumption. The attempt to recover 'business as usual' launched a new wave of (indebted) consumption into the next decade and perpetuated the unstable dynamics of the economy, politics and social relations. Popular responses to the climate crisis emerged, challenging excess consumption, excess production and – with increasing visibility – government subsidies to, and financial investment in, fossil fuels.

In writing this book, I have found myself returning to the idea of an *accumulation* of problems – crises, contradictions, tensions, conflicts and antagonisms – despite dominant efforts to manage or contain them, or even to exploit them. Treating the trajectory of neoliberalism in such terms illuminates one dynamic of the conjuncture – in which the failures of Fordism were succeeded by the failures of neoliberalism, creating an economy that is simultaneously dominated and stalled by rentier capital. Following Piketty (2014), Christophers has examined how rentierism (the seeking of rent from assets possessed or controlled property, monopoly market positions, intellectual property, or even government contracts) became the dominant force in UK capitalism. This produced an economic disposition centred, as he puts it, on 'proprietorialism' rather than 'entrepreneurialism' (2020: xviii). He argues that this asset-focused model has had profound consequences for economic development: 'If investment, and especially R&D investment, is falling, and if growth in labour productivity is also slowing, there can be really only one outcome: a slowdown in the economy as a whole; that is to say, declining growth in economic output' (2020: 35).

This economy was kept afloat by the dominance of international finance and massive levels of consumer indebtedness (despite the 2007–08 experience). Yet it has been unable to provide workers with a living wage, requiring governmental subsidies to manage growing levels of working poverty (Innes, 2021). Nonetheless, this form of capital accumulation has been articulated through a political-cultural commitment to 'wealth'. The *imaginary* of wealth enables an equivalence to be constructed between corporations, billionaires, home owners and pensioners around a projected common interest in the accumulation and preservation of wealth.

As Tony Jefferson pointed out to me in an email about a draft of this chapter, these different temporalities are not just a swirl of shifting issues, facets, developments; they are not a kaleidoscopic arrangement of many things. Rather, each temporality has both its own trajectory and intersects in multiple ways with the others – creating conditions, generating interferences, adding weight to some dynamics while interrupting others. So, it should not be possible to say 'capitalism' without understanding it as always, already 'racial capitalism', even as its forms of racialisation shift. It makes no sense to talk of the economy as a disembedded entity (the fantasy of neoliberal economists and propagandists (Grossberg, 2010: 317)) but as a set of relations and processes that are always social – and socially formed in specific and contested ways.

## New acts in the 'theatre of politics'

*Policing the Crisis* traced the multiple crises in the 1970s, noting that 'where the political struggle issues into the "theatre of politics", it has been experienced as a crisis of "Party"' (Hall et al, 2013: 317). The Conservative Party, reinvented by Thatcher and others as part of an Atlantic New Right, resolved one facet of this crisis, enabling it to both serve as the party of business and respond to the People's (projected) deep desire for the reassertion of authority and moral order. Thatcherism's version of populism involved what might be described as a *moral authoritarianism*, centred on 'traditional values' and sought to both construct and speak for social groups who could imagine themselves as 'middle class' (echoed later in John Major's desire to create a 'classless society'). This was materially enacted through the privatisation of public goods, including the sale of council houses and public share issues to sell off utilities such as gas and water. Such strategies aimed to create a 'property owning democracy' that would bring into being what Christophers (2020: 42–45) describes as *petits rentiers*. Such 'proprietors' were expected to support tax and other policies that would defend their investments (in shares, pensions and, most importantly, property). Despite its external and internal contradictions, the Thatcherite version of the Conservative Party ruled until 1997. The other parties – especially the Labour Party – experienced a much longer drawn out version of the crisis of party. Labour was out of power for 18 years, experimenting with, and discarding, a series of leaders (Callaghan, Kinnock, Foot, Smith) before Blair's invention of 'New Labour' and its mission to 'modernise' Britain (Clarke and Newman, 2004).

In this sense, Thatcherism (and its transatlantic Reaganite shadow) marked a turning point, reassembling economic, social and political forces into new alignments – the nearest we have to a way of describing the shift to a new conjuncture. That reassembling constructs the 'problem space' of the new conjuncture and its elements define the focal concerns that confronted and were worked over by shifting political parties. Such rearrangements generated new fault lines of their own. In the Conservative case, they emerged from the centralising drive to reorganise the local state (abolishing Labour strongholds in the Greater London Council and the metropolitan authorities). This logic brought with it the ill-fated 'Poll Tax' as a regressive system of local taxation, which provoked refusals, resistance and riots and, ultimately, the end of Thatcher, if not Thatcherism (Hannah, 2020). The attempted post-Thatcher renewal of the Conservatives ended in the fiasco of John Major's 'Back to Basics' attempt at a moralising authoritarian populism in 1993.

Major's government attacked rights of assembly (affecting rave culture gatherings and trades unions among others), pilloried 'single mothers' as the cause of moral breakdown and proceeded with the programme to privatise the public realm, including the Private Finance Initiative (PFI) and the privatisation of the railways. The Major government collapsed in a stench of moral hypocrisy, as a series of sex scandals involving members of parliament were revealed. New Labour's 'modernisation' avoided this nostalgic moralism but did little to change either the economic model inherited from Thatcherism (making extensive use of PFI) or the authoritarian use of state power to criminalise those who failed to be either responsible or modern enough, particularly the working class and working-class mothers (see Burney, 2005).

New Labour is often viewed as combining a continuation of social and economic neoliberalism with some 'social democratic' remedial work, in the form of increased public spending on services (health, education, and so on) and significant constitutional changes (in Northern Ireland, Scotland and Wales). It also substituted a model of 'modern' social tolerance of 'diversity' for the moral authoritarianism of Thatcher and Major, promoting a conception of a modern society as multicultural and egalitarian in social norms. However, this does not quite capture the full contradictory complexity of the New Labour project (Steinberg and Johnson, 2004). One critical dimension missing from this view is the extension of coercive state powers, through criminalisation of a range of behaviours and subjects at the intersection of 'anti-social behaviour' and the 'war on terror' after the events of 9/11. The discourses and practices of coercion that had emerged in the 1970s and 80s were extended and put on steroids (Kennedy, 2005; Coleman et al, 2009). What *Policing the Crisis* had called an 'exceptional' – or Law and Order – state became thoroughly *normalised*. The Thatcher and Major Conservative governments and those of New Labour shared a commitment to deploying – and deepening – the coercive capacities of the state. However, the expanding apparatuses of crime control and surveillance failed – perhaps predictably – to reduce public anxieties. On the contrary, such anxiety was constantly revitalised in a vicious circle of popular media and authoritarian populist politics announcing the seemingly permanent crisis of 'law and order'.

This is a critical point of intersection with the growing significance of 'security' as a related figure through which crises, coercion, consent and power were reworked into new formations particularly after 9/11 (for example, Huysmans, 2006). Security names the problem of both external and internal threats – terrorists who may attack the West/ Civilisation/The Free World/Our Country from anywhere, including from 'within' the nation. Policing the security crisis involves external interventions (from wars to 'police actions'), the intensification of borders and their policing (Balibar, 2003; Yuval-Davis et al, 2019) and the deepening of domestic surveillance and interventions in relation to suspect populations (for example, Maskovsky and Ruben, 2008). Given *Policing the Crisis*'s roots in Birmingham, the complexities of this surveillance mode were exemplified in the erection of a proclaimed 'ring of steel' (of security cameras) around the predominantly Muslim areas of Sparkbrook and Washwood Heath in 2010, publicly legitimated as a measure against crime and anti-social behaviour, but funded by, and supplying information to, the government's anti-terrorism programme (Lewis, 2010; more generally, see Graham, 2010). The network was partially dismantled following a public outcry about this wilful conflation of purposes and populations.

New Labour's trajectory reflected the deepening crises of social democracy across Europe and North America, following its exhaustion as the dominant political formation that had secured consent for the development and management of Atlantic Fordism. Social democracy's mutation – in the proliferation of 'Third Ways' – became one of the political forms through which popular consent to the programme of constant innovation – and failures – of neoliberalism was managed, and which led to its second 'exhaustion'. This was also the period in which the UK Labour Party reinvented itself in *organisational* ways, reducing its mass bases, constructing new constituencies (the new middle classes, especially) while losing its hold on its older working-class support. In the same period, Jeremy Gilbert (2015) has suggested that the relationships of consent became more conditional. What he has called the rise of 'disaffected consent' emerged from the limits and contradictions of the New Labour project and the transition to the Conservative-led coalition that came to power in 2010.

The financial crisis of 2008 raised the possibility of different political and economic futures, largely resolved by the view that just as banks were 'too big to be allowed to fail', so capitalism needed to be saved from itself, even at the expense of vast amounts of public financial investment. This investment provided both the material rescue package needed and the ideological ground for a redefinition of the nature of the crisis. It was reimagined as a *fiscal* crisis (of public finances) rather than a *financial* one (located in finance capital). Along with many other states (and vigorously encouraged by international agencies such as the International Monetary Fund (IMF)), the Cameron-led Coalition government of 2010–15 launched itself on a commitment to 'fiscal realism' and 'austerity', while promising to build a 'Big Society' and reforming/dismantling welfare (Clarke and Newman, 2012; Blyth, 2013). As Peck has argued, austerity politics and policies occupied a central, yet fraught, space in the continuing saga of neoliberalism:

> Austerity has become a strategic space for the contradictory reproduction of market rule, calling attention to the ways in which neoliberal rationalities have been resuscitated, reanimated and to some degree rehabilitated in the wake of the Wall Street crash of 2008–2009. ... Beyond its internal contradictions, austerity urbanism has already become a site of struggle in its own right. ... What can be said, for now, is that if austerity defines a new normal, it is a state of normalcy at the very cusp of crisis. (2012: 651)

Cameron's coalition operated in this liminal space – on the cusp of crisis – while attempting to revitalise the dominant political strategy: finding new ways to combine neoliberalism with authoritarian populism, committed to restoring 'business as usual' while leading an assault on the poor and marginalised in the name of social authority, and claiming to 'liberate' them to be both entrepreneurial and responsible (Clarke, 2014; Forkert, 2017). The government's reaction to urban riots in England in 2011 deepened the authoritarian aspect of this combination, with demands for a policing and judicial crackdown, while promising (once again) a 'moral renewal' of British society (Jefferson, 2015). Meanwhile, the British economy failed to progress – in all too familiar ways.

In recent years, the dominant institutions of politics and corporations have begun to shift their stance on the climate crisis from denial and avoidance to regretful acknowledgement, accompanied by promises to change their ways. However, as Carrington (2021) has recently argued, these promises tend to be a strategy of deferral – a 'greenwashing' that 'talks the talk' while continuing to postpone effective action. Perhaps more significantly it has led to mobilisations and manifestations – often involving new actors and new forms of protest, such as the 'schoolkids strikes'. In the UK, Extinction Rebellion (XR) became a dramatic focus for political action – literally, in terms of its performative style of politics that sought to make a drama out of a crisis. These emerging international and national mobilisations in defence of the planet were met by an unstable mixture of praise and support on the one hand, and a revival of authoritarianism on the other. Toby Young, writing in *The Spectator*, argued: 'If children really must wag their fingers at older generations for some imaginary sin, I wish they'd do it at the weekend. Better yet, they could combine it with picking up litter, which really might do something for the environment' (2019). This view was apparently shared by Gavin Williamson, then Secretary of State for

Education, who insisted that children should not be 'bunking off school' (see Evans, 2019).

Meanwhile, the impact of XR (and other forms of activism) was one of the forces leading the Johnson government to develop a substantial increase in police powers to control public protest, especially protest deemed likely to cause a 'public nuisance' (even if that protest involved only one person). The nuisance test in the Police, Crime, Sentencing and Courts Act 2022 created a significant extension of police power (the previous threshold involved the risk of 'serious' disruption, damage or danger). Not for the first time, we encounter the strategy of *policing* the crisis.

## The conjuncture and multiple temporalities

In this chapter, I have argued that it is important to view a conjuncture as composed of multiple temporalities rather than being shaped by a singular line of development. My choice to trace them as separate strands has enabled me to focus on some distinctive trajectories but made it harder to keep their intersections and entanglements in view. Even so, I hope to have shown some of the ways in which the conjuncture has been shaped by the ways in which these strands intersect, affecting and interrupting one another, or coalesce to produce potential turning points. These multiple temporalities certainly have different durations and rhythms: even the longest of *longues durées* – the Anthropocene – has quickened its rhythm and affected the trajectory of the current conjuncture with increasing intensity. Each particular temporality also forms part of the conditions of possibility for others – no 'British capitalism' without the long history of Empire; no British social formation that is not deeply conditioned by the inheritances of colonialism; no systems of 'work and welfare' that are not articulated to imaginaries of the Family (and the multiple realities of its everyday relationships and practices). Similarly, specific temporalities interfere with and interrupt others. So, the Anthropocene's evocation of resistance and reaction has interfered with 'business as usual', generating adaptations and accommodations (if not substantive change) and has evoked responses in the political–cultural field – from new activist mobilisations to the enlargement of government powers to contain and control protest.

In many analyses of the UK, the economy serves as the *normalised* temporality around which other times are subordinated or suppressed. At its simplest, this is the story of the 'British economy' – its trials and tribulations – around which everything else struggles to find a place. This story delivers a particular type of rhythm – what used to be called 'boom and bust' but might better be called the cycle of crisis, retrenchment and crisis renewed. This chapter was deliberately organised in a way that puts other temporalities and their trajectories in the foreground, changing the visibility of different aspects of the social formation, and bringing their effects into view – including the different tensions, crises and antagonisms they create for those trying to govern.

This overview of multiple temporalities has tried to emphasise two things that are vital for understanding the current conjuncture. First, this conjuncture was formed in crucial ways by inheritances from its predecessors, especially the post-war/Cold War conjuncture that preceded it. Although the national and global shifts that marked 1979–80 promised to overcome older contradictions, conflicts and crises, many of them persisted – from economic decline to contestations of the normative social order. Second, the 'solutions' that were proposed – the profoundly unstable combination of neoliberalisation and authoritarian populism – have framed the shifting efforts to resolve, manage or exploit the proliferating crises and conflicts of the following 40-plus years – and remain the preferred choices as I write (in late 2022). The rest of the book explores these dynamics but, first, a brief pause for thought about the challenges of thinking conjuncturally.

# Pause for Thought 1: The Conjuncture as Space and Time

My decision to separate space and time in the preceding two chapters has been both artificial and unsustainable. It proved impossible to write about the shifting arrangements and alignments of places, not least the more or less United Kingdom, without encountering their tendency to shift – as relationships, processes, imaginaries and institutions changed. And it has also been impossible to write about different temporalities without recognising that they 'take place' – happening in particular places and in the relationships between those places. Nevertheless, I think the separation has been useful, given that neither space nor time is simple to discuss. But then the next challenge emerges – how to think conjuncturally in ways that pay attention to both space and time.

For me, it is useful to think of these multiple relationships and dynamics as being *condensed* in the making of the present conjuncture. The idea of being condensed is intended to emphasise something of the effects of compression – the squeezing of this multiplicity into the confines of the 'here and now' brings tensions, pressures, distortions and antagonisms into being in the process. This view also implies treating the conjuncture as being simultaneously overdetermined and underdetermined. It is always *overdetermined* (in the Freudian/Althusserian sense) by the constitutive co-presence of many heterogeneous forces, tendencies, contradictions and antagonisms: there is no singular cause or motive force that makes history move. A conjuncture is always what Hall (2003, following Marx, 1857/1973) called a 'unity in difference', rather than a simple or expressive totality. At the same time, it is necessarily *underdetermined* in its multiple lines of possibility: there are different potential resolutions of the current troubles that might be assembled into political projects and enacted by a political bloc if it can assemble sufficient support or consent. For me, it is exactly this sense of multiplicity and possibility that insists we refuse reductive or deterministic readings of a crisis or its resolution.

This leaves a further question – if conjunctures are marked by this sort of heterogeneity, how do we recognise them? How can we identify what coheres to form a conjuncture, and how do we know when a new one emerges? This is one of the long-running – and unresolved – challenges of conjunctural analysis. My starting point is to resist two obvious temptations: the view that conjunctures can be framed, on the one hand, in economic terms or, on the other, as shifts in the realm of politics. Both rely on reductive views of the conjuncture and marginalise other dynamics. Instead, I think we might turn to Gramsci's observation about the 'life of the state' and his suggestion that it may be viewed as 'a series of unstable equilibria' (1971: 182) – evoking an oscillation between multiple, intersecting and interwoven moments of equilibrium and their destabilisation as contradictions, crises and antagonisms accumulate. Such unsettled and unsettling moments create the *possibility* of movement from one conjuncture to another as new ways forward are proposed, mobilised by political projects, enacted by political blocs and alliances and come to command consent – or fail to do so. This is always the space of possibility in which alternative projects and blocs might be constructed, though there are no guarantees that they will be, or that they will succeed.

In this view, neither the 'economy' nor the 'theatre of politics' exists outside the social formation of which they are part and the other sites of antagonism and settlement that compose it. So, I follow Hart's view (2019) of a conjuncture that was formed in the period 1945–48. This can certainly be imagined in narrowly economic or political-economic terms: it is the moment that inaugurates 'Atlantic Fordism' and its mix of a managed national economy and social welfare. Yet that would be to ignore its other, equally vital, dynamics and settlements – from the inauguration of the Cold War, the tripartite division of 'worlds' (first, second and third), the violent trajectories of decolonisation, or the attempted institutionalisation of a 'normal family' at the intersection of waged work and welfare. Those settlements were, of course, under strain from the very moment of their inauguration – but the crises accumulated and forms of dissent multiplied from the mid-1960s onwards, culminating in the 'crisis of hegemony' that *Policing the Crisis* traced during the 1970s.

In that sense, 1979 can be seen as marking the transition from one conjuncture to the next not because of the arrival of Thatcherism or neoliberalism, but because it marks a profound shift in the larger 'life of the state' – in its apparatuses and their relations to the whole social formation: from the management of migration to the restoration of 'traditional authority'; from the reordering of the relationship between the social and the economic all the way to the programme of 'creative destruction' visited on the thing called the national economy. The new settlements combined neoliberalism with an authoritarian populism in ways that framed the following decades, despite the proliferating crises, the accumulating contradictions, and the multiplication of new and old forms and sites of dissent. That combination of authoritarian populism and neoliberalism certainly shifts as new variants are invented and new compromises or concessions are offered. This long conjuncture has seen continuing attempts to manage consent across all facets of the social formation, combining innovation, incorporation and repression – but always on the basis of distinguishing who will be included in the 'people' (to be rewarded, or at least praised, for being responsible, enterprising, striving, hard-working, and law-abiding wealth creators – or hoarders) and who will be marked for attention from the state's expanding coercive capabilities.

In this view, the Battle for Britain appears as a result of the accumulated contradictions, crises and antagonisms of this conjuncture – as enacted in a particular configuration of space-time. Their promised resolution was expressed in the fantastical claim that everything could be resolved by 'taking back control'. This promise came to fruition (in one sense) in the arrival of the Johnson government in 2019 with its massive parliamentary majority. However, this was simultaneously a moment marked by the deeper entrenching of divisions and antagonisms, the growing accumulation of unresolved contradictions, the growing geopolitical splintering of the UK and proliferating forms of dissent and disaffection. The question is whether the moment of the 'Boris bloc' (Clarke, 2020a) marked the *end* of a trajectory – even before the arrival of the pandemic. Did it represent the exhaustion of a nostalgic, authoritarian, defence of the propertied – the proprietors – against the rest? Or was it a project to construct *new* settlements, built around the promise of binding together the 'left behind' and the 'affluent Eurosceptics' around a fantasy of making Britain Great again? If so, did the government and state have the capacity to stabilise such settlements – to create a new equilibrium? The remaining chapters will explore these questions, although by the time you read them, the answers may be painfully obvious.

3

# Accounting for Brexit

The need to think conjuncturally is nowhere better demonstrated than in the moment of Brexit. Accounting for Brexit has tended to take simplifying forms, ranging from a focus on manoeuvring within the Conservative Party to the grand global explanations centred on neoliberal capitalism. In this chapter I explore three ways of locating and explaining Brexit as exemplifications of the problems of focusing on one dynamic. I address explanations that treat Brexit as one example of a wider global rise of populist politics, explanations that centre on the disruptive and dislocating effects of neoliberal globalisation, and finally, explanations that treat the Brexit vote as the reactions of the 'left behind' in the UK. Each of the lines of argument to be explored here – populism, neoliberalism and the 'left behind' – has provided organising narratives for the phenomenon of Brexit and its afterlife.

These accounts focus on and amplify particular causes for Brexit and have helped to shape popular 'common sense' about what Brexit means. Given how Brexit has shaped the political and cultural landscape, the sheer weight of attention devoted to it is not surprising and nor is the effort that has gone into solidifying particular explanations into narratives of what this means for Britain, Europe, or even the world. Let me be clear: my argument here is not that there has been no rise of populism as a political formation, nor that neoliberalism has not reshaped the world in important ways. But to focus on such dynamics as the explanatory framing of Brexit precisely misses the conjunctural complexity that I have been drawing out in the preceding chapters – and with it the need to think of Brexit as a crucially overdetermined moment within the conjuncture.

## Populism prevails?

We have broken free from a failing political union. We have managed, the little people, the ordinary people who have ignored all the threats that have come from big business and big politics and it has been a huge, amazing exercise in democracy. (Nigel Farage, quoted in Dunn, 2016)

For many commentators, Brexit fits clearly within a wider turn to populist politics, with its celebration of 'the people' clearly captured in Nigel Farage's claims about the referendum result being 'Independence Day'. Brexit lines up alongside many other examples of populist politics: Viktor Orbán's *Fidesz* party in Hungary, the rising appeal of the *Front National*, renamed as *Rassemblement National* (National Rally), in France, the emergence of the AfD (*Alternative für Deutschland*) in Germany; a variety of parties in Italy (Berlusconi's *Forza Italia*, the *Lega Nord*, the 5 Star party, the *Fratelli d'Italia*), the rule of Modi's BJP in India, Jair Bolsanoro's triumph in Brazil and the reinvention of the US Republican party in the form of Trumpism (see, for example, Norris and Inglehart, 2019). Across the vast – and still growing – literature on populism (a genuine academic industry), there are some issues that are significant for my concerns here. The first involves a split between approaches that treat populism as essentially irrational – a disturbance of liberal democracy – and those that treat it as integral to the politics of liberal democracy. There has been a great deal of liberal anxiety – in the media, in political argument and in academic analysis – about the threat that populism poses to 'normal politics'. Such concerns led Jacques Rancière to argue that we are seeing a return of the 19th century's liberal fear (and hatred) of the lower orders: 'It is a reaction that constructs a kind of psychology of the crowd as something dangerous in its ignorance, always prone to listening to troublemakers and fraudsters' (2016).

In contrast, a range of analyses treat populism as either integral to, or a necessary adjunct to, liberal democracy, acting as a sort of corrective where the political system appears dislocated from popular experience. So, Vittorio argues that '[p]opulism is an evolutionary political concept: it warns that the balance has been upset and that a new set of political ideas, plans, and actions is needed' (2017: 137; see also Rosanvallon, 2011). This seems an overly optimistic reading of the self-balancing nature of the political system, but it advances a position that underpins much contemporary writing about populism: the view that it is an expression of things gone wrong. So, for example, Judis claims that:

populist movements arise in times when people see the prevailing political norms – put forward, preserved and defended by the leading segments in the country – as being at odds with their own hopes, fears, and concerns. The populists express these neglected concerns and frame them in a politics that pits the people against an intransigent elite. (2016: 17)

I need to pause here for a moment and reflect on the implications of Judis's formulation because it highlights an issue that will be central to the argument of the book as a whole, involving the *forms of expression* that are at stake in populist politics. Some commentators separate the underlying grievances (the discontent and distress) and the political and discursive forms through which they are expressed – the demagogic, racist, xenophobic and violent repertoire of many contemporary populisms (the attacks on Muslims in the BJP's Hindu nationalist India; the Hungarian government's anti-Roma and anti-migrant politics, and so on). Others pose the question of whether populism expresses authentic popular sentiments rooted in material conditions (Winlow et al, 2017). I think both variants miss a critical understanding of political–cultural work as a labour of *articulation* or *translation*. Judis's view of populist politicians expressing 'neglected concerns' elides a process in which some popular concerns are *selectively* voiced (and, by implication, others are silenced or ignored). At stake here is a challenge to any notion of politics simply reflecting – transparently – popular sentiments, rather than involving the work of translation, articulation and ventriloquism – the discursive practices through which people are 'brought to voice' (see Kipfer and Hart on the 'Gramscian problematic of politics as translation' (2015: 325)). It matters, then, that populism is understood as involving a process of political–cultural *work*. It is crafted by political actors selectively voicing popular grievances as if they were the whole story and ventriloquising them in accessible and recognisable forms.

These practices of articulation include the performance of affect. Academics writing about affect in public–political–cultural domains have used a variety of concepts: Anderson (2009) talks of 'atmospheres', while Ahmed (2014) talks of 'moods'. Wetherell (2013) has explored the idea of 'affective practices' and Grossberg (2018) works with the concept of 'affective landscapes'. I want to stress the large repertoire of affects that has been deployed in populist politics: giving voice to 'rage' against the elites, expressing 'loss' in relation to ways of life, asserting 'pride' in personal, community and national histories and announcing a condition of 'righteousness' (about almost everything). Following Rancière's warning about populism, it is important not to erect a binary distinction between the emotional/affective politics of populism and the realm of 'normal politics', imagined as rational, reasonable and free of emotion. Normal politics operates through a whole range of affective registers: nostalgia, nationalism, the promise of progress or the threat of falling behind, the fear of the other or the desire for self-advancement, and, not least, the various imaginings of 'security'. During the EU referendum campaigns, the 'normal politics' of Remain was dubbed 'Project Fear' by its opponents, as it threatened the grievous harms that would follow on from Brexit. Pankaj Mishra (2020, borrowing from Niebuhr (1959)) talks about the 'bland fanatics' who trumpet the praises of Western civilisation, liberalism in general and neoliberalism in particular. Bland fanaticism neatly captures the paradox of the performance of reasonableness in 'normal politics'.

Here it is important to think conjuncturally about the entanglements of politics, culture and affect. Contemporary populisms (and their articulations with nationalism, nativism, racism, and more) have shifted the affective registers towards more assertively angry and more intensely antagonistic forms. The moment of Brexit involved what felt like a distinctive shift in these terms, involving an articulation of grievance, a sense of victimhood, and a muscular desire to crush all those not at one with the people and the people's will. Earlier I raised the idea that populist politics involve a practice of articulation, bringing social groups to voice, suggesting that this might involve 'ventriloquism'. This term was used by Stuart Hall to talk about Thatcherism, but the following sentence could just as easily have been written about Brexit: 'The press – especially those three popular ventriloquist voices of the radical Right, the *Mail*, the *Sun* and the *Express* – have played here a quite pivotal role' (1979: 18). Those same voices – carefully calibrated with Leave-promoting politicians such as Nigel Farage, Michael Gove and Boris Johnson – were central to the articulation of Brexit populism and, indeed, its Conservative aftermath. There is a distinctive symbiotic relationship between populist politicians and popular media which involves a rhetorical performance of grounding politics in the 'common sense' of the public (as opposed to politicians or experts). In the process, 'ordinary people' are summoned as 'experts of Britishness'. This process might be named *vernacular ventriloquism*, marking a desire to find popular or demotic forms of expression that will add a lustre of 'authenticity' to the thoughts and words of politicians (especially those educated at public schools or elite universities). Political actors and media collude in this dynamic which enables both politicians and media to represent themselves as being 'on the side of the people' and to denounce others as 'playing politics'. Although other media certainly played a part, Zappettini has compellingly described this dynamic as the 'tabloidization of Brexit', arguing that

> a large section of the tabloid press framed the choice over Brexit by providing the public with an imagined sense of empowerment over a perceived threat to the British nation and its popular sovereignty. Most tabloids (namely the Mail-Sun-Express triad) associated this threat with immigration and EU policies which, in turn, were largely represented as adverse to the interests of the (British) people. Within this discursive logic, Brexit tended to be primarily legitimised by tabloids through strategies of fear, resentment and empowerment which relied on antagonistic representations of opposed groups of people (i.e.

the British people and its enemies) and the exclusionary dichotomy of us and them. (2021: 278)

## The People and their Others

As Zappettini suggests, the Brexit campaigns mobilised distinctive versions of the imaginaries that provide populism with its formal architecture. For most analysts, populism rests on a foundational binary distinction between the People and the Elite – or 'power bloc' (for example, Canovan, 1999; Laclau, 2005). The 'cosmopolitan-metropolitan liberal elite' was the main enemy named in the Leave campaigns, variously specified through a range of references: 'big business', the 'political class', 'liberals' and 'experts' among others. However, it is worth thinking about the *multiple* forms taken by the People's 'Others'. Alongside the liberal elite (London-based and out of touch with the country as a whole) the Leave campaigns identified two other enemies. One was 'Brussels' serving as a summative image of the EU in which 'foreign' politicians, Angela Merkel especially, and the 'bureaucrats' who humiliated the UK were condensed (see also Sykes (2018) on Brussels as a spatial imaginary). The second target were the 'Migrants': those beneficiaries of lax immigration policies and 'liberal' social policies. These two threats to the British way of life were conjoined in the EU's commitment to the free movement of labour, even though the 'Migrant' in British populist discourse shape-shifted with fast-moving fluidity between the Muslim 'terrorist', the Romanian farm worker, the Polish plumber and the African-Caribbean migrants who were still understood as being 'out of place' even after 70 years' residence in the UK (Gentleman, 2019). This sort of multiplication of 'enemies of the People' beyond the foundational binary distinction is visible in some studies of populism and has typically been conceptualised as the combination of vertical (anti-elite) and horizontal (anti-minority) axes of antagonism creating a conjunction of populism and nationalism or nativism (for example, Breeze, 2018; Hameleers, 2018). The Brexit trinity (the elite, 'Brussels' and the Migrant), however, is a distinctive formation since it locates 'Brussels' as a hinge between the vertical and horizontal axes, with the EU being portrayed as *both* a hierarchical elite and as enabling the 'foreign' threat to the British way of life.

In the Leave campaigns, the 'People' were represented through classic populist figures, not least the 'ordinary people' and 'little people' invoked by Nigel Farage. Nevertheless, this was hardly a sudden eruption of populist discourse into British politics: rather, the moment of Brexit builds on populist tropes that were established – and polished – by previous UK governments in their anti-welfarist, anti-statist and austerity-promoting politics. For example, New Labour articulated distinctions between 'hard-working, responsible families' and their Others which culminated in Gordon Brown's promise of 'British jobs for British workers' (Anderson, 2013). In 2010, the Conservatives embarked on the construction of a British People ready to face the decade of austerity (Clarke and Newman, 2012). There we gained George Osborne's distinction between 'strivers' and 'shirkers' alongside a deepening antipathy towards migrants in a range of forms: the 'job stealing' Eastern European, the 'bogus' asylum seeker and the 'benefit tourist' (Forkert, 2017). These populist incarnations also remind us of a much longer history of national-popular imaginaries through which the 'fateful triangle' of race, ethnicity and nation has been articulated (Hall, 2017).

This is also the terrain of Gilroy's 'postcolonial melancholia' (2005): the unresolved loss of an imagined past has been a profoundly constitutive element of the current conjuncture, such that debates about 'Britishness' make little sense without it. Meanwhile, the People's Others continued to multiply after the referendum as Brexit's champions pointed fingers at judges and Remain-oriented parliamentarians as 'enemies of the people', while 'Remainers' (aka 'Remoaners') in general were viewed as lacking adequate patriotic commitment and thus no longer counted as part of the People. Indeed, this example points to a significant populist dynamic: the 'true people' are only ever one part of the people at large, a paradox perfectly encapsulated in Donald Trump's 2016 statement that 'the only important thing is the unification of the people – because the other people don't mean anything' (cited in Müller, 2016: 22).

One other critical aspect of Brexit populism involved what Hay identifies as 'a rejection of the politics of expertise, at least in its current form, and *of expert paternalism* in particular' (2020: 199, emphasis in original). This was central to the Leave campaign's rejection of the case being made for remaining in the EU, dressed as it was in the clothes of expert wisdom. A *Daily Telegraph* commentary emphasised the consistency of this theme:

> 'I think people in this country,' declared Vote Leave's Michael Gove, 'have had enough of experts.' His fellow Brexiteers were quick to back him up. 'There is only one expert that matters,' said Labour MP Gisela Stuart, also of Vote Leave, 'and that's you, the voter.' Nigel Farage, the leader of UKIP, suggested that many independent experts were actually in the pay of the Government or the EU. All three reminded voters of occasions when 'the so-called experts' had made mistakes. (Deacon, 2016; see also Clarke and Newman, 2017)

Of course, this revolt against expertise did not suddenly emerge in the moment of Brexit. The rise of forms of technocratic governance, in which 'politics' was subordinated to economic and bureaucratic forms of power, has been extensively discussed as a de-politicising and de-democratising dynamic. For some (for example, Wilson and Swyngedouw, 2015), these developments were linked to the growing complexity of governing and the limited capacity of nation-states to manage domestic economies in the face of global flows of capital and the expanding authority of supranational institutions. More locally, it was shaped by the ideological contours of the 'Third way' governments of the UK, where, in Mallaby's analysis, '[i]f the clashes of abstractions – communism, socialism, capitalism, and so on – were finished, all that remained were practical questions, which were less subjects of political choice and more objects of expert analysis' (2016: 29). This conception of government-as-calculation underpinned the Blairite mantra 'what counts is what works' and the increasing turn to a conception of 'evidence-based' policy-making (Nutley and Walter, 2007).

## Thinking beyond populism

Although the concept of populism is productive, and the ideological-discursive content that it makes visible is important, it has its limitations, not least because of a desire to force too much into this conceptual framing. As Maskovsky and Bjork-James have argued:

> [C]onventional academic debates over populism's exact form and the kinds of politics that are covered by the term do little to help us understand the ways that popular disdain, disillusionment, and disenchantment are taking political form in the world today. Nor does the term *populism* capture the full scope of popular misgivings about the status quo that are expressed in current political formations. (2020: 1–2)

Behind populism stand a range of other political-cultural forms: nationalism, nativism, racism, authoritarianism, and a variety of nostalgias through which the People's past is imagined and celebrated. Hart points to 'the explosive growth of racist and xenophobic expressions of nationalism and authoritarian right-wing populist politics in many different regions of the world, often linked to the rise of religious fundamentalisms and invocations of "family values"' (Hart, 2020: 233).

In terms of the challenges of conjunctural analysis, populism perfectly exemplifies one of the most difficult conceptual and methodological issues: the analytic oscillation between 'methodological nationalism' and 'methodological globalism' that I discussed in Chapter 1. There I argued for the importance of thinking *transnationally* about national phenomena – neither reifying the nation space nor collapsing it into a flattened global realm (see, for instance, Prutsch's (2020) exemplary exploration of the similarities, differences and connections between Trump and Bolsanaro). For me, Brexit populism cannot be adequately understood as either just one more example of a global trend of populist revolts or a uniquely national phenomenon. Rather, such revolts – and their conditions of possibility – interweave national and transnational dynamics and connections. In the case of Brexit, its populism existed in a complex combination with other 'isms' and was mobilised through a distinctive political-cultural strategy. Meanwhile, its protagonists certainly learned lessons from elsewhere (and passed on their own), across the EU and across the Atlantic. Money and knowledge flowed around transnational networks of the Right and Nigel Farage got to ride in Donald Trump's golden elevator (much to his delight). This, then, is why conjunctural analysis matters. Populism only makes sense as a force in the moment of Brexit if we can grasp both its national specificities and its transnational connections, if we can understand its articulation with other political-cultural dynamics and forces and if we can see its relation to other conditions and contradictions that have animated this conjuncture, including the role played by a globalising neoliberalism.

## Revolting neoliberalism?

Many accounts treat neoliberalism as the prime mover of the Brexit vote. However, this simple statement conceals a variety of ways in which neoliberalism is seen to have given rise to Brexit. Here I trace out three variations of this narrative, while raising some problems about how neoliberalism is to be understood to enable a more conjunctural view. The simplest, most direct, view of neoliberalism's involvement in the moment of Brexit is to be found in the claim that the vote to leave the EU was a *revolt against neoliberalism*:

> All the leading publications and official representatives of the expert community unanimously called upon the people to leave everything as it is, threatening all sorts of misfortunes in case of the wrong decision: the people still decided to vote for change.
>
> This means that the Brexit vote was not only a rebellion against the neoliberal European project but also no less a popular uprising against Britain's own ruling elites, including both intellectual and political classes, business and media. (Kagarlitsky, 2017: 111)

Meanwhile, Martin Jacques claimed in the *Observer* that the vote was 'primarily a working class revolt' and Perry Anderson observed in the *London Review of Books* that '[t]he masses who voted for Brexit believed they were striking a blow at Brussels and the neoliberalism under which they had suffered for a quarter of a century' (2021a). There is a difference between the clarity of this vision that Brexit was a popular revolt against neoliberalism and a rather more distanced view of neoliberalism's relationship to Brexit.

In this second view, neoliberalism is understood as having created the conditions for the Leave vote, rather than directly inspiring it. Here, neoliberalism is understood to have generated social dislocations and driven inequalities that underpinned popular disaffection. For example, Powell argues that the 'Brexit "wars" … reflected deep divisions and inequalities that have their roots in 40 years of neoliberalism and have become especially brutal under austerity program assaults on public services, welfare and work security' (2017: 226). She further argued that 'the roots of dissatisfaction and lack of opportunity lie in decades of neoliberalization, that deepened inequalities of class and between regions, and incrementally embedded a consensus around market conformity. That conformity diminished the field of political contestation, as markets were protected from democratic redistributive pressures' (2017: 228).

Neoliberalism, then, created the material conditions and shaped the political consensus which meant that popular discontent could not be voiced within 'normal politics'. Conservative and Labour governments colluded in the management of neoliberalism and its problems (not least the financial crisis of 2007–08 and the ensuing politics and policies of austerity). In the moment of the referendum, however, 'normal politics' was suspended. As Insa Koch argued:

> What made Brexit different from an ordinary election was that they perceived it as an event that would make a difference in their lives in a way that standard electoral processes do not. This is because many saw Brexit as an opportunity to move beyond the current system by saying no to government tout court. (Koch, 2017a)

This view of the alienating impact of neoliberalism has sometimes been focused on the accumulating effects of deindustrialisation (especially in the Midlands and North of England and South Wales). As Winlow, Hall and Treadwell put it: 'It quickly became clear that many of those who occupy the nation's dead and decaying deindustrialised zones had voted to leave' (2017: 198).

This view of neoliberalism as the driver of large-scale social dislocation (and then political disruption) is echoed in the third version of how neoliberalism and Brexit are connected. In this view, Brexit is merely one among many reactions to neoliberalism and its effects. Here neoliberalism is understood not merely as a local, or even European, phenomenon, but as a global force that has generated and spread immiseration, dislocation and despair. Brexit is seen to share an underlying dynamic with many other 'revolts' against neoliberalism or, sometimes, neoliberal globalisation. The means by which this dynamic drove such political outcomes are various. For some, it has been a revolt of the working classes against immiseration and exhaustion. For others (for example, Plavšić, 2019), it has been a disaffection *exploited* by an emergent radical Right (featuring nationalism, racism and more). This more general sense of disaffection underpins the argument by Nancy Fraser that Brexit and the election of Donald Trump represent 'electoral mutinies':

> Although they differ in ideology and goals, these electoral mutinies share a common target: all are rejections of corporate globalization, neoliberalism, and the political establishments that have promoted them. In every case, voters are saying 'No!' to the lethal combination of austerity, free trade, predatory debt, and precarious, ill-paid work that characterize financialized capitalism today. Their votes are a response to the structural crisis of this form of capitalism, which first came into full view with the near meltdown of the global financial order in 2008. (Fraser: 2017)

## Questioning neoliberalism

Identifying neoliberalism as the motive force in the making of Brexit fits with a vast critical literature on neoliberalism that has developed over the last 30 years. However, the sheer scale of that literature presents us with a different problem: the concept of neoliberalism *explains too much* (Clarke, 2008). Indeed, there is hardly anything that has not been explained as, in some way, a consequence of neoliberalism – including tendencies that might be thought to be opposites (neoliberalism underpinned the global marketing of democracy as a political form; neoliberalism is profoundly anti-democratic). Let me be clear: I am not arguing that neoliberalism is not significant or consequential, but I do think that analysis has to move beyond using neoliberalism as what Doreen Massey called a 'capacious, portmanteau, or *zeitgeist* term' (cited by Jamie Peck, 2020: 294) or what Peck and Heather Whiteside term 'a default position' (2018: 191).

One of the problems is whether to understand neoliberalism as an entity, as a dynamic, a political-economic formation, a form of capitalism, an ideology or a political rationality (see, inter alia, Larner, 2000; Peck, 2010b). The term slides all too easily between these possibilities (and others, including Foucauldian usages), creating the appearance of a shared vocabulary that in practice confuses and conflates. This was visible in the midst of Brexit: it is not just a problem of whether the neoliberalism in question was European or British, but about *which* neoliberalism was at stake in the political arguments and imaginaries in circulation. For example, Bell (2019) has suggested that the movement to leave the EU was driven, in some quarters, by a desire to realise a 'neoliberal utopia' (borrowing Bourdieu's phrase, 1998), noting that:

> For Madsen Pirie, co-founder of the neoliberal Adam Smith Institute (ASI) … Brexit has provided the perfect opportunity to take the

Conservative Party back to its neoliberal principles and even to go much further down the road towards the fulfilment of the neoliberal ideal, to allow Britain 'to reboot itself' and to 'do things differently' 'across every area of public policy' [Pirie, 2016]. In this sense, Brexit represents a 'neoliberal wet dream' [Wren-Lewis, 2016]. (Bell, 2019)

Bell traced a number of issues in which the neoliberal dream was to be pursued: the attack on the EU as a stronghold of 'bureaucratic regulation' linked Conservative politicians to neoliberal ideologists and organisations, such as pro-Leave economists like Patrick Minford and think tanks such as the Institute for Economic Affairs (IEA). This poses important questions about *what counts as neoliberalism* (see also Jacotine's (2017) exploration of neoliberal arguments for *and* against Brexit).

Here, though, I intend to concentrate on the question of how we might approach thinking about neoliberalism conjuncturally, rather than epochally. Neoliberalism is too easily understood as a singular and global phenomenon. In that framing, it is easy to neglect historical variations of neoliberalism: Jamie Peck is one of the scholars who has tried to trace different phases and different forms, distinguishing between 'roll back' and 'roll out' neoliberalism (Peck and Tickell, 2002) and between living and 'zombie' neoliberalism (Peck, 2010a). He and Heather Whiteside have insisted that 'actually existing neoliberalism ... can only be found in context specific conjunctures, recombinant forms and volatile hybrids' and must be treated as 'not just contingently but necessarily variegated, mutating, unevenly developed, shape shifting and site shifting' (2018: 181). Others have explored some of the geographical variations of neoliberalism as it takes different forms in particular places. For example, Birch and Mykhnenko (2008) have examined economically variant forms of neoliberal capitalism and warned against 'globalising hyperbole'. This warning is important: there is a temptation to believe neoliberalism's own advocates and publicists who proclaim its universalisation (and naturalisation) as the necessary condition of economic well-being and human progress. It is certainly important to acknowledge that neoliberalism – as an ideology and political rationality committed to the development of market rule – came to be a global common sense, embedded in the international institutions that coordinated global thinking about economic policy and the conditions of economic 'success'. But this is not the same as neoliberalism being the same everywhere or, indeed, being hegemonic everywhere. The 'economies' of neoliberalism do not exist somewhere before, or outside, the social formations into which they were inserted. So, a critical question concerns the forms that neoliberalism takes as an embedded and embodied presence within specific social formations, even ones that are transnationally connected.

Keeping Williams's injunctions about 'actual historical analysis' in mind, it is important to recognise that there are always complex (and messy) political-cultural landscapes that pre-exist the arrival of neoliberalising projects. Some of the formations in these landscapes also tend to persist alongside them, engendering varieties of resistance, refusal and recalcitrance in the face of neoliberal demands to 'modernise'. *Residual* political-cultural forms typically haunt these projects, proving obstructive, refusing to go quietly or sometimes simply sitting sullenly in the way of 'progress'. These landscapes are also transformed – reconstructed – in the process of neoliberalisation, creating new accumulations of contradictions, antagonisms and problems of governing (often overlaid on the unresolved antagonisms of earlier periods). In the process, they also give rise to *emergent* political-cultural possibilities and projects that have to be managed (incorporated, marginalised or subordinated).

Overlaid on these residual and emergent tendencies, we must also reckon with the consequences of neoliberal failures – failures that typically create more crisis-ridden, divided, contradictory and antagonistic social formations. There we discover the political and governmental problems of *managing* neoliberalisation – and its failures. Despite neoliberalism's rhetorical anti-statism, neoliberal projects have constantly reformed, restructured and exploited state capacities in order to install, sustain and manage the instabilities of neoliberal development. State resources have proved essential for reviving capital accumulation (such as subsidies, privatisations, outsourcing and tax reform). States have been crucial to the management of populations, seeking to reform or 'improve' them: teaching them to be entrepreneurial and responsible subjects, and disciplining those who fail, often through increasingly authoritarian measures. Neoliberal projects have also looked to exploit the dynamics of party political competition as a way of creating innovative economic strategies and of managing public consent, especially in the face of crises and catastrophes – charging governments with finding ways of making the world safe for 'business as usual' (as in the aftermath of the 2008 financial crisis).

Ensuring the societal conditions to make neoliberalisation work has placed problematic demands on national governments. These governments – and their states – have attempted to manage the tensions between an unstable regime of accumulation (and its fundamentally transnational and globalising logic) and the need to secure what Jessop (1990) calls its 'societalization': the social and political arrangements necessary to enable its reproduction. Peck's argument that neoliberalism is always 'failing and flailing forwards' (2010b: 7) points to the way that neoliberalism's protagonists have recurrently insisted that only a better, bigger, neoliberalising reform can resolve the problems caused by its failures. Not surprisingly, then, national governments have struggled to manage both the dynamics of neoliberalisation and their economic, social and political fallout. That captures the current conjuncture's unsettled and unsettling character perfectly.

In this section, I have tried to indicate some of the ways in which conjunctural analysis demands that we move from relatively abstract – or epochal – framings of the forces and processes in play towards a more concrete understanding of their particular (and unstable) forms and formations. I have tried to draw out the question of how neoliberalism varies across time and space rather than being a singular entity. That implies taking account of the other conditions, forces and dynamics that neoliberal projects have to cohabit with in particular places (even as they try to dominate them). In this light, how are we to think of those moved to 'revolt' against the neoliberalism of the UK/EU nexus? Who do they think they are? And against what do they think they are revolting? One answer to these questions that has been central to much academic, journalistic and political analysis of Brexit (and beyond) is that they are the 'left behind'.

## The 'left behind'?

> Few things in politics are as fashionable as unfashionable places. The Brexit referendum and Donald Trump's election sent journalists on both sides of the Atlantic scurrying to the margins of Britain and America, in search of the source of disaffection. Academics are making careers interpreting the whims of people who live there. In his first speech as prime minister, Boris Johnson promised to answer 'the plea of the forgotten people and the left-behind towns'. (*The Economist*, 2019)

Few phrases have connected academic work, journalism and politics so compellingly as did the idea of the 'left behind' in the aftermath of the Brexit vote. As this extract from *The Economist* (itself in thrall to the idea) indicates, Boris Johnson promised to put 'left behind' people and places at the top of his 'levelling up' agenda following his 2019 election victory.

The 'left behind' had first emerged as a focus of Ford and Goodwin's work on the rise of new right-wing politics in the UK, notably UKIP as well as a range of nationalist movements ranging from the BNP (British National Party) to the EDL. Despite the shifting national designations (UK, British, English), these are predominantly English nationalist groupings, and form part of a wider revitalisation of English nationalism (as discussed in Chapter 1). For Ford and Goodwin, the support for such parties (subsequently read as a precursor to the Brexit vote) emerged from a double dynamic of change. First, the social and economic changes that resulted in the marginalisation of 'older, working-class, white voters who lack the educational qualifications, incomes and skills that are needed to adapt and thrive amid a modern post-industrial economy' (2014: 278).

Second, generational changes affecting views on social and cultural issues (from immigration to same-sex relationships). They argue that:

> these value shifts have left certain groups of voters behind in a second way, as an outlook that was once seen as mainstream has become increasingly regarded as parochial and intolerant by the younger, university-educated, more socially liberal and financially secure majority who define the political consensus in early twenty-first-century Britain. (Ford and Goodwin, 2014: 279)

They trace the economic transformation of the UK over a 40-year period, noting the impact of deindustrialisation, the rise of service sector employment and the decline of trade unionism as underpinning a sense of political and cultural disaffection. They identify a group of people who have been 'left behind' by the impacts of economic change, by the changing dominant social and political culture, and by their perceived 'natural' political home – the Labour Party (especially during the New Labour years). They argue that 'during the 2000s these left behind groups steadily lost faith in Labour, yet rather than switch to the centre-right Conservatives, they simply stopped identifying with either of Britain's main parties' (2014: 280). In Ford and Goodwin's analysis, the Conservatives and New Labour were seen as equally committed to a market-driven and socially liberal political consensus (though this seems a rather generous reading of Conservative politics) and the 'left behind' were thus likely to either drop out of political activity or find a new home in the restorationist politics of UKIP, which offered a nostalgic imaginary of a once Great Britain that might yet be revitalised.

The rise of UKIP as a home for this group had a double effect on the politics of Brexit. UKIP made the Conservative Party increasingly nervous about the possible impact on its political fortunes – particularly in the Cameron–Osborne austerity years – an anxiety that was intensified by the threat from an increasingly truculent 'Eurosceptic' wing of the Conservative Party. Such political calculations underpinned David Cameron's promise to hold a referendum on UK membership of the EU as part of his campaigning in the 2015 general election. Colin Hay has explored the fragile nature of these calculations and their consequences in examining the political contingencies of Brexit. In particular, he notes that '[t]here needed to be two not just one leave campaign, extending the range of hypothetical (and mutually incompatible) Brexits ostensibly on offer (racist Brexit, protectionist Brexit, 'global British' Brexit and so forth)' (2020: 192).

And, indeed, two leave campaigns emerged: the 'official' Vote Leave (led by Boris Johnson and Michael Gove, two Conservative ministers scenting political opportunity) and the UKIP-driven Leave EU which did a lot of the heavy lifting on nationalism, xenophobia and racism, including the notorious 'Breaking Point' poster, showing lines of Syrian migrants queuing at the border (the border between Croatia and Slovenia, it should be noted). This combination ensured that the 'left behind' were mobilised as Leave voters in significant numbers, as Ford argued shortly after the referendum:

> While immigration was the lightning rod, the divides the Brexit vote has revealed run deeper and broader than a single issue. They reflect deep-seated differences in outlook and values, hopes and prospects, between graduates and school leavers, globalised cosmopolitans and localised nationalists, the old and the young, London and the provinces.
>
> These divides have been building for decades, but were long latent because, before the emergence of UKIP, they lacked a political voice. Now the sheer magnitude of the fracture between the globalised middle class and the anxious majority is clear for all to see. (Ford, 2016)

For Ford and Goodwin, Brexit both reflected and focused these differences in orientation. More generally, the idea of the 'left behind' took hold of academic, political and popular accounts of the moment.

## Problematising the 'left behind'

There are, however, several problems about this view of the 'left behind' and its centrality to the Brexit story. One concerns the class composition of the Leave voting bloc, particularly the dominant focus on the working rather than the middle classes, an issue to which I will return in Chapters 4 and 5. Here, though, I begin by highlighting the *social* and *spatial imaginaries* at stake in conceptions of the 'left behind'. McKenzie has argued that this image of the working class involves a patronising rhetoric which 'relies on the stereotypes and prejudices that the poor white working class are "old fashioned", un-modern, have no mobility, and long for the past' (2017: 208). In a different vein, Sykes has argued compellingly that the Brexit campaign was articulated through a potent range of spatial imaginaries – from the 'insular exceptionalism' of Brexit Britain (contrasted with the overmighty 'Brussels') to the imagery of the 'post-geography world' of global free trade conceived by Brexiteers such as Liam Fox, MP. Sykes suggests that the 'left behind' are enrolled in a powerful spatialised imaginary in debates over Brexit: 'As commentators, politicians and citizens have sought to make sense of the national splintering and convulsion unleashed by the referendum, a potent spatial imaginary and lexicon has emerged – epitomized, for example, by references to "left behind" places and "metropolitan cores"' (Sykes, 2018: 137).

In a subsequent article, Nurse and Sykes argued that the narrative of a Left Behind Britain represents a 'spatio-sociological oversimplification of the referendum geography', suggesting that for the promoters of Brexit it 'cleverly "steals the clothes" of progressives' traditional concern with uneven development and spatial inequality and, in the 2010s, the impacts of austerity' (Nurse and Sykes, 2019: 593). They argue against this reductive spatial imaginary of 'left behind people' in 'left behind places' and contrast such simplifying accounts (of nations, regions and political constituencies) with evidence from the Liverpool City Region which provides ward-level data for voting in the 2016 referendum. They examine correlations between voting patterns (Leave/Remain) and indices of economic deprivation, age and ethnicity, arguing that '[p]arts of this area [the Wirral and Liverpool] are the very embodiment of a "Left Behind Britain" but they do not act in the way that dominant representations of the territoriality of the vote would suggest' (Nurse and Sykes, 2019: 598–599).

Meanwhile, Rhodes, Ashe and Valluvan draw on a study of Oldham to highlight *missing dimensions* in the 'left behind' story. They point to the absence of any role for ethnic minorities except to serve as the object of 'white working class' antagonism:

> [E]thnic minorities are altogether absent in these 'left behind' accounts. The negative impacts of social, political and economic change as experienced by ethnic minorities, alongside the broader histories of racism they encounter, are summarily silenced. Indeed, the formation of the 'left behind' works to re-centre the imputed interests of the 'native' population (itself defined in very specific and narrow terms). Here, the 'White working class' are cast as being uniquely disadvantaged and the primary, if not sole, victims of processes of decline. (2019: 4)

At the same time, they challenge 'increasingly nostalgic' representations of post-war welfare capitalism that treat it as an era characterised by relatively stable, well-paid employment. The generalisation of this picture means that racialised and gendered dynamics of inequality and oppression tend to be marginalised, if not wholly omitted. The years of Fordist welfarism certainly provide one potent referent for 'what has been lost' (alongside an equally potent imaginary of Empire) but it requires reading that history through what might be called the 'core' Fordist working class and its enrolment into a male bread winner/family wage framing of work and welfare. As Fiona Williams (1995 and elsewhere) has insisted, the post-war welfare settlement was forged at the intersection of conceptions of 'Family, Work and Nation' which articulated racialised and gendered orders around this model of waged work. Jeanette Edwards (2019) has argued that:

> We know that the Keynesian-Fordist project, acting here as the benchmark for better times, was short-lived, highly contested and

unequally dispersed. But this has not stopped it looming large in the imagination of a lost, but better, more stable and more secure economic past. Despite its fragility, contested nature and unequal distribution, it has left profound traces and hauntings.

Edwards draws on work by Muehlebach and Shoshan (2012) on this strange affective afterlife of Fordism (what they term 'post-Fordist affect'). They identify a profound and widespread nostalgia for the lost era of Fordism, observing that it evokes different aspects that have left their marks:

> For some, these marks consisted of the promise of relative economic security and well-being, plausible middle-class aspirations, and a sense of linear biographical legibility; for others, it was personal and political futurities that allowed for an orientation toward safety and affluence. ... For others still, it entailed the figure of a strong state, robust unionism, or the normative order of heterosexual patriarchy. (2012: 317)

This rich mixture of elements has been powerfully mobilised in the sense of 'loss' that has been central to many versions of 'angry politics' (Maskovsky and Bjork-James, 2020). Despite its flaws (empirical, conceptual and political), the 'left behind' thesis has been a powerful – and popularised – argument that offers a singular account of how Brexit came about. In doing so, it both simplifies and obscures – not least by leaving out social relations other than class. It relies on a linear history of decline from the 'good old days' of full (male) employment and a 'golden age' welfare state (Huber and Stephens, 2001). Other histories are ignored or occluded, notably the social and political struggles of subordinated or marginalised social groups that only appear in the guise of 'social liberalism' or 'identity politics'. For these reasons and more, it becomes important to locate the moment of Brexit in a wider understanding of the conjuncture in which the complex of histories, social relations and political and cultural conflicts might be located.

## Brexit: turning point or interregnum?

Across these three accounts of Brexit – populism, neoliberalism and the 'left behind' – I have tried to indicate how their limitations and problems create the need for a conjunctural analysis. They provide a springboard for the following chapters that explore the changing social formation of the UK (Chapter 4); the political mobilisation of social forces (Chapter 5) and the accumulating crises that give the present conjuncture its distinctive character (Chapter 6). In thinking about the conjuncture, Brexit forms a distinctive – if long drawn out and complex – moment. For some, it marks a turning point as a new configuration of forces, identities and possibilities is established, captured in Sobolewska and Ford's image of Britain as 'Brexitland' (2020a). They have argued – in the context of the Conservative election victory of December 2019 – that

> [t]he divisions mobilised in the EU referendum have roots going back decades. They are the product of demographic changes which have opened up new fundamental divisions in the electorate over identity and values. These are identity conflicts because they are fundamentally framed around questions of 'us' against 'them'. These are conflicts focused on differing understandings of 'us', different fears and prejudice about threatening outgroups ('them'), and polarised debates about social changes which are shifting who 'we' are and how this should change. (Sobolewska and Ford, 2020b: 4)

While Sobolewska and Ford treat Brexit as the culmination of a long process of change (with 'Brexitland' as its result), others view the moment of Brexit as part of an *unfinished* process, or an 'interregnum' marked by 'a variety of morbid symptoms' that arise 'when the old is dying and the new cannot be born' (in Gramsci's phrase). I will return to this tension between seeing the emergence of a new 'Brexitland' and the idea of an unfinished transition as different ways of thinking about the current conjuncture. But first, I turn to the problem of understanding the social relations that are in play in the conjuncture (Chapter 4) and their mobilisation as political forces (Chapter 5).

4

# Thinking Relationally:
# Class and Its Others

Class became central to debates about Brexit (and the wider conjuncture) in several ways. As we saw in the last chapter, one argument was that Brexit was a 'working-class revolt'. This chapter explores some of the problems associated with this claim before arguing for a more relational understanding of social divisions. The argument ignores evidence about the substantial contributions of the middle classes to the Brexit result. At the same time, there are conceptual questions about the remaking of the working class in deindustrialised times and the contemporaneous remaking of the middle classes. There is a particular issue about the increasing visibility of ideas of the 'white working class' and the chapter explores the conditions for this imagery in the long trajectory from colonialism to post-colonialism. This points to questions of how to understand the articulations of class and other social relations such as racialised and gendered divisions in the current conjuncture – and their shifting social and political *salience* (Williams, 2021). In hard times, there is a recurring tendency for critical thinking to revert to a focus on class, as if the arguments about how class is articulated with other social relations had never taken place. As a result, the final part of the chapter directs attention back to the multiplicity of social relations in the current social formation.

## Rediscovering the working class

In the aftermath of Brexit, the working class was 'rediscovered' as both a social group and a political force. Researchers who had been studying working-class communities argued that people who had been ignored and disdained by Westminster (and politics more generally) had seized the unexpected opportunity provided by the referendum to make themselves heard:

> The sustained attack on working-class people, their identities, their
> work and their culture by Westminster politics and the media bubble

around it has had unforeseen consequences. Working-class people have stopped listening to politicians and Westminster and instead they are doing what every politician fears: they are using their own experiences in judging what is working for and against them. (McKenzie, 2016)

In the aftermath of Brexit, the working class re-entered public discourse in a variety of incarnations. This was often in the relatively dry quantitative analyses of the distribution of the referendum vote (see, for example, Statista, 2016). They were also mapped more sociologically as the 'left behind' in Ford and Goodwin's analysis of political identifications (2014; as discussed in Chapter 3). The 'left behind' often appear as the aggrieved victims of a history that has worked 'behind their backs'. Rather more active conceptions of the working class appeared in qualitative or ethnographic studies such as those by McKenzie (2017) and Koch (2017a). Koch's sense that the referendum was seen as offering an 'opportunity to move beyond the current system by saying no to government tout court' carries an echo of Delanty's analysis of the referendum as a political device that provides the 'illusion of a constitutive moment' (2019: 102). Certainly, the UK's referendum *promised* a constitutive moment, although exactly what was constituted remains a work in progress (six years after the vote).

The working class also appeared as the angrily reasoning subjects of Telford and Wistow's qualitative study on Teesside (2020). The authors challenge what they see as the crudely dismissive and 'reductionist' accounts of working-class Leave voters that treat them as ignorant, ill-educated, racist and 'acting against their own interests'. Such attacks on working-class voters were extensive, echoing Hillary Clinton's dismissal of the 'deplorables' and chiming with many of the liberal responses to populism that demonise 'the people' (see Rancière's critique, 2016). Telford and Wistow explore their respondents' views of the Brexit vote, contextualising them in a political-economic history of the region that foregrounds the combination of neoliberal-driven deindustrialisation and the failure of successive governments from the 1980s to protect the livelihoods of those living there or even to have forms of industrial and economic planning that would have recognised the region. They argue that

[i]t was striking that discussions about Brexit triggered more than anything else a deep and pervasive sense of loss and resignation linked to the inability or unwillingness of politicians to respond to the problems associated with living in an area characterised by long-term industrial decline. Putative rational arguments about Brexit causing further economic damage are likely to fall on deaf ears in regions such as Teesside, because people who feel they have little or nothing to lose are more likely to take a risk on any type of change on offer. (2020: 565)

McKenzie's equally disenchanted respondents (in London and the East Midlands) also felt forgotten or abandoned by successive governments of different types, especially those who had once laid claim to working-class solidarity. She argues for taking the effects of both economic deindustrialisation and the devastating effects of public spending cuts and public service decline seriously as conditions for their disenchantment. She contrasts this with the 'the patronising "left behind" rhetoric' which rather than 'focus on and attempt to genuinely understand the structural nature of deindustrialisation, of class inequality, and of class prejudice ... relies on the stereotypes and prejudices that the poor white working class are "old fashioned", un-modern, have no mobility, and long for the past' (2017: 208). Like Telford and Wistow's respondents, the people in McKenzie's research chose to vote Leave 'not because they thought their lives would be better if Britain was not in the EU. They did so ... because they just couldn't stand it being the same' (McKenzie, 2017: 208).

Each of these studies is an important corrective to two problems: first, the public demonisation of the 'deplorables' as bearing distinctive responsibility for voting the 'wrong' way (both here and in the election of Trump in 2016); and second, the relative neglect of the deindustrialised working class within the social sciences. Yet I think there are other important issues that need to be considered. One concerns the geography of this working class: in most accounts, they appear to be an *English* working class, rather than a British one. As Telford and Wistow acknowledge, this is odd, since 'Scotland (with similarities to the North East of England in terms of deindustrialisation and the influence of neoliberalism over economic and social policy) voted to Remain in the EU' (2020: 557). Given what I argued in Chapter 2 about the different nations and nationalisms of the UK, the English character of *this* working class is important. But there is a further question that demands attention: who are these members of the working class? Although the studies often tell us about their gender, they tend to be unmarked in racial or ethnic terms – an issue of considerable significance given that, as Shilliam (2020) argues, the '*ordinary* working class' in Britain usually turns out to be coterminous with the distinctively racialised figure of the '*white* working class'.

## The making of the 'white working class':

Many studies are concerned to negotiate claims that Leave voters were racist or xenophobic. For example, McKenzie notes that her respondents were upset by accusations that treated

> those planning to vote to leave as 'bigots', 'backwards' and 'racists'.
> The comments had hurt them. They didn't think they were any of

these things and they often commented that 'race' was not part of this referendum. From their standpoint, the decision to vote leave was a way to kick back at an establishment that they felt let down by. (2017: 205)

Meanwhile, Telford and Wistow note that, of their respondents, only 'a small minority were hostile and racist', viewing immigrants as economic competitors and believing that 'immigrants were favoured by national politicians. As a result, they felt forgotten about' (2020: 561).

One recurrent strand in the demonisation of Leave voters (especially those identified as working class) concerned their propensity for racism and xenophobia. What is interesting is that such accusations were predominantly directed to the working class (or those marked as working class by proxy, such as low educational attainment) and not the relatively anonymous middle classes. This follows a well-worn groove in British political culture in which racism has been attributed to the working class in contrast to the more 'liberal' middle classes (see Hindess, 2017). In the process, there has also been a temptation to solidify representations of the working class as white, rather than multi-racial or multi-ethnic, such that a distinction between the 'working class' and 'minority ethnic communities' is recurrently reproduced (see, inter alia, Bhambra, 2017; Virdee and McGeever, 2018).

How, though, did the working class become imagined and represented as white? In an important essay, Alistair Bonnett (1998) points to a significant shift from the 19th to the 20th century. For most of the 19th century, the British working class was not *marked* as white and the 'lower orders' were often imagined in racialised terms, not least as the inhabitants of 'darkest England' (see, for example, Booth, 1890). He argues that the reformation of British capitalism during the first half of the 20th century, including the development of the welfare state, created the conditions for reimagining the working class as part of a racially homogeneous 'national community':

[S]tate welfare helped produce a population ideologically committed to, and capable of participating in 'state managed capitalism'. Thus welfarism both fused and recuperated contradictory and potentially explosively antagonistic social forces into a national project. … As this implies, the benefits of welfare were articulated as a national, and nationalistic, discourse. Welfare came wrapped in the Union Jack. (Bonnett, 1998: 329)

This complex arrangement of welfare, nation and race is filled out in Shilliam's remarkable account of the articulations of race and welfare, especially through the figure of the 'undeserving poor' (2018). He concludes that '[w]hen it came to the EU referendum, immigration was primarily held responsible for the loss of social security and welfare provision which had given the "white working class" constituency an ostensibly "class" interest' (2018: 162). This view is deepened by Bhambra's recent (2022) work on the way in which colonial revenues subsidised metropolitan state welfare while enacting distinctions of nationality, citizenship and access between the British working class and colonial labourers (see also F. Williams, 2022).

The embedding of citizenship in the alignment of state, welfare and nation projected a 'cross-class racial-national community' that came to underpin a proprietorial understanding of 'our' welfare state that needed to be defended against non-national (and non-white) claims on it. Precisely this projection was mobilised in Enoch Powell's racialised nationalism, for example in his argument that:

> 'While to the immigrant entry to this country was admission to privileges and opportunities eagerly sought, the impact upon the existing population was very different ... they found themselves made strangers in their own country, they found their wives unable to obtain hospital beds in childbirth, their children unable to obtain school places.' (Powell, 1968)

This conception of 'our' welfare becomes an increasingly potent symbol as welfare state cuts and changes took place from the late 1970s (Shilliam, 2018). These four decades of change generated a stronger sense of racialised competition for welfare (housing, education, jobs or benefits). This framing of racialised antagonisms as 'competition' shapes Dench, Gavron and Young's account of the 'New East End' (2006, for the Young Foundation), in contrast with their silence about the effects of economic and social transformation, especially government policy towards public services. Michael Keith has argued that their account relies on a simplifying narrative about the 'betrayal' of the white working class, noting that: 'Nostalgia sits in that space after history ends and biography begins. It is always on the move and invariably personally inflected. In the Young Foundation narrative, nostalgia trumps history' (2008).

At the same time, the 'white working class' was itself stigmatised as 'chavs' (Jones, 2012) and was marked as part of the 'demoralised' poor generated by the 'excesses' of liberal welfarism. Such 'poor whites' thus formed part of what the American Conservative policy critic Charles Murray called 'the new rabble' (describing the 'emerging British Underclass', 1990). Later, during a television debate on the 2011 English riots which had largely involved white youth, the historian David Starkey claimed that "the problem is that the whites have become black" (Quinn, 2011). Such denigrations of 'poor whites' intersected uneasily with the emergence of the 'white working class' as a political-cultural identity and potential site for the mobilisation of desires, anxieties and demands. This was the focus of a variety of cultural interventions, including Michael Collins' *The Likes of Us* (2004) and the BBC series *White* (2008) which posed the question of whether the 'white working class was becoming invisible' (see also Sveinsson, 2009 and Ware, 2008). It was also more practically articulated in the realignments of the radical Right in England, especially, as the BNP gave way to a range of new groupings, from UKIP to the EDL (and beyond). There are significant echoes in the US, particularly around the Trump election victory in 2016 which was, in some quarters, associated with the left behind/forgotten/abandoned 'white working class' (prompting an explosion of studies, memoirs and ethnographies: see the thoughtful critique by Brownlow and Wood, 2017).

In the UK, this (re-)emergence of the *white* working class has been extensively discussed, sometimes in the framing of the 'white working class', at others in terms of tracing the fortunes of the 'old' or 'traditional' working class. For example, Winlow, Hall and Treadwell (whose research was completed before Brexit) argue that there is a need to identify the *contemporary* forms of racism that are rising within this white/traditional working class:

> The racism of today is a post-imperial racism rooted in global political economy and the absolute decline of traditional working-class work, security and status in the west. This is not simply the traditional racism that was primarily a product of imperialist colonial ideology. Where that was a racism of imagined superiority, this is a racism of imagined inferiority that each day passes an affirming reality test. There are cultural issues at stake, but these develop in relation to this central economic issue. The sense of community dissolution and the gradual disappearance of the traditional culture are important, and they are experienced as such by millions of ordinary men and women across the country. (2017: 206)

While it is certainly important to attend to the changing conditions of the working class, it is also important to recognise that the 'cultural issues at stake' have to include how people come to see themselves as white (as well as working class) – and how minority ethnic people fall out of class framings. Moreover, the idea of the 'traditional' plays a shifting role in this account, relegating some things to the past ('traditional racism') while valorising other traditions in the present (the loss of traditional jobs, values, communities). This view of a transition from 'traditional racism' to a 'post-imperial racism' obscures the dynamics in which at least aspects of an 'imperialist colonial ideology' have been revitalised and renewed in new configurations. As I suggested above, there is no straightforward identity or identification at stake here: rather, whiteness (however seemingly natural and obvious) has to be constructed, naturalised and made meaningful as a way of thinking about the social world and one's place within it (Back and Ware, 2002; Virdee, 2014).

## Remaking (racial) capitalism, remaking class (and race and more)

In keeping with Bonnett's argument that changing formations of British capitalism were implicated in the construction of a racialised 'white' working class, the shifting formations of British capitalism since the 1970s have been a fertile ground for remaking those representations of the working class and its 'Others'. One profound dynamic of the new conjuncture that formed in 1979–80 has certainly been deindustrialisation, centred on the exporting of manufacturing on a global scale (and the use of that threat to discipline remaining 'national' sectors).

Deindustrialisation went hand in hand with other dynamics: the uneven (re)development of the UK, centred on the hyper-development of the South East/London region, especially the development of the financial sector, accompanied by the rapid deepening of inequalities of both income and wealth (Macleod and Jones, 2018). Deindustrialisation went hand in hand with a systematic approach to what I will call desocialisation and decollectivisation. Desocialisation marks the reversal of the characteristic capitalist development of *socialised* relations of production. Instead, waged work became increasingly fragmented, as traditional manufacturing (and extractive) labour processes were either abolished, exported or automated. Similarly, conditions of employment became more contingent (Leach and Winson, 2002) and individualised as non-unionised labour expanded. At stake in these changes was a tendential shift in the gendering of waged work, with an increasing proportion of women in paid employment (often part time). This shift is connected with the changing sectoral balance of employment as service sector employment grew and extractive and manufacturing sectors declined. This service sector growth crucially involved the commodification of (highly gendered) care work which has also involved its globalisation through the transnational flows of migrant care workers (Ungerson, 1997; Williams, 2010, 2021; Green and Lawson, 2011; Raghuram, 2012).

These changes were the preconditions of deepening economic 'precarity' (Standing, 2011) which is a global dynamic and takes particular national forms. It marks what Ferguson and Li (2018) call 'the end of the proper job', understood as forms of relatively permanent and stabilised employment. They argue that the image of the 'proper job' had been both a powerful organising device for waged work in the global North and an imagined – and widely projected – goal for development in the global South. In the UK, a variety of forms of contingent employment have displaced the 'proper job': internships, zero hours contracts, quasi-self employment, flexible working, unemployment and under-employment. One particular representation of this spread of contingent forms of labour has been the 'gig economy', acquiring a peculiar halo effect from referencing the 'gigging' of performance artists of various kinds. The reality is somewhat grimmer: a zero hours contract for supermarket shelf stacking or delivery driving lacks the implied glamour of the 'gig' (see, inter alia, Friedman, 2014; Manyika et al, 2016). The decline of the 'proper job' also marked a shift in the gendered patterns of waged work as more women entered employment, especially in forms of contingent work.

Behind Standing and others' discussions of deepening precarity lies a more complex dynamic of how the 'proper job' was imagined and distributed. It was associated primarily with the 'core' male working class in the manufacturing base of Atlantic Fordism (and the largely male core of managerial bureaucracies in corporations and states). Fordism, as I argued in Chapter 2, was organised around notions of the 'family wage' and was embedded in principles of work, welfare and family that were articulated through gendered and racialised imaginaries. In global terms, most paid work remained 'contingent' and precarious. Even within the landscapes of Atlantic Fordism, jobs beyond the core were also considerably more contingent and were marked by significantly gendered and racialised dynamics of allocation and reward. More recently, investigations of racialised differences in COVID-19 mortality rates have indicated how such precarious employment in the UK featured significant numbers of minority ethnic and migrant workers – alongside, and indeed interwoven with, the 'white' working class (for example, McIntyre et al, 2020).

Overall, the combined dynamics of deindustrialisation and desocialisation demand a more careful detailing of what – and who – are denoted by concepts of the 'working class'. This mix of changes produced a very *untraditional* working class, as this observation (from an intervention into early debates about a 'working-class Brexit') brilliantly captures:

I am a branch officer of Unite the Union South Yorkshire Community branch who campaigned, as did my Union, for remain. As I type I am sitting on the fault line of the brexit debate. To the west lies the affluent suburbs of Sheffield where there has been much howling and gnashing about losing the vote. To the east lies the working class parts of the city and the wider de-industrialised county of South Yorkshire which voted, with much anger, to leave. The two sides are glaring at each other through the fractures of English society, or so we are told. On one side the educated, liberal progressives, on the other the people who do not know any better; at least according to the likes of the guardian [*sic*]. This is dangerous myth. Most of our members live precarious lives, some are on the dole, some work in fast food joints, some at local universities. You would be hard pushed to tell the difference between the budding academic and the burger flipper, sometimes they are the same person. (James, 2016)

In this remaking of the working class, processes of desocialisation have also gone hand in hand with *decollectivisation*, by which I mean the uprooting of a range of forms, practices, institutional sites and organisations that had provided an infrastructure for working-class consciousness and solidarity at local and national levels: WEA classes, trades unions, local councils and councillors, public services (from libraries to the NHS). I certainly do not mean to romanticise these infrastructural conditions (I grew up with and in them): they were always contradictory, subject to pressures and problems, not least tendencies towards reproducing forms of patriarchal, homophobic and racialised domination. But they were both a connective tissue that underpinned what are often called 'working-class communities' and the sites for struggles against such oppressive tendencies as new conceptions of solidarity were (sometimes) forged. This infrastructure has been the focus of continuing assaults through the last four decades: the curtailing of union rights (and the enabling of non-union employers); and the dismantling and undermining of local government capacities (the abolition of the GLC and the metropolitan authorities; the diminution of powers, such as over schooling, and the 'devolution' of austerity to local authorities). Public services were closed (youth services; libraries), privatised (care for young people, adults and the elderly) or funded on a shrinking basis, evacuating the potential solidarity-forming possibilities of the local. The 'public realm' has not been entirely emptied and, indeed, a range of voluntary organisations and networks have developed in ways that attempt to build connections and cooperation within and across a range of social issues and groups.

Nonetheless, the dismantling of an infrastructure for living together (however constrained and contradictory) was both intentional and systematic. It formed an integral part of the new settlements developed after 1979 as the drive to marketise, individualise and familialise the field of the social gathered pace and required the destruction of what were 'intermediating' institutions, relationships and practices. These dynamics were then accelerated by the austerity programmes of the Cameron governments, driven by his Chancellor George Osborne's fetishisation of fiscal control rather than investment. In the process, it has been harder to both develop and sustain expansive conceptions of the working class and the forms of solidarity that might sustain them. Virdee and McGeever have explored how the category of the 'white working class' was deployed in dominant narratives as a way of framing this decline – naming racialised Others ('migrants') as the driving force of working-class immiseration. As a consequence, they argue,

> the white working class – a descriptive and analytic category whose origins lay in social science research – has over the course of this decade-long crisis been brought to life as a collective social force in the Thompsonian sense (1991), such that some working class men

and women now understand and make sense of the real economic pain they suffer through such a racialized frame of white working class victimhood. (Virdee and McGeever, 2018: 1814; see also Bhambra (2017) on 'methodological whiteness')

It is significant that Virdee and McGeever point to working-class men *and* women, since much of the 'white working class' narrative has been centred on men. As Mondon and Winter note, 'the postindustrial working class is not only presumed to be white, but male. White men are posited as having lost their jobs, earning power, status and ability to support and protect their family and maintain their patriarchal and masculine power' (2019: 517). In Chapter 3, I explored how the 'Fordist' settlement was structured by the idea of the 'family wage' that connected the dominant imaginings and institutionalisations of work, welfare and nation (Williams, 2021). Those articulations are evoked in the nostalgia for a lost 'way of life' (Clarke, 2019). I also highlighted Edwards' argument that the 'left behind' were framed by a potently nostalgic view of the 'traditional' working class, or what Shilliam describes as a 'melancholic racialized nationalism' (2018: 163).

The separation of class, race and gender as axes of social division creates persistent analytic and political problems, often solidifying racialised divisions and rendering invisible the place of black, Asian and other groups *within* the shifting composition of the working class, while simultaneously degendering class itself. However, there is another dynamic involved in the remaking of British capitalism that demands our attention. It is not just the working class that was remade across these decades: the middle classes are also not quite what they used to be.

## Making the middle classes visible

The middle classes have long been a problem for class analysis, whether in sociological or Marxist terms (appearing either below the upper class or as subordinate to the owners of capital). They have been distinguished in occupational terms (white collar workers; the apparently ever-expanding professional and managerial class); in terms of their relation to capital (the petit-bourgeoisie: shopkeepers, traders, rentiers), or even in terms of what Carchedi (1986) called their 'contradictory class location' – positioned uncomfortably between capital and labour. Such arguments became even more complex with the growth of state work during the welfarist expansion of the 1960s and 1970s, as state 'semi-professions' (from teachers to social workers) came to occupy tutelary and disciplinary positions between the state and the public (Johnson, 1972). Acquiring traces of 'professional status' and forms of social capital (as well as getting to exercise forms of state power), these occupations exhibited contradictory tendencies, becoming the sites for new radicalisms in work and beyond, including a revitalised trade unionism in public services. These 'new middle classes' (often 'feminised' and providing a significant route into employment for black and other minority workers) were at pains to distinguish themselves from the 'traditional' middle classes in both political and cultural registers. Indeed, their radicalisms (from progressive educational approaches to radical social work) and political-cultural alignments with new social movements marked them as targets for Thatcherite hostility and were used to legitimate its anti-statism. Virginia Bottomley, then Secretary of State for Health, talked in 1993 of the need to rid social work training of its preoccupation with 'trendy theories' and 'ologies and isms' (Harris, 2003: 107).

This new public sector formation found itself under attack from Thatcherism in the UK (and versions of the New Right elsewhere) as the drive towards the neoliberalisation of the state became coupled with the enunciation of a conservative or traditionalist authoritarianism. In the UK, they became part of the reshaping of the Labour Party and provided a point of articulation between old and new social movements of feminism, anti-racism, and gay/lesbian politics, struggling with the contradictions of how to defend an exhausted social democratic politics and a discredited welfare statism, even as their possibilities and conditions of employment changed (most eloquently explored in the London-Edinburgh Weekend Return Group's *In and Against the State* pamphlet, 1979/2021).

In the Austerity years after 2010, such state occupations became increasingly subcontracted or, indeed, outsourced to voluntary and charitable organisations (see Humphris, 2019). The trajectory of this new state middle class has been in sharp contrast to the renewed rise of a version of the professional and managerial class, as an MBA-fuelled 'new managerialism' took hold in both private and public sectors; the latter as the public sector was subjected to pressures to make it 'more business-like' (Clarke and Newman, 1993, 1997). This class fraction embodied the new 'entrepreneurial self' so essential to the cultural as well as economic dynamics of neoliberalisation (see, for example, the exploration of Wall Street selves in Ho (2009)).

Finally, another new fraction emerged in the cultural industries (sometimes referred to as the 'creative industries'). This sector has been the subject of widely diverging interpretations, from representing a new phase of capitalism (the 'information economy' or 'knowledge capitalism') or the site of new forms of labour ('immaterial labour' or 'affective labour'). Some of these tend to overstate the scale of change (ignoring the export of manufacturing jobs to the global South and to China), or the extent to which working conditions are uniform across the sector. As Gill and Pratt observe:

> While it might be true that most work today is in some sense impacted by information and communications, the grandiosity of such a claim

obscures profound differences between different groups of workers – between, for example, the fast food operative with a digital headset or electronic till in their minimum wage McJob, and the highly educated, well-paid cultural analyst. For many, working in this field has been an experience dominated by much more precarious employment than the managerial cadre. (2008: 9)

An increasing range of work now involves forms of emotional or affective labour, ranging from those whose work centres on the evocation, circulation or management of emotions (cultural practitioners, brand managers, therapists, and so on) to those required to perform emotion in their 'customer facing roles', even down to the burger handler or their equivalent in a range of McJobs (a term first coined in 1986). This form of labour tends to valorise 'feminine' qualities (empathy, warmth, and so on) as Hochschild observed when she conceptualised emotional labour in service work as 'the management of feeling to create a publicly observable facial and bodily display' (1983: 7). This is significant for a range of public service jobs as (some) states have become increasingly interested in governing emotion (or governing through emotion: see Jupp et al, 2017). This 'feminine' attribution has had two consequences: one, that women can be recruited into such service roles (because they are good at doing what comes naturally) and two, that men can be educated (or trained, perhaps) to perform such qualities. In both instances, the feminisation of such qualities tends to have a negative impact on pay and conditions.

As the comment by Gill and Pratt above indicates, the combination of changing sectoral shape and the emerging forms of contingent work blur some of the taken-for-granted distinctions between working and middle classes. This is particularly so where forms of precarious or contingent employment, including the compulsory requirement to be 'self-employed', erode some of the historical differences between working-class and middle-class occupations. In the UK, these dynamics are associated with the expansion of higher education during the 1980s and 1990s. As with the earlier expansion of the 1960s and 1970s, this makes the association between education and class position (and trajectory) more complex – and uncertain, given the shrinking link between degrees and well-remunerated employment. As James (quoted earlier) argued, 'You would be hard pushed to tell the difference between the budding academic and the burger flipper, sometimes they are the same person'.

In brief, the transformations of British capitalism and the wider social formation have not just affected the working class but have also remade the middle classes, producing a formation that is both complex and contradictory. It should be noted that capital – and the embodied forms of capital ownership – have also been dramatically remade into new concentrations of wealth and power. This new formation shares some experiences in common with the emerging working class, not least the proliferation of precarity and varieties of contingent employment, even as differences of wealth, income, security and forms of social capital remain critical for understanding some fractions of this formation. At the same time, as Weiss (2019) notes, the middle classes have remained an object of fascination in both political and wider cultural terms, playing a central role in narratives about social mobility, property owning democracies, the transition to post-industrial societies and, more recently, the problem of the 'the squeezed middle' – a phrase used by Labour Leader Ed Miliband in 2011 and subsequently taken up by Conservative Prime Minister David Cameron (see also OECD, 2019). The middle classes are also characterised by a range of anxieties about status, wealth (and its preservation) and security in many forms (for example, Lucey and Reay, 2002; Dickey, 2012; Freeman et al, 2012) – a theme to which I will return in the following chapter.

## Who wants to leave? The middle classes and Brexit

Making the middle classes visible matters for understanding the moment of Brexit and the wider conjuncture. Responding to claims about a 'working-class Brexit', Dorling (2016) and others have insisted on the centrality of middle-class voters to the referendum result. Kim Moody pointed to the complex polling demography of the vote to leave:

> Polling showed that the 'Blue Collar,' skilled and unskilled lower-paid working class voted by 64% in favor of Leave compared to 51% of 'Middle' class and 43% of 'Upper' and 'Upper Middle' class voters. This is usually the basis for seeing this as a working-class rebellion. But while the working class, defined here as manual skilled, unskilled and unemployed workers, make up 46% of the adult working-age population, they composed only 41.7% of the Leave vote.
>
> Economically well off upper- and upper-middle-class voters compose less than a quarter of the adult population, but counted for over a third of the Leave vote — not that far behind 'the workers.' The 'Middle Class' made up a quarter of Brexit voters, slightly less than their 31% of the adult population, but possibly enough to tip the balance toward 'Brexit.'
>
> In short, the so-called 'Revolt Against the Rich' came heavily from the 'Upper' and richer social stratum itself, reinforced by much of the 'Middle' class. Together, those from the upper half of society composed almost 60% of the Leave vote. (Moody, 2016)

One critical dynamic is a differential propensity to vote: the upper and middle classes (in these terms) were more likely to vote than their working-class counterparts (and they form over half of the voting age population). Mondon and Winter (2019: 518) argue that taking abstention rates into account changes our understanding of the referendum in significant ways. This dynamic is in keeping with a wider trend of working-class political abstention that has emerged as political choices narrowed (Mondon, 2017) and is echoed in McQuarrie's argument about working-class voters in 'Rustbelt' states during the 2016 US Presidential election. His analysis suggests that the Rustbelt swing to Trump combined different phenomena, vote switching and vote withholding: 'Both black and white, poor and working-class Midwesterners rejected Clinton, even if they did so in different ways and to different degrees. For black poor and working-class voters the revolt was expressed most notably in declining turnout, not shifts in partisan sentiment' (2017: S127).

More generally, however, the significance of the middle-class support for Brexit has received relatively little attention (by contrast with the 'left behind'/'white working class' arguments). Work from the National Centre for Social Research (2016) has begun to address this issue, identifying different groups involved in the referendum vote, one of which they describe as 'Affluent Eurosceptics' (later described as 'comfortable leavers', see UK in a Changing Europe, 2021).

In the following chapter I will return to the political-cultural work of building a 'Brexit bloc' from different social groups and examine its subsequent significance for British politics (and culture), but at this point I need to draw out some more general points about the wider concern with 'rethinking class'. Too many discussions since 2016 have tended to take the form of 'class versus race' arguments, as if these were competing social principles in some sort of zero-sum game about explaining social and political developments. Rather, I think it is important to insist that social relations – and the people who inhabit them – are complex, not simple, formations.

## Class and its Others: thinking relationally

> We need to articulate the real class situation of persons who are not merely raceless, sexless workers, but for whom racial and sexual oppression are significant determinants in their working/economic lives. (The Combahee River Collective, 1977)

The question of 'class and its Others' was explicitly posed in a collection edited by Gibson-Graham, Resnick and Wolff (2000). It reflected strains and conflicts around class analysis in which other relations and processes (of inequality, marginalisation, subordination and oppression) were either opposed, or subordinated, to an analysis of class as the primary and even primordial social relation. This has been a well-trodden terrain on which there have been bitter disputes, not least around different claims on 'primacy', involving appeals to both historical precedence and foundational determination. Rather than re-run those conversations, I want to argue for the importance of thinking about the field of *heterogeneous* social relations in which social life is enmeshed and inhabited. The urgency of doing so rests on a significant historical phenomenon: in moments of crisis, the idea of class tends to return in all its (imagined) glory as the central concept, as the singular key to understanding our present troubles. In the process, the long history of trying to think with and beyond class is relegated to footnotes, if it is remembered at all.

Starting from class, though, means thinking about how to move beyond the abstract categories of capital and labour/bourgeoisie and proletariat associated with capitalist modes of production, mainly because no one actually lives in a mode of production. In some versions of Marxism, the concept of the 'social formation' marks a different level of analysis, closer to the social relations that people inhabit. This is typically understood as the combination of multiple modes of production – together with what Althusser and Balibar (1970) called the other levels – political and ideological (this is an abbreviated version of a long and complex story; see, for example, Hindess and Hirst, 1977). I would want to add that social formations are also shaped by the uneasy combination of multiple modes of *reproduction*, including domestic/familial, communal and socialised (there are many versions of, and debates about, social reproduction but in this context see especially Katz (2001a, 2018)).

Most importantly, though, I want to insist that social formations are characterised by the co-presence of *heterogeneous* forms of social relations. These are structured in different forms – as hierarchies; as systems of inclusion, exclusion and subordinated inclusion; as dynamics of integration and marginalisation – and are framed as formations of power and visibility. They are more or less integrated with capitalist social relations but are not reducible to them. In the process of inhabiting these different structures, people occupy multiple, overlapping and sometimes contradictory positions – and live them with different degrees of accommodation and contestation. The Worker is always also gendered, racialised, sexualised, able-bodied or disabled … and much else. Who people feel themselves to be – and who they think they are when they act politically – are therefore complicated issues, rather than simply a matter of the presence, absence or form of class consciousness. Perhaps most importantly, there can be no presumption of conceptual, historical or experiential *precedence*: classes do not come before racialised, gendered or any other formations. As I argued in the previous chapter, the field of the social that has to be reproduced is complex, contingent and contested.

This emphasis on multiple social relations that are condensed together and are contextually variable fits with my interest in conjunctural analysis.

Writing about the importance of thinking through the centrality of race and racialisation to the formation of Europe, Gail Lewis argues that 'race, one of the concepts so central to colonial modernity, remains a key organizing principle in Europe … albeit in multiple and shifting constellations as it is entangled with other axes of differentiation, in particular geopolitical contexts' (2013: 874). Her insistence on the 'albeit' points to the challenge of thinking about shifting configurations and constellations rather than just dealing with the general principle. However deeply embedded the types of relationship may be (and they tend to have long histories), the form that they take varies over time and across space, not least as struggles over them have effects and as the form of their articulations shift. There are echoes here of some versions of intersectional analysis (for example, Crenshaw, 1989; Williams, 2021).

Thinking relationally highlights the constructed and contingent character of that field (and positions within it), treating them as contestable – through particular mobilisations of social forces. At different points, people come to act through different identifications or affiliations – understanding themselves as classes, as black people, as women, as gay or queer … and more. As Williams argues, 'we have to understand the historical, material and cultural specificities of particular forms of social relations: to be aware of the variability in social, economic, cultural, and political *salience* of different social relations at different times and places to the issues we are researching' (2021: 31). But because social formations also involve multiple fields of political-cultural practices, we need to recognise that people may also be mobilised through other points of connection and identification – for example, as members of a nation, or through their attachments to more particular localities (regions, cities, neighbourhoods, and so on). At other moments, they may be summoned to feel themselves members of generations – Generations X or Z, Baby Boomers, the 68 generation and so on. Yet again, they may attach themselves to collective identities formed around affiliations that (supposedly) transcend politics: 'decent, law-abiding people', 'concerned citizens', 'taxpayers', and so on. Put simply, political-cultural mobilisations cannot be – should not be – deduced or read off from singular structural positions.

## Thinking relationally, thinking conjuncturally

I have tried to use some of the debates about class in the context of Brexit as a route to developing a more conjunctural account of the social relations in play. Brexit drove a distinctive 'rediscovery of class' – and of the working class in particular. This working class – what Shilliam (2020) calls the 'ordinary working class' – has featured centrally in both popular political and more abstract sociological accounts. It was recurrently *imagined* as male, and white and was mobilised as a political-cultural subject in conflicts centred on race, ethnicity and immigration. In the process, racialised and minoritised people were systematically 'de-classified' (Kirsten Forkert, personal communication) and positioned outside the imagined structures of class. Two consequences flow from these arguments. First, the (re)discovery of the ordinary/white *working class* has concealed important questions about the middle classes – both about their changing formation and about their distinctive political contribution to the making of Brexit. Second, they highlight a conjunctural question about how people to come to identify and act as particular sorts of subjects – and a related one about how they come to be addressed, summoned and animated as particular sorts of subjects. Debates about Brexit have tended to treat these issues as a matter of class versus race (or the working class versus immigrants). It is important to contest this binary distinction and think about the density of the classed, racialised and gendered identifications and imaginaries that the moment of Brexit has put in play – and which continue to play a role in the wider conjuncture, not least in the remaking of the Conservative Party under Boris Johnson. In the next chapter, I will explore these dynamics of articulation, identification and political mobilisation (and dis-identification and demobilisation) more fully.

In conclusion, then, constitutive social relations of class, race, gender and more produce a field of differences – 'the social' – within which constellations, configurations, solidarities and antagonisms form, fracture and shift, demanding an analysis that is both more relational and more conjunctural. In any concrete social formation, then, there are multiple social relations that produce multiple social groupings and create the conditions for their mobilisation by different political-cultural projects. In the following chapter, I take this forward to pose the question of how such social groups come to act as political forces: when do people act as a class and when do they mobilise through some other political-cultural identification or affiliation? Or, to put it another way, who do people think they are when they act – or, indeed, do not act – politically?

5

# Building Blocs: Towards a Politics of Articulation

The Battle for Britain has generated unusual political turbulence. The long decade from 2010 included a coalition government (Conservative–Liberal Democrat, 2010–15), the rapid rise of an outsider party (the Nigel Farage-led UKIP), two referenda (over Scottish Independence and the vote on EU membership), and a Conservative minority government when Theresa May failed to lead the Conservatives to a majority in 2017. May was replaced by Boris Johnson who then led the party to a landslide victory in 2019, campaigning on the promise to 'get Brexit done' and in 2022 he resigned and was replaced as leader and Prime Minister by Liz Truss – who resigned after 45 days. The accelerating churn of party politics is a feature of the trajectory of this conjuncture and makes it harder to keep the wider dynamics of the conjuncture in sight.

In this chapter, I build on Stuart Hall's idea of *articulation* as a political-cultural practice to think about how social forces are addressed and mobilised conjuncturally. I begin from a critical examination of approaches to politics as structured by social divisions, exemplified in Sobolewska and Ford's (2020a) account of *Brexitland* as embodying divisions between identity conservatives and identity liberals. In contrast, I suggest that it is important to treat people as plural subjects who inhabit a shifting and contested field of social relations. These give rise to different *potential* affiliations, identifications and solidarities. My arguments build on the preceding chapter's analysis of the heterogeneous social relations and the multiple social forces that are active in a conjuncture. This provides me with a route into thinking about the processes of building *political-cultural blocs*, processes that seek to articulate different groups into a temporary unity.

The concept of blocs is borrowed – and adapted – from the work of Antonio Gramsci, for whom it was central to his thoughts about constructing and contesting hegemony. Returning to the moment of Brexit, I explore the political work that went into assembling a 'Brexit bloc', involving the mobilisation of different desires and disaffections through the promise to 'take back control'. I then consider the challenges of maintaining this bloc after the referendum, through the 2017 and 2019 general elections and into the shape shifting formation of contemporary Conservatism.

## Two tribes? The question of political mobilisation

In *Brexitland*, Sobolewska and Ford (2020a) trace the ways in which social and demographic changes generated new political identities – and divisions – in British politics that were crystallised in the Brexit referendum. They argue that two main changes drove these realignments – the expansion of higher education and mass immigration. In the 1990s, established party affiliations began to weaken as parties became more professionalised in their communication, campaigning and choice of candidates. Established distinctions between the two main parties were perceived to shrink: the idea that 'they're all alike' referred to both the social character of politicians and the programmes of the main parties.

For Sobolewska and Ford, the old political divisions had been superseded by a new distinction between 'identity conservatives' (largely white with low or no educational qualifications) and 'identity liberals'. The latter comprise a group of 'conviction liberals' – younger, university-educated people who share 'a general tendency to prize individual and minority group rights and to see diversity as a social good to be promoted' (2020a: 43). This group is often allied with 'necessity liberals', typically members of ethnic minorities who feel vulnerable to 'ethnocentric' politics and policies. As a result, 'ethnic minorities have a strong incentive to align with conviction liberals, even though their views on many other social issues fundamentally differ' (2020a: 45). These groups are at odds with 'identity conservatives' who once formed the 'overwhelming majority of the electorate' (2020a: 46) but found their perceptions of economic and social decline matched by a demographic decline, as identity liberals threatened to displace them. Sobolewska and Ford argue that:

> Before mass migration and educational expansion, ethnocentric white school leavers' views defined the mainstream. From their point of view, it is society that changed and left them behind, their only apparent fault being that that they did not change sufficiently with it. It is therefore not surprising that such voters tend to adopt a conservative stance, seeking to slow down or reverse social changes which they find threatening to their group and which erode its formerly dominant status. Change is perceived as a loss for ethnocentric white voters: a loss of their dominant position, and a loss of the cultural conformity and continuity which they value. (2020a: 46)

At its core, their analysis rests on a claim that 'ethnocentrism' – the 'view of things in which one's own group is the centre of everything' (Sumner 2006[1906]) – played a major role in determining positions on Brexit. However, ethnocentrism is an odd choice of concept for two reasons. First, it is highly abstract: any group defining itself against its other(s) is being ethnocentric. It has no social or cultural substance (how did *this* group come to identify itself as an 'us', using what characteristics, around which issues?). Second, the arguments over Brexit (both political and academic) have recurrently involved questions of racism and xenophobia. Sobolewska and Ford never discuss the first of these, while 'xenophobia' is dismissed in the strange argument that the rising migration of the 2000s activated a 'longstanding but previously latent ethnocentric sentiment which many *mistook* for a surge in xenophobia' (2020a: 151; my emphasis). Ethnocentrism is such an abstract and *empty* concept that it is perfectly compatible with xenophobic or racist content. This emptiness mirrors the book's surprisingly socially and culturally thin representation of Britain, and indeed Britishness. Their analysis examines England and Wales: Scotland is treated as a separate case (structured around the rise of the SNP) while Northern Ireland is not discussed at all. They do not address the formation of 'whiteness', the dynamics through which a society might be racialised, or indeed the dislocating transition from a colonial to a post-colonial society. One might also wonder whether that absence of attention to colonialism is linked to their preference for describing these different groups as 'tribes' (2020a: 237–247; see Lowe, 2001).

The book develops and enlarges Ford's earlier work (with Goodwin) on the 'left behind' to present an analysis of political dispositions and voting behaviour across a decade, drawing on a variety of survey data on social attitudes and political choices. However, Davies' review of the book highlights a critical issue:

> There is also a risk that analyses such as this one contribute to the problems they seek to diagnose. 'Identity conservative', 'conviction liberal' and 'necessity liberal' are categories grounded in careful study of existing data, but much of that data is provided by pollsters and attitudinal surveys, whose entire purpose is to slot people into categories. Inviting someone to either 'agree' or 'disagree' with a given statement strips their experiences – and indeed their identities – of nuance. Various social histories are inevitably obscured by such categorisation, not least that of working class anti-racism, which has owed nothing to attending university, or of the many differing experiences of the 'necessity liberals'. (Davies, 2021)

Sobolewska and Ford's analysis is grounded in forms of data that, rather than simply mapping, actually aim to *produce* coherent framings – ethnocentrism, liberalism and so on. Such attitudinal clusters are then associated (more or less consistently) with both party identification and voting choice. Although the data sets record varying intensities – and their apparent crystallisation into voting blocs in the 2016 referendum – these people do not seem to live very complicated lives or indeed to think about many things other than migration, politicians and whom they would like members of their families to marry. In the process, they emerge as remarkably coherent subjects, untroubled by doubts, confusions and contradictions (Clarke and Newman, 2019).

## Thinking again: beyond the coherent subject

Sobolewska and Ford are by no means alone in taking this view of the political subject. Discussions of both Brexit and the election of Donald Trump regularly turned to such simplifying binary classifications of people and attitudes. Such arguments both rely on, and reproduce, the idea of the singular and coherent subject who can be mapped easily in survey data. One recurrent debate that mobilised such reductive polarisations of political subjectivity centred on the place of racism and other forms of social hatred during the Brexit and Trump campaigns. Supporters of both Vote Leave and Trump were regularly denounced for their racism, misogyny and homophobia (see, for example, McElwee and McDaniel, 2017). Such arguments were equally frequently challenged by claims that a focus on racism and misogyny diverted attention from the other reasons for 'ordinary, decent people' to endorse Trump or Brexit (for example, Frank, 2016). Both arguments rely on the same flawed model of human subjects which treat them as coherent and singular. These subjects can only be *either* 'ordinary, decent people' *or* 'racists', rather than complex, contradictory and contextually mobile people.

Instead, as I argued in the previous chapter, it is more productive to think of people being formed in the articulation of different locations in – and trajectories through – a field of shifting social relations. These intersections expose them to a proliferation of possible identifications and orientations – such that they may take up positions contingently with no requirement that they are coherent or consistent. Other studies have pointed to the complex varieties of racism – and to the complex ways in which people inhabit, refuse and negotiate them (for example, Wetherell and Potter, 1992; Flemmen and Savage, 2017; Jefferson, 2017). It then becomes vitally important to think of subjects who are able to draw on more than one way of thinking. It is vital because it opens the possibility of an escape route (in both analytical and political terms) from this binary separation of subjects into either racist, misogynistic fiends or ordinary decent folk.

I grew up (in a respectable working-class community) among neighbours and family who embodied both dispositions and moved between them contingently and without worrying much about the contradictions. Indeed, most people that I know (either in research settings or in life more generally) seem consistently capable of thinking more than one thing. Indeed, they (we?) seem able to hold multiple thoughts (even about the same topic), and frequently express ones that are at least strained, if not actively contradictory. We may strive for coherence and consistency (since we are all supposed to 'know our own minds', especially when surveys come calling) but we are more likely to express ourselves according to the context, doing discursive work to perform a particular version of ourselves.

So, I want to argue that we are *plural* subjects, containing and able to draw on a wide repertoire of knowledges, feelings and voicings, drawn from the stock of (more or less) 'common culture' that we inhabit. In a Bakhtinian sense (see Holland and Lave, 2001), we are 'heteroglossic', formed in the interplay of many voices, and we know how to borrow and mobilise them in different contexts, in different relationships and in different encounters. Put another way, Sobolewska and Ford's 'identity conservatives' may be addressed (politically and in surveys) as if they are coherent subjects, but they may also have other identifications (home owners, public service users, consumers, parents/grandparents and more) and concerns (such as transport, care needs, house prices or the climate crisis) that demand their attention beyond the survey questions. For example, in one recent survey about climate change (Duffy, 2021) high levels of concern (around 70 per cent) were shared *across* the four generations surveyed (Baby Boomers, Generation X, Millennials, Generation Z).

That Bakhtinian sense of multiplicity – in both the culture and the self – finds echoes in Gramsci's reflections on common sense, which he treats as a *plural* noun, noting that common sense is composed of fragments and traces rather than being a singular entity (that version of 'common sense' which is regularly claimed in populist political discourse). The work of politics then can be seen to involve the *selective* mobilisation of some fragments of common sense and their translation into an apparently coherent and consistent appeal and identity (Kipfer and Hart, 2015; Crehan, 2016).

Let me be clear: this is not to claim that everything is constantly in a condition of flux and fluidity. On the contrary, clusters of attitudes and dispositions may congeal, crystallise and solidify not least because their affective character can prove 'sticky'. For Sara Ahmed (2010: 29), '[a]ffect is what sticks, or what sustains or preserves the connection between ideas, values, and objects'. Such stickiness may also bind subjects or different dispositions into more or less coherent bundles (connecting, for example, varieties of racism, misogyny, nationalism and even anxieties about 'civilisational' loss). Such attitudes and dispositions are also worked on – by political projects, by different media, and by family and friends in dynamics of argument and agreement – and in the process may become 'stuck together' and made to appear more coherent.

As a result, it is important to treat 'attitudes' as the focus of political-cultural work: they are subject to efforts to enable them to 'make sense', make them 'feel right', seem 'obvious' or just 'common sense'. That implies thinking about such crystallisations as an accomplishment that is always potentially vulnerable, at risk of shifting, or being rearranged and realigned in the face of new troubles, new hailings and new possibilities. This approach echoes Hall's view of politics as *articulation* – in its double sense. It involves the practice of 'bringing people to voice', allowing them to articulate, to speak or feel spoken for, including the forms of 'vernacular ventriloquism' discussed in Chapter 3. It also points to the political-cultural task of *building a bloc* – assembling different groups into a (temporary) unity by mobilising a set of concerns that they appear to share. In the remainder of this chapter, I explore the formation of the 'Brexit bloc' (involving not just 'identity conservatives', though they were certainly crucial to its voicing) and its trajectory through to the 'Boris bloc' of 2019. I begin with the question of loss: a 'structure of feeling' (Williams, 1977) at the heart of Brexit.

## Affecting the nation: the politics of loss

Practices of articulation in contemporary politics, notably the vernacular ventriloquism that appears to speak on behalf of others, regularly include the performance of affect or emotion. Here I want to focus on one particular affective thread – the *sense of loss* that is evoked across the moment of Brexit. It is identified by Sobolewska and Ford as a central theme of identity conservatism but attention is needed to how loss is experienced – and articulated. Judith Butler helpfully distinguishes between two aspects of this process, noting that while many political movements are motivated by a sense of loss it can be more 'difficult to read ... how these passions then get transmuted into certain kinds of political claims' (interview in Olson and Worsham, 2000: 28).

Butler indicates the space of possibility for a politics of articulation – the practices through which the 'transmutation' of loss might be accomplished. As with many other affects, loss is a rather generic term but the political-cultural conflicts of a specific moment involve addressing and articulating *particular* senses of loss. Indeed, I will suggest that, in the moment of Brexit (and its afterlives), there have been multiple senses of loss in play, registering different experiences, domains of life and complex entanglements of imagined and material senses of loss. In Sobolewska and Ford's reading, the 'identity conservatives' feel themselves displaced, neglected and abandoned by a political system that has declining interest in 'people like us', a feeling that becomes expressed as nostalgia for a 'lost way of life'.

One crucial dimension of this sense of loss concerns the nature of waged work. This valorises a very particular version of 'work' – and the perceived independence that it brought. As I indicated in Chapter 3, when discussing the 'left behind', the reference point is the experience of the core working class in Euro-Atlantic Fordism – and the associated form of worker that was both racialised and gendered. This experience was some distant from what might be called waged work-in-general, but it has consistently been used as the normative reference point for discussions of 'loss' in the formerly Fordist societies of the global North. These structures of waged work were intimately related to the organisation of the social – around a profoundly classed, racialised and gendered 'normal' centred on a commitment to full (male) employment, with the family (and predominantly women) as the primary source of care and welfare (Williams, 1989, 2021). As I argued in Chapter 2, this structuring of the social became deeply contested during the 1960s and 1970s as its normative principles (and their naturalisation) became the focus for intense challenges. In the process, the taken-for-granted structures – and beliefs – of this model of the social both came under threat and emerged as the focus of 'restorationist' beliefs and politics. These often centred around ideas of people being *out of place*, insisting, for example, that 'a woman's place is in the home' or that racialised minorities should 'go back where you came from'.

The field of the social came to be reorganised in other ways too. From the late 1970s we saw the coincidence of several dynamics: the decline of collectivist organising (in trades unions especially, but in other forms of practice such as the Workers Educational Association and mutuals, cooperatives, and so on); the destabilisation and diminution of public services and public institutions, especially local government; and, not least, the erosion of forms of localised communal support and solidarity, often expressed in the idea of 'community'. Such relationships, institutions and practices became the focus of what Raymond Williams would call 'residual' attachments and identifications, precisely because 'certain experiences, meanings, and values which cannot be expressed or substantially verified in terms of the dominant culture, are nevertheless lived and practised on the basis of the residue – cultural as well as social – of some previous social and cultural institution or formation' (1977: 122).

This complex understanding of the social was powerfully evoked by David Lammy's claim that "people want the social back" (in an interview following the Grenfell Tower fire in 2017 (Adams, 2017)). Lammy's argument connects several threads, but especially drew on ideas of strong communities (although certainly not ones based on racial homogeneity and exclusion) and a local and national 'civic culture' that provides both collective infrastructure and institutions that enable attachment and identification. Above all, this points to a public realm that is both embodied in, and sustained by, public services which have the capacity to enable individual and collective development (as well as providing collective security). This version of the sense of loss brings into view a different process of abandonment – the systematic degradation of the public realm. The public realm was never quite the generous and inclusive collectivity that such nostalgia may suggest, and was, indeed, the focus of constant struggles to overcome its exclusions and subordinations. Nevertheless, the contrast to the contemporary emaciated and impoverished version of the public realm is striking.

This sense of loss certainly contributes affective weight to the feeling that 'nobody is bothered about ordinary people'. All the leading political parties in England have colluded in this dismantling during the decades where they relentlessly pursued the promises of neoliberal growth, market freedoms and the liberation of choice-making individuals. The accumulation of affective and material dislocations engendered by those processes certainly contributed to the profound sense of political disaffection. Although scepticism and cynicism about politics and politicians have long been a significant element of the subordinate condition, the pursuit of the neoliberal fantasy (in its many incarnations) played a decisive role in the spread and intensification of such orientations in popular culture.

In parallel, the deepening contestation of racialised structures of supremacy and domination and the belief systems that undergirded them has been a potent dynamic (rather than just the arrival of increasing numbers of migrants). The struggles around racialised subordination and racism have taken different forms, though often focusing on policing and the criminal justice system. Most recently, the emergence of Black Lives Matter and the drive to decolonise British institutions from museums to universities have renewed those conflicts. Such challenges to various forms of racism have produced a variety of 'morbid symptoms': the denial of race (as in France), the denial of racism, the endless slides between morphological and cultural signifiers of difference, the rise and fall of multi-culturalism, the discovery – and denial – of institutional racism, the collective psychodrama of Gilroy's 'postcolonial melancholia' and the backlash against changes that 'went too far'. Here, varieties of equality politics and policies – around race, gender, disability and sexuality, for example – became the focus for reaction and restoration, standing accused of undermining British values and of neglecting the 'native' or 'indigenous' people (involving a bizarre inversion of colonial categories). In this field of arguments, we might also think of 'anticipated' loss: the sense that these equality movements would – in some future moment – do away with the existing order of things (and its attendant powers and privileges). It may not have happened yet, but if such demands were allowed to go unchecked, British history/culture/society/social order would be destroyed.

The apparently singular 'sense of loss' performs two crucial functions in the political-cultural field of the conjuncture. On the one hand, it provides a convenient – and potent – placeholder term that can be deployed by a range of commentators and activists trying to identify the new politics of populism and nationalism. In this guise, the 'sense of loss' provides a powerful way of connecting those described as the 'left behind' or the 'disaffected' to new political formations, such as the Vote Leave campaign, Trumpism and other nationalist-populist movements across Europe and elsewhere. On the other hand, it serves as a powerful articulatory device for those political projects: they recurrently claim to defend a cherished national, popular, neglected 'way of life'. Part of their success lies in their ability to *selectively* address and give voice to those sentiments of loss. It is important to grasp the double movement in these practices: they are profoundly selective, focusing on some aspects of loss (and some types of cause for those losses). And they simultaneously involve a practice of *articulation* – a way of offering people the chance to see themselves being recognised and spoken for.

## Articulating the 'Brexit bloc'

The underlying point behind this discussion of loss and its varieties is that different experiences, desires and disaffections circulate through the imagery of loss. The selective mobilisation of loss enabled the construction of a 'Brexit bloc' connecting diverse social groups into an apparent unity – attaching them to the identity of Leavers. These social groups have been described in different terms that point to the process of construction *across* differences. For example, Cochrane has suggested that the Leave vote mobilised a

> strange alliance between those in the Conservative heart lands for whom traditional forms of social and political authority were being undermined in the context of 'post-imperial melancholy' [Gilroy, 2005] or 'self-pity' (O'Toole, 2018) and those in the deindustrialized regions for whom post-imperial decay was associated with economic decline while the promise of 'Europe' was always tarnished by the same experience. (Cochrane, 2020: 168–169)

The socially mixed character of the Leave vote has been explored in work from the National Centre for Social Research who found three distinct groups that contributed:

- *Economically deprived, anti-immigration.* Those with least economic resources and who are most anti-immigration and nationalistic. Various labels can be attached to this group, such as the 'left behind' or 'just about managing'. They form the bedrock of UKIP support and have been politically disengaged in the past.
- *Affluent Eurosceptics.* This group are more Conservative than UKIP and more middle class. Yes, they are anti-immigration but they are also interested in Britain's independence and are noticeably anti-welfare.

- *Older working classes.* They are on low incomes and have little in the way of formal qualifications – but do not feel poor or badly educated. They are concerned about immigration and changing identity but are socially different from the first group.

So, the Leave vote was underpinned by the campaign's ability to draw together a broad-based coalition. It is much more wide-ranging than the 'left behind' (Swales, 2016: 27; see also UK in a Changing Europe, 2020, on 'comfortable leavers').

For my purposes, it is important to note that a *bloc* – in Gramscian terms – is more than an electoral coalition. Indeed, the concepts of bloc – and historical bloc – play a significant but complicated role in Gramsci's reflections on political issues and struggles for hegemony (see, for example, Showstack Sassoon, 1987; Gill, 2002). Here I treat the idea of bloc as denoting a (temporary) *unity in difference*, bringing together social groups (or fractions of them) through a mixture of material, affective and symbolic alignments – but under the leadership of (fractions of) dominant social and economic groups (typically fractions of capital) that promise the pursuit of the 'national interest'.

In the moment of Brexit, Leave voters were summoned to join a bloc that was headed by a distinctive alliance: key fractions of rentier capital (often in the form of hedge funds) allied to some more idiosyncratic incarnations of other fractions of capital: Arron Banks (founder of Vote Leave and funder of UKIP), Anthony Bamford of JCB, James Dyson, Jim Ratcliffe of Ineos and Tim Martin of Wetherspoons. They embodied, even if they did not necessarily represent, multiple forms of capital (extractive, manufacturing, service sectors). The bloc included, and was supported by, most of the tabloid press and an elusive network of social media operations – in which the work of Cambridge Analytica has remained a continuing focus of attention for enabling political profiling and targeting (see, for example, *The Guardian*, n.d.) The bloc was fronted by a cast of political figures: Conservative Party opportunists (Michael Gove and Boris Johnson, aided and abetted by Dominic Cummings); long-standing Labour opponents of the EU (Gisela Stuart and Kate Hoey) and, of course, the ubiquitous Nigel Farage (then of UKIP). This cast and their supporting figures certainly enabled the complex 'voicings' – the varieties of ventriloquism – needed to animate the various elements of the Brexit bloc and create the sense of a national project.

Then, as both Cochrane and Swales indicate, the bloc brought together these leading elements with fractions of the working and middle classes, articulated through different identities and registers: loss (ranging from the way of life to imperial greatness), anxiety (about the preservation and transmission of wealth), desire (for progress, for a change, for a chance to be heard) and varieties of nationalism, including racist ones. Material concerns were certainly in play and some commentators have pointed to the significant role that home ownership has played in putting together the Brexit vote (for example, Breach, 2019). More generally in the unfolding conjuncture, home ownership was a critical material and cultural cement constructing the imagined common interest of all rentiers, from transnational corporations to individual private pension holders and home owners (see, for example, Davies, 2019; Christophers, 2020).

Brexit cut across established party affiliations and attachments, dividing the two main UK parties – a shift enabled by its status as a referendum. While most attention was focused on the splits in the Conservative Party which drove Cameron's decision to offer a referendum, there were also substantial divisions on the Left, including within the Labour Party and the Trades Union movement. These centred on the argument for what became known as 'Lexit': a Left Exit from the EU. This built on a long-standing critique of the European Union as a vehicle of globalisation and neoliberalisation in which possibilities for socialist politics and policies had been systematically undermined. Those arguing the case for Lexit pointed to the punitive response of the EU to the Greek debt crisis (Lapavitsas, 2019), while issues of economic and public policy, such as investment in cooperatives or the renationalisation of public utilities were key concerns. Following the Brexit vote, some argued that a future Corbyn-led Labour government should combine Brexit negotiations with a commitment to radical social and economic transformation, focused on the redistribution of power and wealth (for example, Buxton, 2017; Guinan and Hanna, 2017).

Although it is not the focus of my arguments here, it needs to be acknowledged that the Remain vote also involved a fragile coalition constructed from diverse social groups. This bloc was headed by leading fractions of national and transnational capital (industrial and financial); much of the broadsheet press and large sections of most of the political parties. Remain voters tended to come from racialised minorities, from the public sector-based and more socially liberal fractions of the middle classes and some sections of the working class, especially younger voters, and tended to be based in large cities and university towns.

In the same way as the Leave vote, the Remain vote was forged from diverse attachments and orientations. These ranged from an enthusiastic endorsement of the EU as an economic space and marketplace to a more 'cosmopolitan' view of Europe as a political-cultural space, and even from an attachment to the increasingly residualised elements of the EU's 'social dimension'. At this point, it is vital to avoid a simplifying distinction that treats Brexit as the irrational product of a politics of rage and the Remain campaign and vote as the continuation of 'normal' (that is, rational, considered, or even calculating) politics. In practice, the Remain campaign, characterised as 'Project Fear' by its opponents, consistently made efforts to evoke both anxiety and anger about the risks of leaving the EU (and, in the process, tried to marshal lots of heavyweight national and international bodies to underline those risks). The various attachments to both 'Europe' and the EU that mobilised Remain voters were frequently, and sometimes explicitly, weighed against the problems of the 'actually existing EU' (especially after the Greek crisis) and the problems of entering into the unholy alliance that voting Remain involved (which involved siding with the architects of austerity, Cameron and Osborne).

In the end, Leave won, albeit narrowly. Its victory generated new political-cultural alignments and new political and governmental problems. The following few years saw considerable political turbulence as the challenge of making sense of Theresa May's claim that 'Brexit means Brexit' came to occupy much of the political landscape. In the following sections, I explore the unstable trajectory of the Brexit bloc between 2016 and 2022.

## An uncertain trajectory: party politics and the Brexit bloc

The 2016 referendum created new lines of antagonism in British politics as Leavers and Remainers fought over the meaning of Brexit, its conditions and consequences. All of the main political parties experienced both internal turbulence and the challenge of aligning themselves with this new landscape – not least UKIP itself, which was superseded in some ways by the Brexit Party launched by Nigel Farage and others in April 2019 to ensure that the UK left the EU. In the aftermath of the vote, the Conservative Party found itself needing a new leader following the resignation of David Cameron (who went off to write his memoirs (Cameron, 2019), and take up a consultancy career). He was succeeded by Theresa May, who saw an opportunity in 2017 to call an election to capitalise on the referendum result and the emergence of the 'Brexit bloc'. The strategy was not successful. In an election where voting tended to revert back towards a 'two party' model, May increased the Conservative vote (over 2015) by 5.5 per cent but a Labour Party led by Jeremy Corbyn increased its vote share by 9.5 per cent (generating its largest vote share since 2001). The effect of the distribution of votes and seats was to leave the Conservatives without an overall majority in the Commons, necessitating a deal for support from the Northern Irish DUP.

The 'Corbyn effect' (Perryman, 2017) has been much debated but his leadership certainly had a dramatic impact on party membership, more than doubling it from 198,000 in 2015 to 552,000 in 2018 (Whiteley et al, 2019: 81). At a time when most arguments were about political disaffection and withdrawal, the stimulation of membership was a significant development. Whiteley et al suggest that the rise reflected a combination of factors: changing political demography, Corbyn's personal style of doing politics and a 'left-wing' political agenda, although, as Gamble observed, the 2017 manifesto was rather more old style social democratic than socialist (2017: 65). For many, the Corbyn moment promised the possibility of 'politics otherwise' in both style and substance. In particular, the possibility of a politics that was pro-social and pro-public looked radically different from both the depoliticising neoliberal centrism and the government enforced austerity that followed the financial crash of 2008. In this sense, Corbyn spoke to a different sense of 'loss' (a social democratic public realm, with collective infrastructure and welfare) and combined that with the possibility of a different future (in several different registers: economic strategy, political style and a distinctive internationalism). Corbyn and Corbynism appeared as a threat to managed neoliberalism and were subjected to intense attacks within and beyond the Party, including a relentless demonisation of Corbyn in the mass media (Wayne, 2021).

## Under new management: Johnson and the bloc

May's failure to increase or even maintain the Conservative majority was punished: she was replaced by Boris Johnson as leader of the Conservative Party and Prime Minister, promising to 'get Brexit done' – a promise that garnered support from some Remainers suffering 'Brexit exhaustion'. He called a general election in December 2019 on the back of this promise and was rewarded with a landslide electoral victory which revitalised the 'Brexit bloc' and hardened its appeal in the Leave voting towns of the English Midlands and North and Wales. Johnson was able to connect working- and middle-class fractions through a Leave revivalism, a strong English nationalism and, intriguingly, a promise to 'level up' the country. The idea of 'levelling up' appeared as the latest in a series of Conservative concerns about the political and social effects of deepening inequality. Theresa May had previously committed to remedying 'seven burning injustices' when she became Prime Minister in 2016 (for the promises and performance, see BBC Reality Check, 2019). 'Levelling up' remained a theme of the Johnson government, for the most part largely and elusively symbolic, although a cabinet reshuffle in September 2021 created a Minister for Levelling up, Housing and Communities (Michael Gove). 'Levelling up' was combined with what can only be described as 'levelling down' (Williams, 2021: 65, 111) as benefits were cut in the perpetuation of austerity by other means.

Johnson's combination of promises – and the political-cultural nationalism undergirding them – brought a potent electoral bloc into being (aided by the Labour Party's internecine warfare and the public demonisation of Corbyn). The Conservative electoral success was branded as the fall of the 'Red Wall' – a series of Labour held seats across England and Wales from the North East to South Wales (see, for example, Mattinson, 2020; Rayson, 2020). Rayson

(2020) argues that the shift to Conservative voting in such seats marked a change in 'public narratives' in which a collective understanding of the places and people as Labour voting shifted to the view that 'the Labour Party no longer represents people like us'. Others have argued that the 'Red Wall' and its fall is, itself, a political narrative, deployed in the contested political-cultural landscape. Baston (2019) highlights the need to distinguish between a strand of seats that were indeed 'traditionally' held by Labour (largely in declining one-industry towns) and other seats that were historically more volatile in electoral terms (see also Edgerton, 2021).

The issue of the 'Red Wall' matters because it has been central to the arguments about the causes of Labour's failure – and what must be done to remedy it. Indeed, the pollster and author Deborah Mattinson (one of the main proponents of the 'Red Wall' narrative) became Labour's Director of Strategy when Keir Starmer replaced Jeremy Corbyn as Labour leader in 2020. Much of the debate centred around a familiar view of the 'traditional' working class and its historic attachment to Labour. This argument mobilises some very different analyses connected by a profoundly traditionalist view of the working class itself. These arguments about Labour's strategic calculations parallel what Robbie Shilliam (2020) calls the contemporary redemption of the 'ordinary' working class. He traces both the long history of the racialised working class and its contemporary salience in both Conservative and Labour thinking (notably in the intersections between 'Red Conservatism' and 'Blue Labour'). His work reveals the historical, philosophical and cultural threads that underpin (but are rarely visible in) contemporary debates about political strategies and calculations, especially in the juxtaposition of the 'traditional working-class voter' and the younger, socially mobile, and socially liberal groups.

One key political-cultural device central to building and sustaining the 'Boris bloc' (Schwarz, 2019; Clarke, 2020a) has been a form of systematic *historical amnesia*, embodied in promises to overcome the dysfunctional past of the nation (and the errors of previous national governments) as though neither the Party nor the current leaders had any involvement in this history. In an astonishing public lecture, Michael Gove (office holder in Conservative governments from 2010 to 2022) argued that there was "a deep sense of disenchantment on the part of many of our citizens with a political system they feel has failed them". Indeed, he argued that this

'sense that those who had been in power had presided over a growing gulf in both wealth and attitudes, and were no longer working in solidarity with other citizens, was the backdrop for the crises in authority which started during the first decade of this century.

All these factors underlay the revolt against the elites which saw voters desert established parties, withdraw their support for the economic consensus which had underpinned globalisation for at least three decades and, in many cases, they chose to opt for polarised identity politics rather than stay with broadbased national political movements.' (Gove, 2020)

In a similar vein, Johnson recurrently spoke of failures of government and politics as though he was not a member of the 'political class' and had not been a part of, and indeed minister in, several Conservative governments. Instead, this 2019 Conservative Party presented itself as the new broom, ready to make things different. This amnesia was central to the populism of the Leave movement (as practised by both Gove and Johnson) and was a foundation point for the Johnson government, enabling its promises about restoring public services, putting an end to austerity and, more generally, putting the Great back in Britain. It is a strangely establishment form of populism, denying its own history and location in favour of celebrating the people and their 'common sense'. This historical amnesia also makes possible the sheer heterogeneity of the Johnson-led party: mixing 'One Nation' Conservatism with a renewal of globalisation, combining 'levelling up' with the commitment to reduce taxation, aligning the promise of progress with the celebration of nostalgia, practising racism and at the same time – and very selectively – condemning racism.

This heterogeneity of Johnson's Conservatism (or what might be deployed at different moments for different audiences, since it was nothing if not performative) was central to the building and maintenance of the bloc. Writing shortly after the 2019 election, Ken Spours (2020) drew attention to the 'shape shifting' character of British Conservatism and its importance in Johnson's remaking of the Party. Although the Conservative Party had a long history of political innovation and an ability to switch its 'political personae' to maintain power, Johnson made it a defining feature of his leadership, having reset the Party in his own image (clearing out older One Nation and/or Remain-inclined MPs for the 2019 election). In the process, he tried on a range of political masks and voicings, ventriloquising different constituencies without much attention to issues of coherence or consistency. Bill Schwarz has suggested that there is a profound and paradoxical class character to Johnson's engagement with power and politics: 'We know that Johnson himself, personally, relishes the enticements of destruction … [In this] he was following a long line of upper-class men drawn to the erotics of taking apart the social system they'd long been tutored to conserve, and allying themselves to the perversities of power' (2019: 14).

Johnson's public persona also centred on a distinctive performative style, with him being variously described as showman, clown, orator and a Fool in the Shakespearian tradition (Docx, 2021). This tendency to play to the crowd made it hard to identify his political character (as if politicians should be singular and coherent subjects) but it may be more productive to emphasise and explore his capacity to be multiple and mobile in political-cultural terms. Spours also speculated about the likelihood of this shape shifting continuing as a Johnson government encountered new challenges and possibilities in practice. This expectation was borne out in practice as a sort of neo-Keynesianism, or what Gerbaudo (2021) calls conservative 'neo-statism' (especially after the arrival of the pandemic), was combined with deepening anti-democratic and authoritarian concentrations of power and a commitment to the pursuit of 'culture wars' (discussed further in Chapters 7 and 8). Faced with increasingly unsettled – and unsettling – economic, social and political conditions, the *pace* of shape shifting increased as part of a political-cultural strategy that simultaneously proclaimed innovation and promoted further attacks of amnesia – exemplified in a recurrent tendency to make new funding announcements that involved recycling funds which had already been committed (see, for example, Hargrave, 2021).

Spours suggested a range of areas in which 'Johnsonism' might encounter problems. These ranged from the consequences of its selective alignment with fractions of capital (some sections of finance capital, rather than manufacturing), through its international isolationism (pivoting on a Trumpian US), the challenges of new politics, especially around the environment, to the implications of profoundly English-centric understanding of the Union (Spours, 2020: 11–12). It is fair to say that all of these emerged in practice as sites of strain for the Johnson government, even before the arrival of COVID-19, threatening the coherence of the bloc. However, rentierism proved an exceptionally persistent foundation for the bloc as both capital and housing markets remained buoyant despite the other accumulating crises and, as I suggested earlier, provided one organising thread of the cross-class bloc attached to Brexit and the Conservatives. Writing before the 2019 election, Davies argued that we could 'look at the new conservative coalition as an alliance of rentiers. The "no deal" supporters are not classic rentiers. ... However, they are at a point in life where they have paid off their mortgages, and are living off the assets held by pension funds'. Davies went on to argue that:

> What this group shares with the Johnson/Farage backers is a lack of any immediate interest in labour markets or productive capitalism. What's the worst that could happen from the perspective of these interests? Inflation or a stock market slump would certainly harm them, but they may have forgotten that these things are even possible. Jeremy Corbyn terrifies them even more than Remain, as they believe he will tax capital, gifts and inheritance into oblivion (they are less concerned with income tax as they don't pay it). Where productivity gains are

no longer sought, the goal becomes defending private wealth and keeping it in the family. This is a logic that unites the international oligarch and the comfortable *Telegraph*-reading retiree in Hampshire. (Davies: 2019)

This view of rentierism requires an understanding of its double character. It is both a cluster of material interests and a political-cultural representation that naturalises and universalises 'Wealth' – especially its possession and transmission. It sustains an imaginary unity between the oligarch, the hedge fund manager and the home owner and asserts their common interest in a government that will preserve the conditions of their wealth. Davies' understanding of these fractions' *fear* of loss suggests the potential affinities and points of articulation with other senses of loss. Adding a further thread to this analysis of the 'Boris bloc', Nesrine Malik has argued that the resulting Conservative government rested on an implicit contract in which the protection of wealth and the protection of the (imagined) nation are combined. In this contract,

> Johnson is a contracted private service provider – as long as he delivers, then as clients, his supporters don't really care what he gets up to outside of the tasks he has been hired for. Those tasks are broadly Brexit and a shiny, prosperous country where jobs and funds have been cut or confiscated from those less deserving.
>
> The sub-clauses in the contract that flow from these two headline items all, one way or another, are about preserving the *financial and cultural assets* of Conservative voters. Maintaining an economy built on protecting private capital and property values, shifting the blame for low wages and unemployment on to immigrants rather than poor regulation of employers, and forging a synthetic supremacist national identity through relentless culture war posturing on colonial history, statues, flags and national anthems. (Malik, 2022a; my emphasis)

At stake here is an imagined nation (that is, these strata *projected* as a nation) which is both anxious and aggrieved and desires the restoration/maintenance of the proper order of things (and their place within it). Johnson's fall in July 2022 (following accumulating crises and shrinking trust within the Party) exposed how fragile the unity of the Party and the wider bloc might be. His replacement (Liz Truss) offered neoliberal zealotry in pursuit of 'growth, growth, growth' but crashed the economy within days, split the Party, fractured the electoral coalition and undermined the bloc – with only hedge funds (the extreme wing of finance capital) and libertarian think tanks remaining on side. Her resignation, after 45 days in office, triggered another scramble to fix a party dissolving before the public's eyes.

## Building blocs: the dynamics of mobilisation and demobilisation

In this chapter, I have tried to argue for a view of politics as centred on the political-cultural work of articulation. Stuart Hall always stressed its double sense: articulation as the process of bringing to voice and articulation as constructing linkages and connections between different groups as they are brought into a political assemblage – a bloc or alliance. I have shown how the idea of loss – and the structure of feeling that it evokes – formed a critical point of articulation in the building of the 'Brexit bloc', enabling different groups to feel themselves being 'spoken for' (in the performance of vernacular ventriloquism by the Leave campaigns). At the same time, the heteroglossic character of the idea of loss enabled different losses to be assembled together as if they formed a unity. In the process, the different groups feeling those losses (of very different kinds) were drawn into a unity: a bloc of 'Leavers'. Three other issues flow from this argument.

First, people are not coherent and singular subjects: they think multiple thoughts, feel multiple things and express them in diverse registers and through different identities and identifications. Articulation is always a *selective* practice, drawing out some views, some experiences, some dispositions, some identities while ignoring or actively silencing others. The blocs that are formed are, therefore, always contingent assemblages – however coherent and natural they may appear to be.

Second, such blocs are consequently vulnerable to being dis-articulated and dis-assembled as other voicings circulate, as other desires, fears and frustrations are brought to voice, and as other identities and identifications are made available. For all its limitations, the Corbyn moment of 2017 stands as a reminder that other articulations, other mobilisations and other blocs are possible.

Third, these processes of articulation and assembly have parallel dynamics in which social groups find themselves *de-mobilised*, feeling themselves not spoken for by political movements. Although they are often described as 'withdrawing' from politics, it may be more accurate to say that the versions of politics on offer have withdrawn from them, not offering ways for them to identify or come to voice. McQuarrie (2017) argued that this was the experience of many poor and working-class black people in the US 2016 election, an experience that contrasted with the significant Democrat attempts to find ways of mobilising them in 2020. Both withdrawal and engagement are possible depending on the combination of political-cultural repertoires on offer, the party political infrastructures and the prevailing regulation of electoral processes (as the recent fierce contention in the US and UK over voter registration, proof of identity and accessibility of voting demonstrates). These shifts provide an important reminder that the realm of the political is not exhausted by party politics and the act of voting.

People may exist in various states of disaffection – passive dissent, deploying weapons of the weak or actively engaging in what Roth (2018) calls 'counter movements' – that exist alongside, and often outside, the narrow field of formal politics.

In the chapters that follow, I explore the accumulating crises, contradictions and conflicts that Johnson and the 'Boris bloc' have had to confront – and consider some of the strategies developed to manage them. These troubles range from the continuing problems of 'getting Brexit done' even after the UK formally left the European Union, to the deepening economic crises, the pandemic, the political-cultural antagonisms around racialised divisions, struggles over violence against women and conflicts over the advancing climate catastrophe. Subsequently I examine the deepening crises of the party, the bloc and the state as these strategies failed and consent evaporated.

# Pause for Thought 2: Thinking Articulation

In Chapter 3, I approached the significance of conjunctural analysis by exploring some of the accounts that have been offered for 'Brexit'. Across the many accounts, I focused on three themes in particular – populism, neoliberalism and the 'left behind' – because they exemplify two concerns that have preoccupied me since the Brexit vote. First, they tend to frame events and their causes epochally (in Raymond Williams' terms), treating the event as part of an era or period dominated by one condition – populism or neoliberalism. Second, they tend towards a singular view of explanation, relegating other dynamics or forces to subordinate or marginal roles. In contrast, I have been developing the view that conjunctural analysis requires ways of thinking *contingently* and thinking *complexly*. Conjunctures are formed through contingent – and contested – arrangements of times, places, people, possibilities and powers. There is, as I tried to show in Chapter 2, always more than one dynamic in play – and it is the complexity of their entanglements that both forms the conjuncture and creates its unstable trajectory.

Chapters 3, 4 and 5 have been devoted to thinking about the UK as a complex *social formation* that contains heterogeneous social forces. That idea has its origins in a distinction within Marxism between modes of production (made up of the forces and relations of production) and social formations, understood as the more concrete arrangements in which multiple modes of production are combined with their other elements – such as politics, ideology and (in some versions) processes of social reproduction. These are not just the 'superstructures' (in the old base versus superstructure distinction) but form the necessary conditions of existence for production (and the extraction of surplus value) to take place. But it will be clear that I want to make the idea of 'social formation' do rather more work than that.

My view of the social as a field of complex and shifting relationships is central to this. Such relationships are structured by divisions, hierarchies, forms of domination and subordination that certainly include class divisions (and sub-divisions) but extend well beyond those. In the current conjuncture, they certainly involve the legacies and continuing effects of colonialism (and the racialised imaginaries of the world that emerged from there); they involve the patriarchal and heteronormative orderings of gendered divisions (and the preferred form of the nuclear family as the way of organising them). More than that, they involve the many distinctions based in the productivist division between able-bodied and disabled people, as well as differences around sexuality and sexual identities. The list is long, precisely because the social is a field characterised by shifting and contested 'mappings' (Catherine Hall's phrase) of difference through which inequality and power are ordered – and challenged. As a result, social reproduction is also always complex (and contested) given that it involves the reproduction of heterogeneous social relations, even as they are being contested. This matters because it is in the field of the social that people live their lives, imbue them with meanings and affects, come to adapt, succumb, refuse and resist – all in unsettled combinations of material and imaginary relations.

Other relations, processes and practices are threaded through the social. People work at things, sometimes for wages. They form relationships, engage with others in multiple ways. They become animated and join groups, develop movements or engage in the formal practices of politics. They live in and through time – passing it, spending it, or, as Sarah Marie Hall (2021) suggests, doing a lot of waiting. They make sense of things (including describing them as senseless or beyond understanding). They invest themselves affectively in positive and negative ways, attributing value to all sorts of activities and relationships while regarding others as not worth the time or effort. I deliberately used the phrase 'threaded through the social' at the start of this paragraph because much social analysis marks out a series of different sites, domains, fields or levels. Here is the economy, where people make things, including money. Over there is politics, where people make decisions or choices, or perhaps just vote (or not). Then there is the field of culture, in which meanings are produced, circulated and consumed. Sometimes, this field is called ideology. This splitting of life into different domains feels odd but is very convenient for the organisation of academic work because most fields are imagined to belong to one discipline (Economics, Political Science, Sociology, and so on). For me, cultural studies disrupted these tidy divisions and offered a route into thinking about how ways of thinking and feeling were always entangled with forms of power and ordering – which were always contestable. This brings me to the significance of articulation in this approach.

I have been concerned with the ways in which meanings and affects are publicly, collectively articulated – how they 'come to voice'. At one level, this is a constant everyday process: people think, talk, exchange views and make statements about things (including 'I don't know'). It is both banal and complicated, since everyday life is always *heteroglossic*: it is composed of many different possible voicings, ways of thinking and ways of feeling and people have to negotiate that complexity. But it is also the focus of what

I have insisted on calling political-cultural work as parties, movements, networks and organisations strive to address aspects of everyday thinking and feeling and make them 'come to voice'. I have talked about this as a form of *ventriloquism* – the practice of trying to speak on behalf of the 'people', crafted through a vernacular style, that is central to contemporary forms of populist politics. But this process is integral to mobilisation. Articulation names the moment of connection or recognition: the sense of feeling recognised, addressed and being 'spoken for'. I emphasised how this is necessarily a selective process (given the complexity of people as social subjects and the heteroglossic character of the cultures that they inhabit). In the present conjuncture, nationalist, authoritarian, populist political projects have been effective in the selective voicing of popular frustrations, grievances, forms of despair and anger. But, as Gramsci understood, the practice of articulation is also integral to progressive politics, striving to find and bring to voice what he called the 'good sense' that lies within the mixed bag of 'common sense'.

Such political-cultural work is the precondition for the other meaning of articulation that I want to underline here. The practices of speaking to and speaking for segments of the population enable their mobilisation and potential articulation into a 'bloc' – a temporary 'unity in difference'. The differences matter – political-cultural work aims to suppress or marginalise differences for the sake of constructing a felt unity of interest or identity that can be linked to a leading (or oppositional) group. As we have seen in relation to the 'Brexit' and 'Boris' blocs (and the threads that connect them), the work of assembling, mobilising and performing the unity of such blocs is substantial – the connecting of common identifications and commitments, and the work of ventriloquising that projected unity are demanding tasks. But as I insisted earlier, one reason that Stuart Hall made articulation so central to his approach was that it emphasised contingency: that which had been articulated into a unity in difference could always come apart or be dis-articulated.

In the following chapters, I explore some of the emerging sources and sites of strain that have unsettled the dominant bloc and its attempts to create a trajectory through the conjuncture. The accumulating crises, contradictions and conflicts of the present moment – this distinctive phase of the conjuncture – have threatened to outrun the capacity of the dominant bloc to sustain its rule.

6

# An Accumulation of Crises

This chapter explores developments in the present conjuncture that have shaped the terrain on which the Battle for Britain is being fought. Building on the arguments about heterogeneous social relations and the possibilities for political mobilisation and demobilisation in the preceding chapters, I turn to the accumulating crises that have shaped the current dynamics of the conjuncture. In Chapter 2, I argued that the UK (and the Euro-Atlantic system) had taken shape around two different conjunctural formations. The first, formed in the post-war/Cold War period, was articulated around the end of colonialism, the rise of Atlantic Fordism and the political-cultural formations in which it was embedded (centred on imaginaries of work, family and welfare within a distinctive national framing). The post-war settlements connecting these different domains were, of course, under strain from their very beginning and the dynamics of the conjuncture centred on the proliferation of contradictions, conflicts and crises that culminated in the crisis of hegemony of the 1970s traced in *Policing the Crisis* (Hall et al, 2013).

I argued for treating 1979 as marking the transition from that conjuncture: a transition marked by a shift in the larger 'life of the state' and in its relationships to the whole social formation. The new settlements that were assembled then combined neoliberal desires with an authoritarian populism in ways that framed the following decades. That combination was constantly reworked as new challenges appeared and new economic, social and political-cultural concessions were extracted. Consent, as Jeremy Gilbert has argued, centred on consumption as the form in which promises of inclusion and progress were made (for example, Gilbert, 2015; Gilbert and Williams, 2022). But this fragile and conditional consent was always intimately interwoven with emerging forms of authoritarianism, expanding the state's coercive capacities in multiple ways.

The Battle for Britain has been taking place on the landscape of the accumulated contradictions, crises and antagonisms of this conjuncture. Just as Thatcherism promised to 'set people free', so the promised resolution of these continuing and deepening troubles was expressed in the fantastical claim that everything could be resolved by 'taking back control'. By this point, the UK was marked by the growing geopolitical splintering of the UK and proliferating forms of dissent and disaffection. This chapter – and those that follow it – explore the attempts to construct and enforce new settlements in the face of what some have called the 'polycrisis' (see, inter alia, Juncker, 2016; Zeitlin et al, 2019; Alexander, 2022; Lawrence et al, 2022; Tooze, 2022a).

This chapter focuses on the accumulation and intersections of crises as they have been experienced in the UK (though the Unitedness of the UK is also one of the crises). Chapter 7 explores some of these developments through the lens of 'race' given that – not for the first time – key aspects of the current troubles have been framed and refracted through dynamics of racialisation and racism. Chapter 8 then turns to the political-cultural dynamics of crisis in another way – examining what *Policing the Crisis* framed as the expanding crises of the ruling party and the dominant bloc. Chapter 9 turns to the state and explores how these dynamics have generated a crisis of the state itself. Throughout, I am concerned to examine the current *sense of crisis* alongside the accumulation of crises.

## The afterlives of Brexit

The Johnson government took office in 2019 on a wave of secessionist optimism, expressed in the promise to 'get Brexit done' and thereby liberate the United Kingdom from the European Union. The pitch appealed to both Leave voters and some Remain voters, exhausted by the continuing Brexit saga (and the vituperative political-cultural climate it had brought with it). The phrase 'why don't they just get it done' was heard with growing frequency between 2016 and 2019, usually concealing a profound ambiguity around what exactly might be involved in 'it'. Turning projections of imagined sovereignty into political and inter-governmental arrangements proved to be a difficult process. Political-cultural projects that seek to remake sovereignty, and the scalar and spatial orders in which sovereignty is embedded, articulate themselves through imaginaries: representations of a desired ordering of things. However, such projects also face the challenges of making those imaginaries come true in practice. These challenges include dismantling the existing institutionalised arrangements, embodied in treaties, maps, legislation, sets of habituated relationships, practices and places, as well as the everyday forms of affiliation and attachment. The process also requires the new order to be assembled in those same institutionalised formations (Clarke, 2020b). In the event, the efforts to make Brexit materialise brought about new disorders of space, scale and the challenges of inscribing sovereignty in a variety of social, political, governmental and constitutional forms proved contentious.

At the time of writing (October 2022), the problems of making 'Brexit mean Brexit' have ranged from the constitutional crisis of Johnson's efforts to prorogue Parliament in December 2019 (overturned by the Supreme Court), through recurring 'fishing wars' to the struggle to win new trade agreements. Perhaps most problematic have been the contradictions of the Northern Ireland protocol. This protocol was negotiated with the EU in order to avoid a 'hard border' between the Republic of Ireland (within the EU) and the North (within the UK) which, it was feared, would undermine the Good Friday agreement. Instead, the protocol created a border in the Irish Sea, between mainland Britain and Northern Ireland which proved difficult to manage – both practically and politically. Those who had negotiated the exit deal for the UK side tried to undo the protocol (notably Lord Frost, sometimes known as 'Frosty the No Man': see Kelly, 2021). It is difficult to tell whether these problems are a tribute to the UK government's incompetence (not reading the draft treaties or being unable to work out their implications) or are part of a long-running political–cultural strategy to find, and then recycle, 'enemies of the people' as a foundational element of the bloc's politics. The protocol was a continuing reminder of the marginalisation of Northern Ireland in the trajectory of Brexit – despite regular efforts, not least from the Republic, to remind people of its significance (O'Toole, 2021). Beyond this Northern Ireland-focused dynamic, Brexit has also been implicated in the growing pressure for a new Scottish independence vote and an increasing sense of Welsh distance from English dominance.

Brexit effects also contributed to a range of 'economic' crises, from labour shortages (farming, care work, HGV drivers) to supply chain problems (gas and fuel interruptions, food shortages) that became a focus for ritualised claims and denials about whether they are really 'global' issues or distinctively 'UK' problems. They were also visible in problems for exporting businesses (apparently borders work both ways) and a decline in overall UK exports. Meanwhile EU citizens in the UK have found themselves part of the UK's 'hostile environment' after the UK required them to apply for 'settled status' if they (and their family members) wished to remain in the UK (for example, Jablonowski, 2020).

Brexit was also heavily implicated in the deepening crisis of care. The social care sector had been heavily dependent on migrant workers who staffed the low-waged sector of care work (especially in care homes). The 'crisis of care' had been looming for some time (Dowling, 2021) and certainly not just in the UK (see, for example, Williams, 2018, 2021). In the UK, emerging problems of care provision had been assessed by the Dilnot Commission which in 2011 recommended (among other things) the 'capping' of care costs that individuals might face. The proposal was eventually accepted and legislated upon in 2015 but was then postponed in the face of Treasury worries about 'affordability'. Since then, the Treasury has, of course, continued to worry about affordability in ways that have stalled the urgent need for reform. There is nothing new about the crisis in care – except its deepening intensity and its global and transnational dynamics. The crisis has haunted the governments of the last decade. The Coalition government of 2010–15 promised to act on the Dilnot Report – and didn't. The Cameron government that came into office in 2015 also promised to reform social care – and didn't. The Johnson government of 2019 also started with a promise to reform social care – and didn't (Charlesworth et al, 2021). The crisis in care was to intersect – in terrifying ways – with the arrival and spread of COVID-19.

Fiona Williams argues that the crisis of staffing social care services has to be understood in the context of the global movement of care workers, as people (mainly women) travel to become carers in the nations of the global North. She makes visible how these flows have become entangled with the political strategies of the deinstitutionalisation and commodification of care, with unsettling consequences:

> The transnational movement of care labor intersects with other global crises. First, the effects of austerity following the global financial crisis have intensified states' search for more cost-effective care provision. … Second, the dependence of higher-income countries on migrant workers co-exists with a rise in anti-immigration xenophobia. The political debates about the refugee crisis are shaping changes in immigration policies which affect migrant care workers. These policies are becoming more restrictive not only toward 'unskilled' workers (into which category care workers fall) but also in limiting migrant eligibility to basic welfare provision. (Williams, 2018)

The complexly racialised and gendered dynamics of the care crisis were brought starkly into view following the arrival of COVID-19.

## Pandemic problems: 'following the science' or 'following the money'?

Several things were notable about the UK's encounter with COVID-19 beyond its self-proclaimed 'world leading' features. Many centred on the sluggish responses of a government which originally failed to pay much attention to the emerging pandemic (believing it to be a 'flu-like' problem). Subsequently, lockdowns and other interventions were constantly delayed, incurring extra infections, hospitalisations and deaths in each phase. Calvert and Arbuthnott (2021) have traced the unfolding saga of the Johnson government's approach from the original pursuit of 'herd immunity', through the disasters of delayed lockdowns, to the failures of 'track and trace' systems. They point to two devastatingly interlinked tendencies. First, Johnson himself seemed inattentive to the crisis, unwilling to be distracted from the triumphs of Brexit and painfully reluctant to introduce measures that would curb individual freedoms. Second, he inherited a state whose infrastructure had been hollowed out, privatised (notably testing laboratories) and impoverished materially and intellectually by a decade of Conservative austerity policies (themselves following on two decades of privatisation, contracting out and managerialisation). Calvert and Arbuthnott observe that 'contrary to the official line, Britain was not in a state of readiness for the pandemic' (2021: 8).

The deepening pandemic was to intersect brutally with the 'crisis of care' at the point when the government became anxious about the capacity of the NHS to cope as the rate of infection increased. The resulting efforts to empty hospital beds meant that up to 15,000 'medically fit' patients were to be discharged from hospitals. With no obligation to test, many infected patients were delivered to care homes, creating new waves of infection (in settings where PPE was typically non-existent). In response (and in denial), Matt Hancock (then Secretary of State for Health) frequently claimed that: 'Right from the start, it's been clear that this horrible virus affects older people most. So right from the start, we've tried to throw a protective ring around our care homes' (Press conference, 15 May 2020). This was one of many Hancock claims that proved unsustainable, and deaths in care homes (among both residents and staff) increased rapidly.

The impact of COVID-19 in the UK was crucially shaped by the collapsing state infrastructure that it encountered: an understaffed and underfunded NHS, a 'rationalised' and undernourished public health system and local authority services suffering from a decade of austerity-driven cuts, on top of decades of public sector 'reform'. It also was enmeshed in the differentiated and devolved governmental structure of the UK, with each of the nation regions having responsibility for aspects of policy and practice while the usual conflation of England and the UK continued. Each of the subordinate nations felt rarely consulted or even ignored in the centralising trajectory of the Johnson government, exacerbating political-cultural fissures.

Meanwhile, care provision for both adults and children encountered increasing difficulties, while the lengthy hospital waiting lists that had grown before the arrival of COVID-19 increased massively as beds were sequestered for coronavirus victims and planned operations were cancelled (often several times). Warnings had been issued after a pandemic planning exercise held in 2016 which

> uncovered crucial gaps in the UK's ability to plan and prepare for a
> pandemic at the local and national level. The recommendations from
> the report on the exercise appear to have been largely overlooked

by the Government which meant the UK started out at a significant disadvantage, with inadequate resources and resilience mechanisms. And cost-cutting and austerity can only have exacerbated these problems. (Blackburn, 2020)

In the moment of the pandemic, crisis and contradiction were intimately entwined. The decline of public capacity owed much to the decade of Conservative austerity as all public services were hit by reductions in funding and public service workers' salaries were effectively frozen. But the decline was also shaped by the effects of outsourcing and privatisation as both the private and voluntary sectors were enrolled into 'serving the public'. This notably diverted resources into the service of capital accumulation – whether providing infrastructure (such as the PFI for hospital building) or delivering services, such as care homes. By 2021, over three-quarters of care homes for older people and people with dementia were run by for-profit organisations (Quarmby and Norris, 2021).

## Business as usual?

The pandemic deepened this contradictory dynamic as the UK government saw the crisis as an opportunity for further contracting out – notably in the provision of PPE and the process of tracking and tracing potential cases of COVID-19 infection. Contracts were awarded with minimal scrutiny (as the government argued that urgency meant overriding due process), generating accusations of 'crony capitalism' where profitable contracts were allocated to contacts and friends of MPs and ministers. As Geoghegan (2020) has argued: 'Covid-19 has revealed the depth of cronyism and clientelism in British public life. More than almost any comparable state, Britain – or, more accurately, England – has outsourced swathes of its pandemic response, often to companies with strong links to Conservative politicians but little obvious relevant experience.'

Subsequently, investigations by the National Audit Office and others into pandemic contracting and business support indicated both the extent of fraud and systemic mismanagement of contracts (NAO, 2021, 2022). Even more striking was the decision to contract SERCO (a well-known outsourcing beneficiary) to provide test and trace services. The contract was issued in May 2020, via the NHS Test and Trace programme, originally headed by Baroness Dido Harding (friend of then Health Secretary Matt Hancock). The performance of this service (delivered by Serco) was damningly criticised in a Select Committees' report in October 2021 for having failed to achieve most of its objectives. However, as the *Financial Times* reported in November 2021, 'Serco has raised profit forecasts by millions of pounds as the outsourcer expects demand for the UK government's controversial

Covid-19 test and trace services to last longer than originally anticipated' (Plimmer and Provan, 2021).

In parallel with the pandemic, a major parliamentary row arose in 2021 over evidence that (privatised) water companies were discharging very high levels of untreated sewage into rivers and seas around the UK (see Allen and Pryke (2013) on the financialisation of water services). Conservative MPs (except for 27 rebels) backed the government's decision to reject a House of Lords amendment to an environment bill that would have placed a legal duty on water companies to reduce such outflows. Instead, following a wave of public protest, the government presented a revision that required such companies to 'take reasonable steps' to prevent such discharges and minimise their impact, with targets stretching to 2040 (*The Guardian*, 8 November 2021). The discharges and the mobilisations against them continued – and increased – during 2022. The old juxtaposition of 'private affluence and public squalor' (coined by J.K. Galbraith in 1958) has been repeatedly cited – and remade into the image of the 'effluent society'. The (non-)treatment of water-borne waste was only one element in a larger problem of the UK as a *non-regulatory* state across a range of environmental degradations (Monbiot, 2021a).

Central to these two examples (but visible in many others) is the extent of the entangling of capital and the state. Such entanglements are, of course, nothing new: what changes is the form of relationships that connect them. During the pandemic, the relationships became denser, more intimate (personalised in crucial ways) – and substantially more profitable. Their contribution to the public health of the nation is a rather different question.

## Governing the pandemic: denial, deferral and 'the science'

The dynamics of trying to govern the pandemic UK-style (and note that Wales and Scotland have had partly independent trajectories in these processes) have revealed government tendencies to defer and deny. Calvert and Arbuthnott's detailed account (2021) of the first year of the pandemic reveals the absolute centrality of *deferral*, with decisions constantly postponed and avoided. PPE, care home protections, international travel constraints, test and trace, lockdowns – all followed a distinct pattern of decisions postponed long past the critical moments. There was also a consistent pattern of *denial*: that things had happened or that statements had been made. The most notorious example centred on the trip to Durham made by Dominic Cummings (then the Prime Minister's chief of staff) and his family during lockdown and in breach of the lockdown regulations. However convoluted the various explanations of the trip eventually became, its most important impact was on levels of public trust in pandemic policies. Research had shown that levels of public compliance with lockdown and related rules had been much higher than anticipated, but Cummings' travels triggered a steady decline in compliance, often evoking the claim that he had demonstrated that 'there's one rule for us and one for them'.

In the meantime, public concern was also growing about reports of parties having been held at Downing Street in the Christmas period, 2020, when such gatherings were banned under pandemic rules (aka 'partygate'). As usual, denial came first: no such parties had taken place ... and if they had, all the rules had been followed. As John Crace observed, 'We were now in the realms of Schrödinger's Night Out. One that had both taken place and not taken place' (Crace, 2021). Denial was shortly followed by deferral – to an inquiry to be chaired by a senior civil servant who then had to be replaced when it became clear that he may have been at one of the parties (that had or had not taken place). The number of parties to be scrutinised (by this inquiry and an eventual Metropolitan Police investigation) multiplied. Public outrage focused on the disjuncture between Downing Street, ministries and the Conservative Party hosting such parties at a time when government regulations banned indoor socialising while many people had had relatives die without being able to visit them in hospital or care homes. Once again public anger crystallised around the sense that 'there's one law for them and one law for us': power and privilege trumped any claim that 'we are all in this together'. This issue was to dog Johnson until the end of his leadership in September 2022.

One central feature of pandemic governance was the claim to be 'following the science'. This was a strange claim for a Brexit-driven government closely linked to the Vote Leave campaign, which had been notably sceptical about expertise, equating it with liberal elitism. Its dismissal of the expert was perfectly captured in Michael Gove's claim that 'people in this country have had enough of experts', along with its attempted qualification: 'from organisations with acronyms saying that they know what is best and getting it consistently wrong' (later further qualified to claim he was referring to economists). It was the short version of the claim that stuck, not least because it was the counterpart to the populist logic of trusting the 'common sense' of the people (see Clarke and Newman, 2017).

However, what is most striking about Gove's claim is not the subsequent turn to expertise and science in his governmental work, but the *historical amnesia* that underpinned the claim in the first place. Gove had been a minister in the Coalition and Conservative governments that had deployed austerity as the articulating principle of government policy after 2010, relying on 'scientific' judgements from experts in 'organisations with acronyms', notably the IMF's belief in 'expansionary fiscal consolidation' or 'expansionary austerity' (see the critique by Guajardo et al, 2011). Other acronymic organisations played their part too: including the OECD, WTO and ECB (the Organisation for Economic Cooperation and Development, the World Trade Organization and the European Central Bank). I remarked on this historical amnesia in the previous chapter and it will appear again, as it forms one of the foundational epistemological conditions of contemporary UK Conservative politics, enabling each new strategy to be launched without any historical 'baggage'. It became a central thread in the claim made by Johnson and his supporters and fans that, despite it all, he 'got all the big calls right'.

Of course, the pandemic changed the place and value of 'expertise' as the UK government adopted the rhetorical device of insisting that, in all matters, it was 'following the science'. This claim begged a number of questions. First, which sciences and scientists constituted 'science' at any particular moment in time? The composition of the government's Scientific Advisory Group on Emergencies (SAGE) and its various subgroups was the subject of some controversy (once they were eventually de-anonymised). There were arguments about which sorts of science were included, notably the relative lack of global public health expertise and virology (Parliament Science and Technology Committee, 2021), and elsewhere about the thin involvement of social scientists. By May 2020, an Independent SAGE had been established with a different membership, committed to informing the public debate about the pandemic and proposed solutions.

Second, the 'Science' in the UK was crucially mediated by government officials – particularly the Scientific and Medical Officers who fronted many of the televised briefings alongside the Prime Minister and other members of the government. Calvert and Arbuthnott (2021: 181–183) point to important roles played by them in translating discussions taking place within the NHS and the SAGE committee meetings for the public, including the interpretation of scientific evidence about the use of face masks and the risks attached to large-scale events in the early days of the pandemic. Public policy scholar Paul Cairney noted that 'when UK government ministers describe being "guided by the science" they mean "our scientists". They rely on a small group of science advisers employed as insiders loyal to government and possessing the skills and networks to retain core insider status' (Cairney, 2021). This distinction was important for the public presentation – and consumption – of pandemic 'science', with debates *among* scientists receiving relatively little attention.

Third, the 'following the science' slogan (attributed to Dominic Cummings) was notably opaque about the temporalities at stake in 'following', while concealing the moments of political choice. 'Following' was represented as meaning decisions being directed by scientific judgements. In practice, it tended to mean lagging as far behind as possible, as the government constantly delayed critical decisions (for a detailed account, see the timeline developed by the Independent Sage (2021)).

Political dispositions and calculations were central to the UK's pandemic trajectory as choices were framed by calculations about cost ('can we afford to …?'), efficiency ('getting people back to work'), political principle (personal liberties versus compulsion) and the economic emergency (health *versus* the economy). Despite all these issues, 'following the science' remained a governmental mantra throughout 2020 and 2021, usually accompanied by muscular conceptions of 'wrestling with the virus'. Ministers and their staffs were claimed to be 'striving day and night' while making 'unceasing efforts' and 'straining every sinew', as though the promise of exhausted political bodies would be reassuring.

## And then ... the climate catastrophe

As I noted in Chapter 2, the climate crisis has both a long history and a distinctive temporality: long drawn out but with quickenings of pace and intensity. This generates a disconcerting rhythm as the crisis is dragged into view as an object of concern, only to disappear beneath the waves of everyday politics (and indeed 'business as usual'). The growing forces of scientific expertise and activist insistence have combined to demand not just public and political attention, but action. The pandemic and the environmental crisis are not, of course, separate problems. They are enmeshed through the ways that forms of environmental degradation have made pandemics more likely (for example, Tollefson, 2020).

As with the pandemic, the climate crisis is simultaneously a global crisis and takes distinctive local forms, whether that be the prospect of being driven from Pacific islands, suffering the consequences of the deforestation of the Amazon (intensified under Bolsanaro), having lives and livelihoods swept away by floods or being driven out by forest fires. Despite the growing urgency, dominant strategies continued to focus on ways to defer and deflect the demands for change. *Denialism* – a crucial articulation between right-wing politics and carbon capital – may have receded since the moment of peak-Trump (though it lingers in many forms and places) but a range of strategies for *deferral* have emerged that combine public acknowledgement of the crisis with the avoidance of doing anything too urgently. One strategy has involved varieties of 'greenwashing', a term coined by Westerveldt in 1986 which has gained increasing purchase as corporations (and others, including governments) try to add a 'green sheen' to their products and activities. Greenwashing has come to refer to a range of practices that seek to incorporate the imagery of environmental consciousness while obscuring continuing environmentally hostile processes and practices.

Other strategies have grown in prominence. A second critical route to deferring action (while claiming to contribute to developing solutions) has been the mirage of the 'technological fix' in which as-yet-undeveloped technologies (for example, carbon capture) are folded into government and private sector strategies. Deploying the future as a strategy for deferring action in the present is a common way of using the promise of technology to organise political time. This was central to the promise of 'net zero carbon' that came to dominate public discourse around the COP26 conference held in November 2021. As Dyke, Watson and Knorr (2021) argue, the *promise* of carbon capture technologies has played a critical role in enabling the use of what could then be represented as 'climate friendly coal'. They suggest that 'the mere prospect of carbon capture and storage gave policy makers a way out of making the much needed cuts to greenhouse gas emissions'. This is a particular version of what Levidow and Raman call 'sociotechnical imaginaries' (2020, following Jasanoff and Kim, 2015). They conclude an examination of the UK government's waste and energy strategies by suggesting that they recurrently evoke 'a techno-market fix [that] emphasizes several market-type elements: financial incentives as the main policy instruments, market competition as the means to stimulate technological improvements and strengthen global competitiveness' (Levidow and Raman, 2020: 632).

The discursive framing of these issues as 'economic' and/or 'technological' displaces them from political domains: 'letting the market decide' on the one hand, or 'following the science' on the other. These framings aim to insulate the issues from popular pressures in both discursive and temporal ways. Discursively, problems are inscribed in forms which value (and reproduce) certain forms of expertise. Temporally, the issues are bundled into a form of techno-futurism (Lo, 2018), in which resolutions are always about to be found and where we, the people, should have faith.

There is a third strategy of deferral in play – what Mann (2021) calls 'climate inactivism' – as politicians, corporations and thinktanks articulate reasons to *postpone* difficult choices. In the UK, Shenker has suggested, such tactics are being bundled together with 'culture wars' and 'social justice' discourses in claims that the poor need to be defended against the environmental avant-garde (another 'elite' set against the 'people'). Shenker highlighted Conservative MPs challenging net zero targets, including Craig Mackinlay who insisted that 'sooner or later, the public will rebel against this madness', while Steve Baker 'dismissed the Committee on Climate Change, which advises the government, as "unelected and unaccountable"' (Shenker, 2021).

Just as crises are interwoven and entangled, so are dominant strategies for responding to them – and to the social movements demanding action. Delay and deferral play a central role in the political-cultural struggles around crises: they are a part of 'chronopolitics' – the conflicts over time in the face of multiple temporalities (Huebener et al, 2016: 246). As I suggested in Chapter 2, the capacity to 'tell the time' is a central political objective: at stake is the orchestration of conceptions of past, present and future such that they point to the one and only way forward that can represent 'progress'.

## From Shropshire to Moscow: the tendrils of corruption

Meanwhile, back at the heart of government in the UK, other crises were in motion. Rapidly deepening concerns about corruption – in the business of government (for example, about COVID contracts) and the workings of the Party (for example, selling peerages) – intersected with concerns about the conduct of ministers and MPs. These concerns crystallised in the case of Owen Paterson, MP for North Shropshire. In 2022, the Parliamentary Standards Commission judged that he had breached lobbying rules and recommended a 30-day suspension from the Commons. Instead, the Prime Minister backed a campaign by a number of Conservative MPs to deflect the judgement (and the suspension) by turning the issue into a question about the reform of the Parliamentary Standards process itself. Conservative MPs were whipped (that is, required to vote by the Party) to support this manoeuvre which saved Paterson temporarily. However, the resulting parliamentary and public outrage was such that the vote was overturned the following day, and Paterson resigned as a member of parliament. His seat was subsequently lost to the Liberal Democrats in a massive electoral swing.

Some argued that this moment was the most visible example of corruption creeping into the British state:

> Collusive corruption is a term usually applied to other fields – such as companies colluding with public officials to fix tendering procedures for their mutual benefit – but it is a term that seems appropriate here as well.
>
> Perhaps this is a very British form of corruption: colluding to defuse the storm around a corrupt act, implicitly denying there was any substantial wrongdoing, changing the rules to benefit a friend, proposing a wholly inadequate alternative in order to get a better outcome – and all of this with the underlying suspicion that a future beneficiary of a neutered standards regime might be the Prime Minister himself. (Barrington, 2021)

This dynamic of political corruption was intimately connected with the 'relaxed' regime of financial governance that had made the UK an attractive destination for capital flows, not least from oligarchic, kleptocratic and criminal sources. The rise of the City of London as a major financial centre – and symbol of London as a 'World City' (Massey, 2007) – rested on its capacity to attract money at precisely the point where growing concentrations of wealth were looking for safe havens (that is, protected from governments and their taxation policies (see Bullough, 2022)). London also became a space for investing such wealth, in real estate, art and luxury goods. There had been growing concern about these processes and their economic, political and social consequences, with the *Financial Times*, among others, calling for the 'London laundromat' to be cleaned up (2018). However, the flows of wealth into the UK, London, and the Conservative Party's finances continued until their uncomfortable intersection with another crisis – Russia's invasion of Ukraine in 2022. The reaction across the West, which led to the imposition of economic sanctions on Russia – and the members of the Putin regime – was followed, albeit somewhat sluggishly, in the UK. Nor did the Conservative Party relinquish money from Russians linked to Putin that had been donated to party funds (Rowley, 2022).

The war in Ukraine contributed to a deepening global capitalist crisis and instigated some all too familiar routes of it: the expansion of the arms industry and the military-industrial complex more generally; and a panicked search for non-Russian oil and gas, despite the nominal pursuit of zero-carbon. The UK was enmeshed in these general dynamics (as new oil and gas exploration licences were granted and 'fracking' returned to the policy agenda after a brief moratorium). But the UK was also marked by some distinctive dynamics as the impact of Brexit was felt in reduced trade, including export delays as regulations changed. All of these were framed within the dominant discourse as problems of low or slow 'growth', almost as though politicians, economists and economic commentators had never heard of the environmental catastrophe and the problems of pursuing permanent growth.

In April 2022, these intersecting dynamics came to a head with the return of inflation on a massive scale, driven by rapidly rising energy and fuel charges alongside increasing food and other prices at exactly the moment when the temporary uplift of Universal Credit benefits was stopped. Described by some as a 'perfect storm' of pressures bearing on 'ordinary families', the emergent cost of living crisis embroiled an unsettled government in calculations about how to respond, even as it embarked on a leadership contest in July 2022 when Johnson reacted to deepening divisions in the Party by resigning as Prime Minister. I will return to this set of crises again in Chapter 8 but here it is important to locate Conservative flailing about the cost of living issue in a wider set of political and policy dynamics.

The strategies established at the start of this conjuncture (in 1979) have produced a sustained deepening of inequalities of both income and wealth. Reviewing recent decades, a Resolution Foundation study – *Stagnation Nation* – observed that '[h]aving surged during the 1980s, and remained consistently high ever since, income inequality in the UK was higher than any other large European country in 2018' (2022: 9), while the rate of growth in real wages 'fell to below zero in the 2010s' (2022: 8). Meanwhile, levels of wealth have grown rapidly as have the absolute gaps between different groups. The rising value of wealth relative to income means people are more dependent on what they inherit, rather than what they can do themselves through earning pay rises and saving (2022: 42). The Foundation also highlights the way in which taxation policies have benefitted wealth holders: while 'wealth has risen from three to almost eight times national income since the 1980s ... wealth taxes have not risen at all as a share of GDP' (2022: 10–15).

Writing about contemporary social policies, Fiona Williams has pointed to two potent dynamics at the heart of UK approaches. Borrowing from Lister (2018), she argues that a range of policies – from the treatment of refugees to the systems of income support – have been characterised by a systemic 'institutional indifference' to the effects of these policies on everyday lives. As long as the policies can be narrated in the dominant framings (creating 'hostile environments' of various kinds that will dissuade people from exploiting the British state's generosity), their actual effects are of little concern. Those effects have, however, been dehumanising and have caused 'purposeful impoverishment' (Williams, 2021: 86). Although Mayblin, Wake and Kazemi (2019) use the phrase 'purposeful impoverishment' to describe government policies towards asylum seekers, Williams is surely right to see it as a more widely active principle.

In all of these tendencies, inequality flows along grimly familiar tracks. It is shaped by regional unevenness, organised along the axes of gender and disability, and profoundly structured by racialising processes. As the Runnymede Trust reported in 2022: 'Black and minority ethnic people are 2.5 times more likely to be in poverty than white people' (Edmiston, Begum and Kataria, 2022: 2) and were most affected by the economic consequences of both the 2008 financial crisis and the pandemic.

Across these scenes, local, national and global dynamics of crises become transnationally entangled and enmeshed. As I argued earlier, though, crisis/crises are not the only significant dynamic in the forming of the conjuncture. They are entangled in multiple ways with other conditions. They are notably entwined with long-running contradictions – about the state of the state (and the degradation of its capacities); about the stresses produced by the different privatisations of care; and about the impossible tension between the infinitely expanding desires of capital accumulation and the physical limits of the planet. For good reason, these crises are also entangled with a variety of sites and forms of social antagonisms, whether the backlash to feminism in defence of male power and privilege, or the constant revival of the hierarchies embedded in colonialism.

## Crisis talk

Like many other books, articles, blogs, podcasts and more, this book is part of a rising tide of crisis talk: identifying, naming, classifying and working out what to do about crises is a contemporary condition. Although concern about crisis is nothing new, two features of the present stand out. On the one hand, there is a paradoxical sense of what has been called *permanent crisis* or *permacrisis* (for example, Chesney, 2018; Heifetz et al, 2009) – paradoxical, given that crises are typically understood as moments or, at least, turning points. Now, we are invited to think about living with crisis as a persistent condition that resists resolution. On the other hand, there is a growing use of the idea of a *polycrisis* to draw attention to the interconnectedness of the many crises that have developed. Polycrisis was attributed to Jean Claude Juncker in 2016, when serving as President of the European Union. In a speech in Greece, he observed that

> 'I have often used the Greek word "polycrisis" to describe the current situation. Our various challenges – from the security threats in our neighbourhood and at home, to the refugee crisis, and to the UK referendum – have not only arrived at the same time. They also feed each other, creating a sense of doubt and uncertainty in the minds of our people.' (Juncker, 2016)

The term has proliferated – coming to refer to the intersecting dynamics of the multiple crises that commentators identify (see the overview by Alexander, 2022). The crises invoked in specific accounts vary, but polycrisis insistently points towards a multiplicity of interconnected crises whose interconnections may be mapped (see, for example, Tooze (2022a), who argues that '[a] polycrisis is not just a situation where you face multiple crises. It is a situation … where the whole is even more dangerous than the sum of the parts').

I would not want to dissent from either the idea of a multiplicity of crises, nor the sense that they are interconnected in important ways. Yet, the idea of a polycrisis tends to conceal other problems and I will focus on two here. First, the crises identified tend not to include either political-cultural directions set by dominant blocs (globally, regionally, nationally – for example, the EU was itself implicated in many of the crises mentioned by Juncker) or the condition of the governmental apparatuses attempting to manage them. Second, the discussions of crises tend to take their meaning as self-evident. Yet to identify and name a crisis is itself an act of political-cultural work.

From a cultural studies perspective, it is important to recognise that 'crisis' itself is a somewhat elusive concept – even as the number of crises being identified multiplies. We might begin from Gramsci's famous warning about assuming that crises have direct consequences: 'It may be ruled out that immediate economic crises of themselves produce fundamental historical events; they can simply create a terrain more favourable to the dissemination of certain modes of thought, and certain ways of posing and resolving questions' (1971: 184).

This points to one way through these issues: treating the 'immediate crises' as facilitating the circulation of particular 'modes of thought' makes it possible to consider how crises create possibilities that may be worked on and developed by political-cultural projects (for one striking example, see Naomi Klein's (2008) work on disaster capitalism and the 'shock doctrine'). There are many examples – ranging across economic, political, social or moral crises – in which a particular form of order or stability is declared to be at risk and demands exceptional measures. Crises are *made up* – in the double meaning of that phrase: they are *imagined and projected* as matters of social concern; and they are *assembled* as objects of political action. From this point of view, crises are variously anticipated, predicted, discovered, denied, calibrated, managed, resolved and more: they are always objects of political-cultural fascination and the focus for intensive political-cultural labour in the effort to make them productive. This is true for a variety of political standpoints: a crisis is understood as potential political-cultural capital that can be put to work. Boletsi, Mika, Robbe and Dekker put it more formally: 'Crisis is also, significantly, a speech act, that is, a declaration that issues a judgement or diagnosis of the present fraught with implications for meaning-making, subject-formation, temporal and spatial orientation, infrastructures and the livability and survival of people and/or the planet' (2021: 4).

It may be productive to link their view of crisis as a 'speech act' to Ien Ang's conception of a 'sense of crisis', since something more than a definitional moment is at stake. She has argued that: 'the multiplicity of other social, political and environmental crises erupting around the world, large and small, [is] giving many people a sense that "the world is falling apart" – a more profound *sense of global crisis*' (2021: 599; my emphasis). Ang offers different registers through which to think about crisis, connecting the profound dislocations – environmental, cultural, political – that are in play alongside a more affective orientation: the 'sense of crisis' (what Raymond Williams might have called an emergent 'structure of feeling'). This 'sense of crisis' – experienced as traumatic, alarming or enlivening – is a vital condition for such moments to have political-cultural consequences (whether leading to mobilisation or paralysis). Political movements regularly recognise – and try to mobilise – the potential productivity of such affective dynamics of crises. Dangers or threats can be narrated, dramatised and represented as 'crises' in order to bring about either the restoration of the 'proper/normal' order of things or the transformation of the disorder into something new and better.

In this sense, crises are pedagogic devices: they teach us lessons about how things went wrong and what needs to change (on learning from crises, see Jessop and Knio, 2019). More accurately, perhaps, crises are made to speak: they are *ventriloquised* by different social and political actors, in order to tell us what lessons we should be learning. One critical part of this pedagogic politics is the articulation of a 'sense of crisis' – the feeling of risk, danger or things 'being out of order' or 'out of control'. One potent example of this has been the 'migrant crisis' in which Europe and the US are (said to be) enmeshed. The 'migrant crisis' names a disorder (people 'out of place'), dramatises the situation (images of people approaching borders by land or sea), evokes feelings (of the collapse of the nation – in all its senses) and summons 'us' (the People) to a defence of borders, territory and the 'way of life' contained therein (see, for example, Cantat and Rajaram (2018) on the Hungarian version).

Crises are certainly enmeshed in the efforts to sustain and multiply the power and reach of capital – manifested in the shifting forms of proletarianisation, immiseration, neocolonialism and racialised exclusions (even as selected strata of subordinate classes are invited to feel themselves 'at home' in these relations). Yet other antagonisms have appeared to unsettle the social peace of neoliberalised social formations – the revolts of disabled people, the disruptions generated by queer politics, and most recently, the challenges mounted to heteronormative framings of gender, sexuality, identity and safety by trans activists and their allies. Such 'counter movements' do not easily or readily align, although Roth has argued that they have arisen, both in Europe and the United States, in response to '[t]he rise of far-right movements, anti-gender movements, and populist movements from the right' (2018: 501). More pessimistically, Ang has argued that '[t]his is a political crisis affecting the world at large, but it is experienced on the ground at the level of the everyday, where prospects of a shared, liveable and equitable future for all are fast receding, amplifying a cultural paralysis which is hard to overcome' (Ang, 2021: 599).

Ang also highlights the spatial complexity of this moment, combining a sense of the specificity of where things 'take place' (bushfires in Australia, the killing of George Floyd in the US) with a more dispersed sense of space associated with the pandemic – a crisis without spatial limits, even if it has geographical trajectories and differential 'landings' in particular places (see also Balibar, 2021; Boletsi et al, 2021; Williams, 2021).

The pandemic has been both global and local. COVID-19 has connected and separated – literally as borders were closed and people were 'locked down' in privatised spaces (or public institutions). The coronavirus formed a common threat but was differentially distributed within and between societies (the more so as 'vaccine nationalism' came into play). Despite the temptations of the 'global' and the 'planetary' as ways of framing them, I want to return to ideas of the transnational, which (as I argued in Chapter 1) open the possibilities of thinking about movement, connection, disjuncture and unevenness. So, for example, COVID-19 travels, connects, disrupts and conjoins people and places in different and destabilising ways. Similarly, the climate catastrophe is both general and differentially distributed in its causes and consequences. So, for me, it makes sense to think of the conjuncture as formed through a cluster of connections (and disjunctions) that are *transnational* in their dynamics.

## Crises and the conjuncture

In brief, the current conjuncture is characterised by an accumulation of crises of different kinds, operating across multiple scales (local, regional, national, transnational and planetary) in ways that demand political attention – to either control or exploit them. There is no singular foundational crisis but nor can the accumulation of these multiple crises be understood in additive terms – rather, they become entangled with one another and thus have multiplying dynamics, exacerbating, intensifying and creating the conditions for other forms of strain, tensions and social antagonism. Some of them have a predominantly economic character, driven by the failures and desires of contemporary capitalist organisation (or disorganisation). Others have an environmental focus – lodged in the rapid worsening of conditions of life on the planet – though this dynamic is intimately linked to the endless search for growth and to the conditions that enable and create pandemics at increasing speed. The contemporary crises are also political and governmental, shaped by political desires – and failures – as well as intimately related to the 'hollowed-out' state form driven by neoliberalising projects. Finally, the crises are also social, driven by the phenomenal accumulation and concentration of wealth and its obverse – the purposeful impoverishment of millions. Wealth – and impoverishment – flow along well-worn channels of social difference and division, exacerbating conflicts over scarce resources (from employment to public goods) in their wake. But naming them in this way and attributing different sites to them risks losing sight of their most significant quality – their entanglement – in the dynamic disturbance of the world and particular places within it.

This condensation of crises, contradictions and conflicts will reappear in the following chapters, alongside the strategies that the dominant bloc has developed to contain, manage and exploit them. This is the necessary double dynamic of crises: they have a material presence and they also have to be discovered and defined – given meaning and made to matter. Dominant, as well as oppositional, political projects are engaged in these practices of making crises matter. In the midst of these condensed crises, the pandemic stood out for many reasons. It illuminated the eviscerated condition of public services and the UK state more generally, it was greeted with familiar claims about 'British exceptionalism' and it demonstrated the complexly transnational dynamics of the present. Not least, it highlighted questions of inequality within the UK, particularly those associated with racialised divisions as disproportionate numbers of people from minority backgrounds died from the virus. In the next chapter, I explore this issue and its entanglement with other racialised dynamics at the heart of these accumulating crises.

7

# 'The Best Country in the World': Race, Culture, History

In the previous chapter I argued that the trajectory of the present conjuncture was forged by a distinctive – and accelerating – accumulation of crises, while insisting that crises are also the focus of political-cultural efforts to define them, give them meaning and make them matter to audiences. The pandemic was the focus of such definitional struggles from the beginning, as the government strove to use it to articulate versions of British exceptionalism ('world beating' responses) while others sought to draw attention to failures and hidden dynamics. Not for the first time in recent British history, crisis and questions of race became entangled. In the 1970s, the deepening crisis of hegemony was displaced into a projected crisis of 'Law and Order', embodied in the threat of young black men – 'muggers' – roaming city streets (Hall et al, 2013: 240–242, 268–271). The pandemic saw different articulations of crisis and race, as the racialised inequalities of the pandemic intersected potently with the global reaction to the murder of George Floyd. This chapter explores these connections and their relationships to both longer standing anti-racist campaigns (especially around policing) and to emerging challenges, particularly around the history of British colonialism and imperialism. It then examines the political responses to these emergent mobilisations, involving strategies of denial, deferral and deflection.

These political-cultural strategies to contain and deflect invoked a distinctive version of the 'culture wars' in which efforts were made to reframe the question of racism. Exploring this strategy opens a wider discussion of the significance of culture wars for an analysis that treats politics as the site of political-cultural articulations, in which discursive framings, historical narratives and potent symbolisations of the nation and its people occupied central places.

## Who can't breathe?

As I suggested in the previous chapter, COVID-19 embodied many of the distinctive features of contemporary crises – formed in transnational processes and relations with spatially differentiated consequences (across and within countries) and inextricably linked to other crises, notably those of the current nation-state form. Its trajectory was both familiar and distinctive: it encountered national and international organisations ill-prepared for its demands; it flowed along well-worn routes of circulation, tracking deeply embedded structures of inequality (globally and within nations). In the UK, it encountered a British government with its attention elsewhere and a hollowed-out public infrastructure. It also entered a media ecology characterised by short attention spans, violent mood swings (each day a triumph or a disaster), and a propensity to divide the world between friends and enemies of the people (see, for example: Cinelli et al (2020) on social media's 'infodemic'; Theocharis et al (2021) on different social media platforms; Thomas et al (2020) on Australian news media). British media seemed prone to reproduce government confidence, exemplified in the recurrent use of the phrase 'world beating' (Rutter, 2020) and the culture of British/English exceptionalism (Sim and Tombs, 2022).

Alongside frequent promises that our responses would be 'world beating', government approaches to the pandemic assured us that 'we are all in this together' (a well-established Conservative trope from the austerity years). But COVID-19 turned out to be anything but an even-handed pandemic. Rather, its impacts (social, medical, psychological) were profoundly uneven – and in grimly predictable ways. In the UK, it disproportionately affected older people, poor people, people with 'pre-existing conditions', people working in low-paid but 'essential' occupations (from health and social care to the food chain), and people classed as something other than 'white British' (in census category framings). These are, of course, not separate categories: racialised minorities in the UK are more likely to live in poverty, to be concentrated in low-paid employment and to form a disproportionately large part of the health care and social care workforces. As Gamlin, Gibbons and Calestani put it, 'Populations and biopolitics also collide in the colonial patterning of care provision by Britain's NHS, the centrepiece of the UK's epidemic response, an institution sustained in large part by the combined labour of EU and colonial diaspora communities' (2021: 109). The NHS was itself part of a wider dynamic of labour market deregulation combined with the weakening of unions that, in the words of Nesrine Malik, 'led to a generation of precarious workers having to choose between their health and their income when they should be isolating' (2021a).

Campaigns drew attention to the distinctive vulnerability of racialised minorities to the virus. While certainly not unique to the UK, the racialised distribution of COVID-19 deaths in the UK became visible at the intersection of two framings. On the one hand, the early weeks and months of the pandemic in the UK centred on distinctive urban concentrations (London, areas in the West and East Midlands which had significant racialised/minoritised populations). On the other hand, media reporting of the deaths of 'front line' health and care workers revealed – not least in the accompanying gallery of photographic images – that they were disproportionately not 'white British'. One consequence was that the UK became familiar with a distinctive acronym as these fatalities were named as 'BAME [Black, Asian, Ethnic Minority] deaths'. BAME offered a broad umbrella categorisation in place of multiple racialised ethnicities. For many reasons, it has been a contested term and has not been adopted as an active identity or form of self-naming (see, inter alia, Aspinall, 2002; Okolosie et al, 2015). But it came into its own during the pandemic as an administrative category for naming coronavirus-related inequalities.

A picture of systemically skewed mortality rates emerged in the UK and in other Western countries and a story began to take shape about who was dying from COVID-19, centring on its disproportionate effects on racialised minorities (for example, the Centre for Evidence Based Medicine, 2020). These concerns eventually drove the government to establish an inquiry into BAME death rates. The report (PHE 2020a) revealed what was already known: BAME people were twice as likely as white people to die after contracting COVID-19. It received an angry response for its failure to address the causes of the disparities or propose solutions. A range of critical reactions – from the British Medical Association to the Muslim Council of Great Britain – led to the government publishing the responses and suggestions collected during the consultations undertaken for the report (PHE 2020b). This second report was received with rather more enthusiasm, not least because the suggestions included references to 'historic racism' and 'social inequality' as potential contributory causes of BAME mortality rates. Faced with pressure to implement this report's recommendations immediately, the government opted instead to set up a further review to be led by Equalities Minister, Kemi Badenoch. To many, this looked like yet another *deferral* – an approach well established in governmental responses to questions about systemic or institutional racism.

By this point, the killing of George Floyd by Minneapolis police officers on 25 May 2020, had triggered new Black Lives Matter protests across the globe. One effect was that the issue of BAME coronavirus deaths became folded into a wider politics of 'race' and death. As many recognised, George Floyd's last words struck uncanny echoes in the moment of coronavirus as "I can't breathe" condensed different forms of systemic oppression and vulnerability. Bue Rübner Hansen has captured these echoes:

Suffocation is the suffering of the day. There is the stifling atmosphere of pandemic isolation, the breathlessness of anxiety, the stress of work, debt and unemployment. There is the literal suffocation of the lungs of COVID-patients slowly filling with fluid and of George Floyd, at the knee of a police officer. There is the orange sky over California, the grey smog over industrial belts across the world, the airborne pollutants of asthma and early death. There is the suffering of people who simply cannot take it anymore, who push back police with placards paraphrasing Fanon: 'We revolt because we cannot breathe'. (Hansen, 2020: 109; see also Okri 2020)

In the UK, the intersection of COVID-19's racialised effects and George Floyd's murder mobilised people on a wholly unexpected scale. The moment made visible the connections between health inequalities, racism and the simultaneous movements to decolonise British institutions, from universities to public memorialisations (dramatised in the toppling of slave trader Edward Colston's statue in Bristol harbour on 7 June 2020 (Beebeejaun, 2021)). Further struggles were taking place around the 'hostile environment' policies directed at people judged to be 'out of place' (Gentleman, 2019) and against the Home Office's deportation flights (especially those to Jamaica). All these overlapped and intersected with current versions of long-running struggles about the policing of black communities in the UK. 1970s' campaigns against the use of 'Sus' laws (section 4 of the 1824 Vagrancy Act, permitting police officers to stop anyone on the grounds of 'reasonable suspicion') had mutated into campaigns against the 'stop and search' powers enacted in the Police and Criminal Evidence (PACE) Act of 1984: powers used disproportionately against young black men (see, for example, Maggs, 2019). And there were continuing campaigns around deaths in police custody or during police operations. Although such practices and the campaigns against them were concentrated in London (as part of the continuing problem of the 'institutional racism' of the Metropolitan Police), they existed elsewhere too. In 2016, Dalian Atkinson, a former footballer, died after being tasered multiple times and then kicked twice in the head by a police officer outside his father's house in Telford (BBC, 2021a).

Despite the attempted deferral of the issue to the new review (the Commission on Race and Ethnic Disparities – CRED), questions continued to be asked in public and in parliament. In one debate, Kemi Badenoch (then Minister for Equality) insisted:

'[L]et us not in this House use statements like "being black is a death sentence", which young people out there hear, don't understand the context and then continue to believe that they live in a society that is against them. When actually this is one of the best countries in the world to be a black person.' (quoted in Brewis, 2020)

This claim was greeted with some scepticism, as was the deferral of the issues to the new Commission. Critics pointed to the long list of previous investigations, studies and reports in which racialised inequalities had been enumerated and discussed to little or no effect (Lammy, 2020). Concern also focused on the government adviser charged with establishing the new Commission: Munira Mirza was the head of the Prime Minister's policy unit at Number 10 and had worked for Johnson while he was Mayor of London (Fletcher, 2020). Mirza had previously insisted that claims of 'institutional racism' were 'a perception more than a reality' and that anti-racist lobby groups and diversity policies encouraged people to 'see everything through the prism of racial difference' (Stone, 2020).

## Investigating race, avoiding racism

A preliminary report (in October 2020) from the government's Race Disparity Unit, located in 10 Downing Street, refused the claim that systemic or institutional racism could be implicated in the 'BAME' deaths. On the contrary, they argued that:

> After taking into account the COVID-19 mortality rate in each local authority, controlling for population density, and adjusting for deprivation and socioeconomic position, household composition and occupational exposure, health and disability at the time of the 2011 Census – the *excess risk of mortality* from COVID-19 compared with that of the White ethnic group was reduced for all ethnic minority groups, especially for Black and the combined Pakistani and Bangladeshi ethnic groups. (Race Disparity Unit, 2020: 54; pages un-numbered in original, my emphasis)

This is a frequently used method for minimising the significance of racism, reducing it to what is left over after 'controlling' for a variety of other factors. In contrast, analyses of structural racism view such 'factors' as population density, deprivation, and socioeconomic position, household composition and occupational exposure, health and disability as integral elements of the racialised dynamics of the society. These factors come to be concentrated in distinctive ways on racialised and minoritised groups. This counter view was articulated in a different report, commissioned by the Labour Party from Baroness Doreen Lawrence, which argued that:

> Covid-19 has thrived on structural inequalities that have long scarred British society. Black and minority ethnic people are more likely to

work in frontline or shutdown sectors, more likely to live in poor quality or overcrowded housing and more likely to face barriers to accessing healthcare. Biological factors do not explain the disparity in deaths and infections; Black, Asian and minority ethnic people have been overexposed to this virus. (Lawrence, 2020: 24–25)

The government's CRED report was published in April 2021 and claimed that there was little evidence of structural, systemic or institutional racism in the UK. On the contrary, it suggested that young people from 'ethnic minority' backgrounds fail to progress because of 'family and culture' issues. Worse still, the misplaced 'idealism' of 'well-intentioned' young people had led them to protest inappropriately. This report was characterised by a combination of an evasive approach to evidence and elusive conceptualisations of racism. It was also conditioned by a distinctive understanding of *political-cultural* practice, especially the political advantages of agenda setting and the careful cultivation of outrage. The report's authors made the most of the chance to reassure its target audience that Britain is not a racist society:

> Put simply we no longer see a Britain where the system is deliberately rigged against ethnic minorities. The impediments and disparities do exist, they are varied, and ironically very few of them are directly to do with racism. Too often 'racism' is the catch-all explanation, and can be simply implicitly accepted rather than explicitly examined.
>
> The evidence shows that geography, family influence, socio-economic background, culture and religion have more significant impact on life chances than the existence of racism. (CRED, 2021: 8)

The report generated predictable effects, attracting widespread criticism and condemnation from many quarters. The arguments played out along familiar lines: claims about the UK's progress and the absence of institutional racism were met with further evidence and analyses demonstrating the persistence of systemic inequalities. The report was described by one critic (Maurice Macleod, chair of Race on the Agenda) as 'government level gaslighting' (quoted in Walker et al, 2021). The relative success of these tactics meant that later 'clarifications' passed by quietly, even the admission that the Commission had indeed found evidence of 'persistent race-based discrimination' (White, 2021). Such practices give a tactical advantage to what *Policing the Crisis* called the 'primary definers' (Hall et al, 2013: 60–63) – in this case, led by the Prime Minister's office which had carefully provided a media briefing note the day before the full 258-page document was published.

In sum, then, the potent entanglement of racialised inequalities, anti-racist movements and the brutal impact of COVID-19 generated intense political pressures to which the dominant bloc responded with a triple strategy of *denial*, *deferral* and *deflection*. Denial relies heavily on the temporal dynamics and difficulties of challenge and refutation, as in Badenoch's claim that Britain 'is one of the best countries of the world to be a black person'. Although the claim was indeed contested, its value lay in the claim itself and its affinity with two other sentiments: an intensely racialised scepticism about black people claiming to be 'victims' and the endemic 'British boosterism' of the Johnson style. Deferral, as I argued in the previous chapter, draws on the control of time as a governmental resource: delaying issues to a 'more suitable time' (also used in relation to demands for a public inquiry into the management of the pandemic) and agreeing to set up an inquiry as a way of postponing controversial issues are both well-established temporal tactics.

In some ways, though, deflection was the most innovative approach since the Commission (and many of the arguments preceding its report) tried to find new ways of framing racialised inequalities. This framing shifted the issue to already familiar 'culture wars' terrain, in which the response to 'counter movements' (Roth, 2018) involves their simultaneous diminution and demonisation. They are framed as not *representative* (set against the constantly recycled figure of the Nixonian 'silent majority' in its many incarnations). 'Sensible', 'law-abiding' people need to be insulated from the wild claims of extreme minorities, and that insulation is recurrently renewed and refurbished by authoritative statements denouncing the extremists (renamed as the 'woke' in a borrowing from the American Right). Anti-racist, decolonising, feminist, environmentalist and anti-homophobia movements were denounced as extreme and disruptive and positioned as a threat to law and order. They were often contrasted with the 'reasonable' outliers of such movements whose arguments and demands could be taken on board by governments (especially when they required no action beyond positive statements). At the same time, the denunciations of extremists were framed through a classic dominant distinction between the dangerous minority and a supporting cast of the well-meaning but easily led astray: exemplified in the Commission's view of 'well-intentioned', idealistic young people being led into inappropriate protests (the same framing was applied to school pupils taking part in climate school strikes). These are all well-established elements of the dominant repertoire (for example, Hall et al, 2013: 218–222). So, is there anything distinctively different about culture wars?

## Culture wars, UK-style?

Like so many others, the term *culture wars* is an import to the UK from the US. It has been used to talk about deepening political polarisation in the US across a wide range of issues that appear outside of the conventional range of 'political' issues and framings. In a political science framing, Lindaman and Haider-Markel argued that: 'The conflictual nature of issues such as black civil rights, abortion, environmental protection, pornography, gun control, and gay civil rights appear to intensify the partisan environment, which may gradually lead to long-lasting shifts in the demographic and ideological groups defining party coalitions' (2002: 92). This approach seems to underestimate the challenge of understanding how some issues come to be the focus of conflict and the role of 'ideological groups' in constructing and animating those focal points. Meanwhile, accounts such as Hartman's formulation of 'a war for the soul of America' (2015) treat it as a cultural conflict between the 1960s counter-culture ('liberation') and the reaction from the neoconservatives locked in a struggle over different ideas of America. In this context, though, it is worth pursuing a more cultural studies approach to the integral connections of politics *and* culture rather than their juxtaposition.

Larry Grossberg's work on the long remaking of the American Right provides a route to such an approach, in particular his analysis of the way in which Trump was able to both benefit from *and* animate this remaking. In *Under the Cover of Chaos* (2018), he traces the transformations that two key strands of the Right – the *conservative Right* and the *reactionary Right* – underwent across the second half of the 20th century. Grossberg highlights Trump's capacity to forge connections between the conservative Right, already well entrenched in the Republican movement, and 'the constituencies, voices, practices and projects of the reactionary right' (2018: 88), in the process pulling the Republican Party further rightwards. Both strands had an interest in culture wars issues as sites through which 'liberal' advances (from abortion to civil rights) might be reversed and a white Christian nationalist vision of America might be promulgated (see also Bjork-James, 2020 and 2021). Grossberg develops a compelling argument that, in the current (US) conjuncture, it is *culture* that occupies the dominant position in organising social life – mediating and reorganising the relationships between politics and the economy:

> Trump's politics are cultural: the problem space [of politics] is reconstructed so that matters of both economics (reduced largely to the lived immediacy of jobs and taxes) and democracy (the relations between majorities and minorities) are displaced into the relations of nationality and difference, and political polarization is translated into cultural polarization. (2018: 115)

For Grossberg, the field of culture is contested by different articulations of meanings, identities and affective intensities that combine to produce 'mattering maps' that articulate both what is at stake in the present and why we should be affectively invested in these things. This is the character of what we might call 'culture in general', but the moment of Trump marked a reworking of the relationships between culture and politics, such that culture became the dominant register in which politics was conducted.

Some of these strategies flowed to the UK along transnational networks that provided a conduit for political learning. The transatlantic Right had been nurtured by flows of money, personnel and ideas between the US and the UK (going back to the moment of Thatcherism), often institutionalised in the form of think tanks. In this period, the articulation of new forms of nationalism was inscribed in tropes such as the clash of civilisations, the 'great replacement' thesis and its equivalents (see, inter alia, Bromley, 2018; Bracke and Aguilar, 2020). These had permeated European politics, circulating widely through far Right networks, and emerged as a critical thread in the 2022 French presidential elections. Similarly, the central role of social media enabled rapid flows of ideas and images to take place, connecting different national constituencies into a series of virtual global associations.

Despite the rise of the EDL, Britain First, National Action and other organisations, the UK was marked by the *relative* absence of two other forces compared to the US. The anti-statist militias and the Christian nationalists had provided enthusiasts for Trumpism and substantial organisational infrastructures for their connection and mobilisation. In the UK, the rise of UKIP had exerted a rightward pull on Conservative politics and created a space in which more fiercely nationalist (as well as racist and misogynist) politics could be explicitly articulated. The Conservative Party shifted its centre of political gravity rightwards to accommodate a variety of nationalist (mainly English) positions. Some of these were certainly mobilised in culture wars formulations – often borrowing focal points and discursive devices from the US, especially around history, education (texts and practices) and cultural institutions (such as museums). The strong ties between the party and the bulk of the print and digital media (alongside emerging sites such as GB News) enabled the wider circulation of such 'culture wars' tropes. These included attacks on 'woke' politics, as in Johnson's speech to the 2021 Conservative Party conference:

'We should never forget, people around the world admire this country for its history and traditions. They love the groovy new architecture, and the fashion, music, and all the rest of it.

They like it for the way it emerges organically from a vast inherited conglomerate of culture and tradition. And we Conservatives, understand the need for both, and how each nourishes the other and we attack and deny our history at our peril.

When they began to attack Churchill as a racist I was minded to ignore them. It was only 20 years ago BBC audiences overwhelmingly voted him the greatest Briton of all time. He helped to defeat a regime after all that was defined by one of the most vicious racisms the world has ever seen.

But as time has gone by it's become clear to me that this isn't just a joke, they really do want to rewrite our national story starting with Hereward the Woke.' (quoted in Learmonth, 2021)

Such defences of 'our history' against decolonising and anti-racist challenges were interwoven – in familiar fashion – with other elements, notably the insistent defence of 'freedom of speech' and attacks on 'cancel culture'. 'Culture wars' interventions were not merely rhetorical; they were addressed to aspects of institutional configuration in education, the voluntary sector and the arts. A range of charities were publicly criticised and challenged by ministers and MPs (Butler and Siddique, 2021; Grayson, 2022). They included the National Trust (for researching and publicising the historical connections of its properties to the slave trade), Barnardo's (over a blog on racial inequality) and the Royal National Lifeboat Institution (RNLI) for rescuing migrants attempting to cross the channel. The outcomes of such attacks proved contradictory. Certainly, the RNLI became the subject of subsequent assaults including cyber hacking, verbal abuse of crews and physical attacks on two volunteers working at the St Ives station (*The Fishing Daily*, 2020). The RNLI was also denounced by Nigel Farage who described them as a 'taxi service' for illegal immigration. However, this criticism appeared to improve the organisation's public standing (Shakespeare, 2021) and created a substantial increase in donations to the charity (R. Hall, 2021). It also led to a crowd funding campaign to buy a hovercraft for the RNLI which would be named the Flying Farage (Cooney, 2021).

Elsewhere, Arts bodies and the BBC found themselves subjected to a mixture of criticism, admonition and interventions into appointments, especially to governing bodies. For example, then Culture Secretary Oliver Dowden wrote to the Arts Council and other funding bodies to emphasise that 'I would expect arm's-length bodies' approach to issues of contested heritage to be consistent with the government's position' (quoted in Higgins, 2021). Dowden's replacement as Culture Secretary, Nadine Dorries, demanded a 'less elitist' and 'more representative' approach from the BBC, alongside attacking 'left-wing snobbishness and elitism' more generally in the cultural sector (BBC, 2021b). Dorries later went on to promise the end of the licence fee funding model for the BBC and the privatisation of publicly owned Channel 4. At the same time, institutional remaking included the appointment of a chair of the BBC governing body (banker Richard Sharp) who had given over £400,000 in donations to the Conservative Party and a BBC Director-General Tim Davie who had previously been a Conservative political candidate.

Culture wars framings of issues were both rhetorical devices directed at an audience of the dominant bloc's members (attacking the 'liberal elite') and ways of changing the calculations that public and voluntary organisations have to make about the work they do and how it can be justified. They form part of a strategy to shift the institutional landscape, in terms of both personnel and practices – affecting what, to borrow from Foucault, might be described as a struggle to define the limits of the thinkable, sayable and doable. As Nesrine Malik has argued:

> We are already seeing a chilling effect on the work of charities and voluntary organisations which are legally required to be impartial. The head of a migrant rights charity recently told me that, when taking on new projects, he doesn't just weigh up whether he has the resources, but also whether it will expose his organisation to claims of political bias. Worse still, he worries for the safety of his staff following [then Home Secretary] Patel's attacks on 'activist lawyers'. (2021b)

Key phrases from the cultural populist glossary of terms were also put to work (in December 2021) to introduce changes to the Human Rights Act (long a target for Conservative anger, in part because of its European lineage). As Dominic Raab, then Minister for Justice, prepared to introduce a bill on the subject, a Ministry of Justice source claimed that the government felt changes were necessary because 'free speech and democratic debate had been whittled away "whether by wokery or political correctness"' (Siddique and Syal, 2021). These culture wars are not merely cultural – they are entwined with projects to remake the state, both enabling and enforcing changes of structure, form, personnel and practice (see also Clarke and Newman, 2022).

## Constructing 'our history': which 'we' is this?

As with other varieties of populism, the cultural populism of culture wars combines some generic trends with some distinctive national variations. In part, this reflects the central role allocated in these discourses to the national – what is at stake is the *national* culture (from the 'groovy new architecture' to 'our history'). A national culture is full of virtues that may, on occasion, need to be rescued by a government committed to their defence, even as that same government and its allies carefully construct the imaginary coherence of that culture. Such commitments to militantly defending and preserving the national culture have been shared by a range of contemporary populist parties, from Fidesz in Hungary to the BJP in India. The celebration of national culture – and its deployment by governments – has a long history in the UK, especially around questions of citizenship and immigration (Fortier, 2021).

The virtues of the English-British national culture have been increasingly recounted in the form of 'our history' that needs to be defended against anti-racist and decolonising moves. At the heart of these conflicts is a question about which 'we' is being imagined in claims about 'our history'. The campaigns around Brexit featured continuing attempts to claim – and proclaim – versions of 'our history' that marked Britain's place in the world, with frequent references to World Wars (especially the second), defeating fascism, and experiences of leading the world. Reynolds shows how such campaigns – and their aftermath – deployed a proliferation of such 'island stories' in which British exceptionalism was celebrated, as both separate from an imagined Europe and its recurrent rescuer from attempts to unify and homogenise it, ranging from the Roman Empire to Nazism and, of course, the EU 'superstate' (Reynolds, 2019: 3–4). Such stories became more visible and audible in response to the growing challenges to core elements and key absences in dominant accounts of 'our history'. Both the development of Black British history (for example, Olusoga, 2016; Adi, 2019) and rising demands to decolonise curricula and educational practice (for example, de Sousa Santos, 2017; Bhambra et al, 2018) made both British and global histories more contested. Despite these developments, some of the most dramatic rewriting of British history took place in government publications aimed at would-be citizens of the UK: *Life in the United Kingdom* (Home Office, 2019). The historian Frank Trentmann has examined the 2019 version (and compared it with earlier ones) and concluded that the history chapter (entitled 'A long and illustrious history') 'is not only riddled with factual errors but amounts to a distortion of the past that does violence to our basic understanding of history and raises fundamental questions for a liberal society' (2020: 1).

These contested histories constantly return what Hall (2017) called the 'fateful triangle' of race, ethnicity and nation in relation to Empire. A variety of movements coalesced around these questions: challenges to racist policing and exclusionary formulations of citizenship – both in law and in practice – encountered demands to address the colonial history of British institutions, from museums to stately homes. Not for the first time, a British crisis took shape through the figure of 'race' and posed, in increasingly contested terms, the question of *whose* history this was.

Sivamohan Valluvan has argued that European national histories are inextricably linked to nationalist imaginaries that are themselves founded on an exclusionary dynamic: nations defined against their (racialised) Others. Valluvan locates a desire for closure – of the imagined national community against its Others – in a period where the idea(l) of 'the European nation and ideas of race both began to find their proper historical definition at the same historical moment' generating a conception of the nation as a community which is centred on a 'normative "we" [that] has no inevitable political complexion other than that of its exclusionary ethno-racial desires' (2019: 14). For Valluvan, then, European varieties of nationalism are always political-cultural formations that have racialised exclusion as their founding principle: the 'we' they celebrate can never be innocent of these foundational conditions (consequently he is profoundly sceptical about the possibilities of any 'progressive' nationalism (2019: 58–60)). This analysis underpins his powerful account of the contemporary entanglements of race and nation in the UK, not least the temporalities of loss in play in conservative appeals to the nation.

Some of Valluvan's themes are echoed in *Empireland* (Sanghera, 2021), where Sathnam Sanghera explores how combinations of selective nostalgia and amnesia sustain an attachment to an imagined Empire. He draws out the distinctive positioning of himself and many others as 'outside' the nation (by virtue of their non-whiteness) despite being British. But he also makes an attempt to reimagine the 'we' of the nation, arguing that

> [t]he way we fail to acknowledge that we are a multicultural society because we had a multicultural empire makes our national conversations absurd and tragic. The manner in which our imperial history inspires a sense of exceptionalism results in dysfunctional politics and disastrous decision-making. Our collective amnesia about the fact that we were, as a nation, wilfully white supremacist and occasionally genocidal, and our failure to understand how this informs modern-day racism, are catastrophic. (2021: 217)

By laying claim to 'we' and 'our' in this way, Sanghera unsettles the established presumptions about the ways in which they are populated. If 'we' are, indeed, this multicultural and entangled people, then whose history is being preserved and protected against decolonising challenges? It is precisely this issue that is at stake in contemporary Conservative claims about the need to defend 'our history'. The 'we' in question is inescapably that of a Britain imagined as white, as the organisers and beneficiaries of Empire (rather than its 'victims'). This viewing/speaking position is deeply inscribed in the institutional arrangements – as well as the politics – of British life: I find it hard to imagine writing opinion poll questions that ask people if they would be happy for their daughter to marry a black person or a Muslim, as though some of those to be surveyed might not be black and/or Muslim. As Gary Younge has argued, racism works systemically:

> Bequeathed through history, embedded within our institutions and entrenched in our political economy, racism is sustained as much, if not more, by compliance than intent. ... This is the system that left

non-white people more vulnerable to Covid, and less able to survive it. In marked contrast to the brutality of the murder of George Floyd, Covid illustrated the banality of societal inequalities: the familiar, quotidian, bureaucratic complicity that results in far more deaths, even if they are far less dramatic. (2021)

COVID-19 and culture wars were entangled in such ways through the persistence of racialised divisions and attempts to counter – or confirm – them. But culture wars have also been fought over many other topics, not least around the desire to restore 'traditional' versions of gender and sexuality and the normative orders associated with them. Such desires became entangled in arguments over sex, gender and the recognition of 'trans' rights. There, the question of whether 'biology is destiny' returned to centre stage as some feminist groups and a larger array of right-wing forces demanded the differentiation of Women and Trans Women, with only the former to be allowed access to single-sex spaces (Hines, 2020). This particular culture war played out across a range of sites – universities and 'freedom of speech', legislation (especially about gender recognition) and sporting participation, for example. As Zoe Williams (2022) noted, the question of whether a woman is defined by the possession of a vagina emerged as a charged question in public discourse – and a stick with which to beat political opponents (and featured in the first 2022 Conservative Party leadership campaign).

Nonetheless, there are arguments about the extent to which culture wars have been central to the divisions and alignments of British politics. For Sobolewska and Ford, culture wars express (and mobilise) the 'identity politics' that were key to the Conservatives' 2019 election success and to Brexit before that: 'The Leave side has won the long and divisive post-referendum tug of war, at least for now. But the deeper identity divides which the Brexit vote mobilised remain in place, and could easily flare up again over other issues' (2020a: 6–7). In contrast, Duffy (2021) argues that headline divisions between what he identifies as 'Traditionalists' and 'Progressives' – the contending forces in the culture wars – conceal a more complex landscape in which two other groups account for at least half of the population. These other groups are the 'Moderates' (32 per cent) and the 'Disengaged' (18 per cent) who are less committed to key issues in the culture wars debates. All groups tend to think that, while deep differences exist, such differences have been exaggerated and have been fuelled by both the media and politicians (2021: 22–24). Meanwhile, McNeill and Harding (2021) argued that 'culture wars' have been relatively undeveloped in the UK by contrast with the US, but have been increasingly used as a political strategy by the Conservative Party, raising the question of how progressive forces should relate to culture wars.

## What's the culture in culture wars?

For the Left (broadly defined), the rise of culture wars poses both conceptual and practical problems (and the two are connected). Are culture wars a way of deflecting attention from 'real' politics? Are they invented or 'confected' by the Right as a divide and rule tactic? Do they drain energy out of political movements by demanding replies, rebuttals and refusals? Or do they try to occupy and disrupt the political terrain that progressive movements had created (social justice, anti-racism, anti-misogyny, anti-homophobia, and so on)?

There is no doubt that some focal points for these controversies were indeed 'fabricated', such as the controversy over not singing 'Rule Britannia' at the Last Night of the Proms in 2020 (O'Connor, 2020). But more generally, the scepticism about culture wars reflects deeper controversies about what 'culture' means for the Left. Nesrine Malik has argued that refusing to take culture wars seriously misses their significance:

> [b]ecause culture war is not about winning a debate about what constitutes England through factual disputes about its character, its statues, its football team or its history of empire. It is not a peripheral indulgence, or a mere confection. Culture war is an aggressive political act with the purpose of creating new dividing lines and therefore new and bigger electoral majorities. It aims to create its own truth, and its own England, through what Nietzsche called a 'mobile army of metaphors'.
>
> In the right's mobile army, race and identity have played a central role, painting an England that is under assault from uppity minorities and their woke backers who can only be kept at bay by the Conservatives. (Malik, 2021c)

The resistance on the Left to taking culture wars seriously draws on concerns that connect Marxist scepticism about 'superstructural froth' with Labourist desires to rebuild their relationships with 'traditional' working-class Labour voters, symbolised in the loss of the 'Red Wall' (as discussed in Chapter 5). This issue involves an inner party struggle (albeit one often conducted in public view) about whether the Party has fallen too much into the hands of a cosmopolitan middle-class tendency leading it to neglect the older and 'ordinary' working-class voter. Jon Bloomfield (2020) wrote of the tendency within Labour to demand a focus on national identity, patriotism and culture; or, as the original Blue Labour slogan put it, 'flag, faith and family'.

This antipathy towards a progressive culture builds on an older scepticism on the Left about 'culture', social movements and 'identity politics', treated as distractions from the business of 'real politics' (which are defined by being about the material substratum of life and class inequalities). One exemplary account of this proclaimed split between proper politics and the froth of culture appeared at the heart of the historian Tony Judt's diagnosis of the crisis of social democracy in the 1970s and 1980s. In *Ill Fares the Land* (2010), Judt argued that the withdrawal from state welfare, the collapse of public services and the rise of Thatcherism (and neoliberal politics more generally) was a disaster for which much of the responsibility lay with the social movements of the 1960s which had undermined the solidarities of social democracy.

> The *new* Left, as it began to call itself in those years, was something very different. To a younger generation, 'change' was not to be brought about by disciplined mass action defined and led by authorized spokesmen. Change itself appeared to have moved on from the industrial West into the developing or 'third' world. Communism and capitalism alike were charged with stagnation and 'repression'. The initiative for radical innovation and action now lay either with distant peasants or else with a new set of revolutionary constituents. In place of the male proletariat there were now posited the candidacies of 'blacks', 'students', 'women' and, a little later, homosexuals.
>
> The politics of the '60s thus devolved into an aggregation of individual claims upon society and the state. 'Identity' began to colonize public discourse: private identity, sexual identity, cultural identity. From here it was but a short step to the fragmentation of radical politics, its metamorphism into multiculturalism. (2010: 87–88; emphasis in original)

This betrayal (aided by the 'rhetorical awning' of Marxism (Judt, 2010: 89)) created the terrain onto which the new Right came to play. As Dylan Riley has argued 'For Judt, the crisis of the welfare state was therefore largely a matter of ideas – selfish ones on the part of the 60s radicals, and counter-arguments … from the Hayekians. If things had been otherwise, the post-war consensus would presumably still be intact' (Riley, 2011). Riley pointed out that Judt provides little or no explanation for the crises of social democracy in political-economic terms; a point echoed by Maisano (2010) who emphasises Judt's failure to recognise that 'by the early 1970s, social democracy reached its political and economic limits'. Nonetheless, there is a further argument to be made about Judt's analysis that goes beyond this political-economic framing. These social movements arose precisely from the exclusions, subordinations and forms of exploitation that were characteristic of the social democratic version of managed capitalism (and the transitions from colonialism to neocolonialism on a global scale). They were not the cultural froth that concealed the deeper truths of its political economy but were formed from profound dynamics within it.

Nevertheless, the distinction between culture and political economy has remained a frequently deployed distinction that underpins dismissive terms such as 'cultural politics' or 'identity politics' and was dissected by Judith Butler in her 1999 essay 'Merely Cultural'. Butler identified consequences attributed to the cultural turn: the fragmenting of the Left, the abandonment of materialism and the loss of a common political project. Through a critical examination of Nancy Fraser's (1997) distinction between recognition and redistribution in political struggles, Butler mounted a compelling argument for escaping from treating politics through such a binary material-cultural distinction (see also Rao, 2020: 152–153). Nonetheless, the binary distinction has persisted.

While I would agree that a narrowly identitarian conception of social movements *may* lead to a narrowing and fracturing of the political field, such arguments tend to rest on a lazy equation of political outcomes with political intentions. There is no reason to assume that such social movements are reducible to their subsequent identitarian framings; any more than older working-class movements should be directly equated with either Labourism or bureaucratised trade unionism. In contrast to such reductive equivalences, Lisa Duggan's analysis of equality struggles (2003) emphasised the dynamics of *selective* co-option of parts of social movements (and their political demands) into a neoliberal framing (see also Rao, 2020: 152–154). This view of the entanglements of politics and culture might take us back to Raymond Williams' insistence that emergent forms and practices are always at risk of selective co-option by the dominant bloc (1977: 122). He offered a suggestive commentary on the dynamics of emergence and incorporation: '[t]he process of emergence, in such conditions, is then a constantly repeated ... move beyond a phase of practical incorporation: usually made much more difficult by the fact that much incorporation looks like recognition, acknowledgement, and thus a form of *acceptance*' (1977: 124–125; italics in original).

From such a starting point, culture wars might be best understood as a shift in strategy *within* the dominant bloc, moving from incorporation to contestation, and from acceptance to refusal. Where the New Labour period, and even some aspects of Cameron's conservatism, emphasised the 'tolerance' of difference within a framework of liberal 'diversity', the recent period has seen efforts to stake out differences as contestable. This strategy opened up new terrains in the Gramscian 'war of position', as the dominant bloc sought to revitalise and secure its alliances. Borrowing from the US enabled a repertoire of potential fractures to be imported, translated and rearticulated into British terms. Some of these lines of division travelled better than others: many in the UK puzzled over 'woke-ness' or the apparent threat of 'critical race theory', but the translation of 'our history' found rather more traction.

More generally, the commitment to taking culture seriously as the form through which identities and possibilities are forged, imposed, contested and transcended remains a vital concern. This is the space that Cultural Studies tried to create out of its borrowings from Gramsci's concern with hegemony, consent and common sense – and the concept of articulation as the practices of connecting and mobilising social forces into a temporary unity (Jefferson, 2021: 119–135; see also Rao, 2020: 207–208). This implies thinking about culture wars as one particular strategy for inhabiting and acting on this political-cultural landscape. It is not a shift from 'politics' to 'culture' but about how their articulation is being reorganised. In that sense, culture wars formed one element in a large and mobile repertoire of strategies that were deployed to build and sustain a particular bloc. But it is important to insist that the pursuit of culture wars was constantly entwined with new strategies for institutional reconfiguration, for centralising power, in particular the development of anti-democratic policies, and new forms of authoritarianism that return us to the problematic of '*policing* the crisis'. In the next chapter, I explore some of these other strategies in the context of the deepening fractures and fissures with the Conservative Party and within the wider bloc.

## Rearticulating politics and culture: the return (again) of race

Questions of race – racialised inequalities, racism and their long history – are rarely far away from the shape that crises take in the UK. This conjuncture – and the moment of the pandemic within it – have been no exception to this recurring logic. As always, different temporalities and multiple transnational flows combine – and are condensed in – the way in which race comes to figure. The long histories of British colonialism both shaped the British social formation in vital ways and became the object of explicit mobilisations and contestations, notably around colonial memorialisation and the institutions of education, as demands for decolonising them gathered momentum. The pandemic put new, yet grimly familiar, racialised distributions of vulnerability into play in the UK and elsewhere which intersected fiercely with the spread of Black Lives Matter-centred anger in the wake of the killing of George Floyd.

Such developments encountered characteristic forms of governmental displacement – denial, deferral and deflection – as new movements mobilised and public anger rose. In the midst of these strategies, government attempts to minimise and contain the question of race merged with the strategies of culture wars, borrowed and translated from the US. While race was by no means the only focus of culture wars, it was a central focus, notably around questions of 'our history'. I have tried to show how culture wars are by no means simply a confection or a distraction from 'real politics' but involve a distinctive reworking of the entanglements of politics and culture and seek to organise both politics and institutional arrangements. In moving to the next chapter, it is important to stress that culture wars do not exist on their own: they form part of a much larger repertoire of strategies deployed by the government in trying to control the proliferating crises and conflicts and to stabilise the political-cultural unities in difference of both party and bloc.

# Holding It Together? The Coercive Turn and the Crises of Party and Bloc

In this chapter, I explore the contradictions, crises and conflicts associated with the 2019 Conservative government's attempts to manage the trajectory of the conjuncture. Building on the discussion of culture wars in the previous chapter, I turn to other elements of the governmental repertoire, with particular attention to the simultaneous expansion of coercive capacities and the centralisation of power in the hands of the ruling party. Just as culture wars were never 'merely cultural', so these strategies were both material and symbolic, evoking a variety of legitimating devices for their introduction, including the continuing deployment of the imaginary of 'wealth'. I then consider these strategies in the light of the emerging fissures and fractures within the Party and within the wider ruling bloc. The problems of maintaining these two 'unities in difference' dominated the life of the Johnson government (2019–22), culminating in the overthrow of Johnson by the parliamentary Conservative Party and his replacement in the summer of 2022 by Liz Truss. Her arrival and departure as party leader and prime minister coincided with the last phases of writing this book but have already contributed to the expanding proliferation of crises, contradictions and conflicts. The chapter ends with some reflections on the arrival of what might be called 'zombie Thatcherism' (to borrow from Jamie Peck).

## Law and order politics (again)

In the UK, the public reactions to Brexit, political dislocations, COVID-19 and Black Lives Matter became entwined with campaigns of environmental activism and challenges to violence against women (particularly after the kidnapping, rape and murder of Sarah Everard by a serving Metropolitan Police officer). The aftermath of this case intersected with continuing investigations into undercover police spies, particularly those who had infiltrated social movements and, in some cases, formed relationships and had children with members of those movements (McFarlane, 2020). Indeed, the Metropolitan Police were rarely out of the headlines as policing problems, failures and disasters accumulated – from a series of highly publicised racialised stop and search actions to the policing of a vigil to commemorate Sarah Everard, which itself resulted in the sexualised trolling by police officers of one protester who was arrested at the vigil (see, inter alia, Rodger, 2021; Topping, 2021). By April 2022, the Commissioner of the Met (Cressida Dick) had resigned, following a declaration by Sadiq Khan, the Mayor of London, that he had lost confidence in her ability to reform the force. Shortly afterwards, the force was placed in 'special measures' by HM Inspector of Constabulary, as a result of 'systemic' failings (Dodd, 2022). Its misconduct system (for dealing with professional misbehaviour) was also the focus of a scathing (interim) report by Baroness Louise Casey which concluded that the system was failing both the Force and the public (Casey, 2022).

Meanwhile, other counter movements posed political – and policing – challenges. Extinction Rebellion (XR) protests dramatically interrupted city life (in London especially) while Insulate Britain activists took to blocking roads, including the M25 motorway. Others renewed tunnelling and tree-sitting tactics to interrupt and delay the environmental destruction associated with the building of HS2, a high-speed rail line planned to link London and the North (although the North later turned out to be a less comprehensive destination than was first thought (Hotten, 2021)). Such movements intersected with demonstrations against the government's Police, Crime, Sentencing and Courts Bill that sought to control protest and extend police powers, notably enabling them to prevent demonstrations that might cause 'disruption'. Demonstrations – organised under the suitably ambiguous title 'Kill the Bill' ('the Bill' also being a popular nickname for the police) – were often acrimonious and turned violent in some places. These events highlighted a deepening crisis of what in the UK has historically been celebrated as 'policing by consent' (see, inter alia, Reiner, 2010). Policing and protest were once again entangled in the crises of the British state and re-emerged at the heart of legislation introduced in 2021.

The Police, Crime, Sentencing and Courts Act (2022) significantly extended police powers, particularly in relation to those dealing with protests and demonstrations, creating very low thresholds for criminalising behaviours. During the passage of the Bill the then Home Secretary, Priti Patel, clearly thinking it was all a bit underpowered, added amendments that made it illegal for protesters to attach themselves to another person or an object (the widely used tactic of 'locking on') and to obstruct transport infrastructure works. At the same time, the Act extended police 'stop and search' powers where they believed an illegal protest might be taking place (Monbiot, 2021b).

This extension of coercive capacities combined with the extension of criminalisation was accompanied by familiar 'public interest' justifications: coercion is always culturally encased in potent symbolic wrappings. The government legitimated the measures with a characteristic denunciation of how 'some protesters' disrupted everyday life: 'The measures in the Police, Crime, Sentencing and Courts Bill will improve the police's ability to manage such protests, enabling them to balance the rights of protesters against the rights of others to go about their daily business, and to dedicate their resources to keeping the public safe' (Home Office, 2021).

In such ways, the practices of 'retooling the state' (Jones and Novak, 1999) via reorganising its capacities and machinery was entwined with the symbolic business of reaffirming the 'People' (the hard-working majority going about their daily business) imagined as (always) in need of better protection. A similar blend of symbolic and institutional elements was visible in the Nationality and Borders Bill. This was a response to the Conservatives' continually failing promise to control migration, dramatised in repeated images of small boats bringing migrants across the Channel. Lucy Mayblin argued that the Bill was a piece of political theatre and contained many proposals that were likely to prove either unworkable or illegal (or both, simultaneously). However, she insisted:

> Even if none of the plans come to fruition, the idea that boat arrivals in the Channel are a crisis of criminality which can only be solved with draconian laws and military rhetoric creates a toxic politics of fear and hostility. Some of the plans also will come to fruition, and those that do will see more people drowning in the Channel, more people imprisoned and deported rather than their asylum claim heard, more housed in squalid prison like accommodation. (Mayblin, 2021)

This issue of channel crossings had haunted politics since David Cameron promised to get immigration under control in 2011. This promise put into play a perverse dynamic in which numbers would always be too high, and 'public discontent' would always be ready to be summoned to demand new measures. Such summonings continued, focusing particularly on Channel crossings. The exit from the EU added further intensity to the issue and manifested itself in the Johnson government's recurrent attacks on the French government for failing to prevent people leaving the French coast in the hope of arriving in the UK. This focus on migration culminated in proposals by the Home Secretary (in April 2022) to outsource the management of 'illegal' migrants to Rwanda – a proposal certain to attract legal challenges for its breaches of national and international law. The resulting interstate agreement may or may not be used to manage migrants arriving in the UK but it certainly mobilised perceived popular anxieties about immigration and desires to see action being taken. More than that, legal challenges were turned into political capital in government attacks on 'lefty lawyers' attempting to thwart the 'will of the people'.

The Johnson government also embarked on a programme of what might loosely be called constitutional reform. Changes to the election process and practices, steps to weaken the arrangements for judicial review of decisions by the government and other public authorities, and plans to reform the law on human rights were all launched in 2021. The Elections Act included the demand (borrowed from the US Republicans) for Voter ID and proposals to subject the Electoral Commission to government control. In addition, the Act made changes to forms of political involvement and participation, especially in relation to 'third party' campaigners. The Act also gave government increased powers to register, remove or change the descriptions of such organisations, potentially ranging from Trades Unions to Black Lives Matter (Howarth, 2021). This change would add substantial administrative burdens to charities and other civil society organisations seeking to register as Third Parties. Finally, the Act also restricted the capacity of parties to form electoral pacts: an increasingly significant issue given the arguments for 'progressive alliances' to work around the limitations of the first past the post parliamentary voting system (see, for example, Lawson, 2021). Provisions to limit the process of judicial review were also significant. Judicial review had consistently been a target for the Johnson-led Conservative Party, given that two reviews had challenged the Brexit process (judging that it was parliament, not the executive, who could take the decision to leave the EU, and that the attempted prorogation of parliament in 2018 as a device to 'get Brexit done' was illegitimate).

Ferdinand Mount summarised the shifts in power at stake in 2022's five Acts (The Dissolution and Calling of Parliament Act – ending fixed term parliaments; the Judicial Review and Courts Act; the Elections Act; the Nationality and Borders Act; and the Police, Crime, Sentencing and Courts Act):

> These five Acts of Parliament were all in force by the end of April. Each of them is intended to increase government control: over Parliament, over elections, over the courts, over immigrants and over public demonstrations. ... For Johnson, the outrage that these Acts have generated in lefty circles is not a drawback but a brilliant success. The whole thing is a deliberate strategy to enthuse his core vote and heighten their sense of imperilment. (Mount, 2022)

Many of these strategies have a grimly familiar quality. From the demonisation of protest to the extension of coercive powers, and from the centralisation of power to the deepening of political-cultural fractures, they have at least a genetic resemblance to the UK's descent into crisis in the 1970s. This is, though, not a simple repetition: in the 1980s the UK entered a new conjuncture, built around the projects that promised to resolve the crises of the 1970s. But the *failures* of those projects – and the subsequent accumulation of new crises, contradictions and conflicts – have combined to produce a new moment in which consent evaporated and the recourse to authoritarian and populist modes of governing was becoming increasingly central.

The current political-cultural bloc and its strategies build on the ruins of the old and are enlivened by new transnational dynamics. The strategies put into play were always *both* material and cultural. They reorganised state capacities and reach while reinforcing the narratives, representations and symbols of the nation that were central to the dominant bloc's formation. But they also point to the ways in accumulating crises, contradictions and antagonisms had unsettled the bloc. This unsettling turbulence has been lived, in part, in the body of the Conservative Party – as it has been headed by five different leaders in the space of six years (Cameron, May, Johnson, Truss and Sunak).

## Under tension: strains in the Party

All political parties are, in some sense, coalitions of interests and perspectives, temporarily united in the search for political power – or the drive to maintain it. The Johnson-led Conservative Party was no different, although its character certainly differed from earlier incarnations of the Party. Johnson and his allies had purged a range of people – the bearers of traces that were no longer welcome in the post-Brexit world of 'Britannia Unchained'. 'One Nation' Conservatives and a number of Remain-leaning MPs (and former ministers) either resigned or were de-selected in time for the 2019 general election. This tilted the balance of the parliamentary party towards a mixture of libertarian, nationalist, Brexiteer and globalising free traders, seeking – in the words of the 2019 Manifesto – to 'unleash Britain's potential'. The result was a landslide victory, giving Johnson an 80-seat majority. However, this was not exactly a united party. The 2019 parliament saw an efflorescence of Conservative parliamentary groups, presumably modelled on the achievements of the pro-Brexit European Research Group (ERG) in the previous decade. They included the COVID Recovery Group (CRG), the Common Sense Group (CSG), the New Social Covenant Unit and the Northern Research Group (NRG) while the ERG continued to supervise Brexit and demanded much else besides. A profile of its chief organiser, Steve Baker, described him as a Christian Conservative, small stater and a fan of Austrian economics (Gimson, 2021). The ERG also described themselves as 'the Spartans' (Francois, 2021).

Although memberships overlapped, the groups had significant differences of orientation. The CSG proclaimed its commitment to 'authentic conservatism', rejecting both the 'liberal elite' and 'subversives' such as Black Lives Matter, Extinction Rebellion and others. They were committed to a 'culture wars' stance, arguing that 'The business of politics is values – it's about place, purpose and pride. The Battle for Britain has begun, it must be won by those who, inspired by the people's will, stand for the common good in the national interest' (quoted in Lester, 2021). A rather different tone is represented by the NRG, mainly composed of MPs who had benefitted from the fall of the Red Wall. For them, a central concern was to ensure the delivery of the 'levelling up' agenda. As the chair, Paul Berry, put it during an interview in the *New Statesman*, they saw Johnson as a leader for 'levelling up', committed to low tax and regulation, while willing to use state intervention to fix broken markets (Hayward, 2021). This speaks to an older Conservatism in its view of the uses of the state but it was the state – both its uses and costs – that became a major focus for intra-Party tensions as the pandemic continued.

Aspects of this older Conservatism were also visible in the New Social Covenant Unit, a self-described mix of 'old–new ideas'. Committed to 'Family, Community and Nation – the associations that make people free and safe', they proclaimed that 'we need a new social covenant for the 21st century' (New Social Covenant Unit, n.d.). Ten MPs (all from the 2019 intake) published a report in 2021, entitled 'Trusting the People: the case for community-powered Conservatism' (Baillie et al, 2021).

The CRG, founded by MPs Steve Baker (as above) and Mark Harper pressured the government to limit interventions against COVID-19, attacking lockdown plans and vaccinations for children, for example, as state over-reach and infringements of personal liberty. The CRG was the beneficiary of substantial external funding from established Conservative donors, including a private equity firm and a former oil company executive, while also receiving support from an 'unincorporated association' called the Recovery Alliance. The pandemic exposed multiple (and intersecting) fault lines within the Party. Conservative MPs were consistently reluctant to support interventions such as lockdowns. Some opposed measures to enforce vaccination (equating obligatory vaccination with 'fascism') and other measures directed to control the spread, denouncing the use of 'vaccine passports' as 'communism' (echoing US Republican claims). In the process, these MPs generated a sort of organisational drag on the government's capacity to take action during the third phase of the pandemic, further slowing down decisions. However, this self-declared 'libertarian' wing of the Party offered no resistance to the range of legislation discussed earlier, from the criminalising effects of the Police, Crime, Courts and Sentencing Act to the changes to Judicial Review: some freedoms count more than others, or some people's freedoms count more than others.

At the same time, criticisms of the government adopting a high tax, large state position began to multiply, within and beyond the Party. The *Economist's* Bagehot complained that:

> The conservatives have undergone many transformations in their time: from the party of the landed squirearchy to that of the industrial bourgeoisie; from the post-war consensus to free-market radicalism. Now they are undergoing another. For 40 years, from the choice of Margaret Thatcher as its leader in 1975 to David Cameron stepping down as prime minister in 2016, Tories stood for small government. Today they are the party of big-government conservatism.
>
> The budget provided a vivid illustration. By the mid-2020s public spending will be the highest, as a share of GDP, since the mid-1970s. By the same measure, taxation will be its highest since the early 1950s. But there is more to big-government conservatism than the size of the state. There is the philosophy of the state as well. And under Boris Johnson, the Conservatives have set themselves aims they think can be achieved only by big-state activism. (Bagehot, 2021)

This was echoed by the ever-busy Steve Baker, who announced that he was planning to set up yet another group within the Conservative Party that would "provide a vehicle to unleash the potential of the United Kingdom and redefine a free market conservatism for the future" because "I'm looking at a party which is going in the wrong direction" (quoted in Politics.co.uk, 2021) The same issues also drove the resignation of Lord Frost as chief Brexit negotiator in December 2021, driven by 'concerns about the current direction of travel' and his wish to 'move as fast as possible to where we need to get to: a lightly regulated, low-tax, entrepreneurial economy, at the cutting edge of modern science and economic change' (BBC, 2021c).

The factional splits within the Party contributed to a sense of instability that was compounded by the deepening problems of Johnson's leadership. Anxieties gathered around the issues of 'Partygate', as Johnson's claims that he 'didn't know' the events he attended (glass in hand) were, in fact, parties (and thus illegal at the time) and around questions of sleaze, corruption and collusion. Mostly these were held at bay during the first half of 2022 by reaffirmations of Johnson's vote-winning popular style and (somewhat bizarre) claims that he 'had got most of the big calls right'.

## Crises, corruption and consent: fractures and fissures in the bloc

The internal tensions of the Conservative Party were certainly important but their relationships to the wider bloc were equally significant. In Gramscian terms, this may be posed as a question of leadership, referring to both the leading sections of the bloc (the dominant fractions of rentier capital in its widest – and transnational – sense) and the role played by the Party and Johnson in producing and performing the coherence of the bloc. By early 2022, there were multiplying strains and tensions within the bloc, pointing to emerging lines of fracture within its conception of the British people. Some of these arose from the long-running English dominance of this version of Britishness which generated new varieties of scepticism, anger and distance across the other three nations. Others were emerging in the fraught relations between the commitment to rentierism and the mixed fortunes of other fractions of capital, some of whom had not forgotten Johnson's 'fuck business' when he was asked about industry concerns about Brexit in June 2018. The *Financial Times* reported:

> 'Fuck business.' Never was the Brexit manifesto more succinctly captured than in Boris Johnson's impromptu aside. As slogans go, it has everything. It surfs the populist wave of anger towards elites. It is easy to understand. Hell, it's even shorter than 'take back control'.
> … After two years of failing to offer up even a scintilla of a plan, relying on magical thinking and the belief that if Britain just held its nerve, Europe would fold, this is all he had left – a petulant explosion. It is only a few weeks since Mr Johnson was caught saying much the same thing about Ireland as its complexities threatened the simplicity of his Brexit. (Shrimsley, 2018)

This troubled relationship to industrial and commercial sectors was replayed during the gathering energy and supply chain crises of 2021–22. The government appeared ill-prepared (again) for the emergence of these problems. Johnson's response was to insist that there was no crisis and that any problems could be solved by British business moving away from its dependence on 'cheap foreign labour'. He insisted that the UK as a whole needed to move away from a 'low wage, low cost' economy (an interesting variant on the deferral strategy). Ross argued that

> the 'fuck business' attitude of the Brexit wars is back, along with the debate over the UK's immigration regime. It is a stance that is shaping the government's response to the shortages of workers in sectors including hospitality, manufacturing and logistics. Industry leaders want more workers but Johnson says he is refashioning the economy to wean it off an addiction to cheap foreign labour. (2021)

The same cluster of problems also appeared in the agricultural sector, as vegetables rotted in the fields in the absence of seasonal migrant labour to pick them, while pigs were culled because of a lack of butchers. Farmers had been a relatively strong component of the Brexit bloc (as well as having long-standing affinities with the Conservative Party) but in this sector, as in others, a certain sense of 'buyer's remorse' was setting in (especially as problems emerged about replacing EU financial support). Similar sentiments were expressed in the fishing industry (another strongly pro-Brexit sector).

Meanwhile the carbon-centred extractive sector was posing different problems for maintaining a coherent – or even apparently coherent – alliance. Close to government in many ways, and certainly among the consistent donors to the Conservative Party, the sector continued to benefit from government support. However, government decisions to back the sector emerged as a focus of increasing public concern, driven by decisions to license new North Sea drilling operations, proposals to open new coal mines (in Cumbria and Wales) and even the mooted return of fracking. All indicated a failure to take the carbon issue seriously and highlighted the power of the extractive sector to influence government. Coinciding with the UK's hosting of COP26, such initiatives generated claims of hypocrisy.

There were troubles elsewhere in the bloc. The petit-rentier sections of the middle classes had been largely locked in by the double movement of rising property prices (and the associated imaginary of wealth – its creation and preservation) and the cluster of traditionalist/nationalist sentiments promoted by the government (from stopping immigration to defending 'our history'). But even here, the return of inflation in 2021–22, driven by rising energy and import costs, threatened the perceived value of savings – subsequently accelerated by the combination of rising inflation and the disastrous Truss/Kwarteng budget of October 2022, with its effects on interest rates and threat to pension finds. Historically, inflation has been a frequent feature of middle-class anxieties, often associated with populist or even fascist enthusiasms (not least the desire for a 'strong leader'). Meanwhile, concern about 'standards' threatened to bite into this traditionalist attachment, with the swirl of sleaze, corruption and lying being perceived by some as undermining cherished 'British values' or merely confirming their scepticism about politicians. Such concerns were associated with arguments about whether the unwritten British constitution could survive the absence of 'good chaps' who could be trusted to behave properly (see, inter alia, Hennessy, 1994; Blick and Hennessy, 2019; Saunders, 2021). In the end, though, it was what became known as 'Partygate' (lockdown rule-breaching parties in Downing Street and elsewhere in government buildings) that crystallised many of these doubts and anxieties. As I observed previously, they were widely understood as demonstrating that there was 'one rule for them, another for the rest of us'.

The mix of material and ethical issues cut into aspects of working-class support for the bloc. At the same time, racialised minority fractions of the working class were exposed to the continuation of the 'hostile environment' and were particularly at risk from COVID-19 (as discussed in the previous chapter). Women's wages declined during the pandemic, relative to men's, while domestic violence spiralled with particular consequences for those trapped 'at home'. Young people's disaffection from the Conservatives continued to deepen, motivated by a variety of economic, political-cultural and social concerns, that included problems of housing and the planetary crisis.

After the 2019 election, there was much talk about 'Red Wall' votes being 'on loan' to the Conservatives and that generation of Conservative MPs have become increasingly anxious as polling in the later months of 2021 showed voters turning away from the Party, naming a variety of issues from 'sleaze', MPs' second jobs, and the failure to deliver on levelling up promises (Shaw, 2021). On 16 December 2021, the by-election in North Shropshire resulting from Owen Paterson's resignation saw a massive swing of 34 per cent in this hitherto safe Conservative seat to the Liberal Democrat candidate Helen Morgan. The result contributed to declining performance in national opinion polling, both for the Conservative Party generally and for Johnson as Prime Minister.

Liberal/progressive social groups were, of course, mostly not part of the Brexit and Boris blocs and the transition to the Johnson government accelerated their disaffections on multiple fronts, ranging from pandemic failures to the proliferation of racist, xenophobic, patriarchal tropes that appeared in government statements. Although the competition was fierce, this was perhaps best exemplified in the Minister for Justice, Dominic Raab, not knowing the meaning of misogyny when asked if the government would make it a hate crime (BBC, 2021d). Anger continued to mount as inequalities deepened, crises worsened and violence against subordinated and marginalised groups increased during the first years of the Johnson government.

## Performative politics in the face of fractures and fragility

In a conjuncture characterised by proliferating crises, contradictions and conflicts, how could the 'Boris bloc' be held together? A variety of strategies were deployed, ranging, as we have seen, from mobilising 'culture wars' to strengthening the coercive capacities of the state and the grip of the government on the machinery of the state. None of these prevented the fissures and fractures deepening as confidence shrank in the government's capacity to fulfil its promises: from managing Brexit to levelling up, or from ensuring global free trade to ensuring collective security in pandemic times. Instead, by the start of 2022, Brexit was still enmeshed in fraught negotiations with the EU and the French; levelling up was the subject of deepening scepticism in the north of England (and elsewhere, it should be added); global trade deals had been in short supply (and nothing had prepared the UK for interrupted supply chains) and the fourth wave of the pandemic (omicron variant) found a characteristically underprepared and slow to act government doing its usual thing. Indeed, 2021 had ended with the unimaginable coming true: the Labour Party under Keir Starmer had taken a substantial lead in opinion polls.

By the beginning of 2022, the accumulation of mishaps and missteps had taken a toll on Johnson's popularity and MPs and party members were having doubts about his leadership. Questions proliferated: about the costs of decorating the Downing Street flat, the evidence of pandemic corruption and 'crony capitalism', the selling of honours, the breaches of lockdown rules ('partygate'), the mishandling of the Paterson case and the subsequent by-election loss in North Shropshire (explained by Johnson as the result of the media focusing excessively on 'politics and politicians' (Mason, 2021)). One particularly telling moment was a speech to the CBI (Confederation of British Industry) in which Johnson lost his place, became confused and embarked on a long digression about Peppa Pig – a children's cartoon character (Nicholson, 2021).

Johnson had been crucial to the shaping of the Brexit bloc and its conversion into a Conservative-supporting coalition. His leadership in both settings was highly personalised and performative, offering a distinctive embodiment of a politician unlike other (British) politicians: more lovable rogue that competent technocrat. This style undercut established political habits – marking them as too solemn, too elitist, too uncool – and promised (not unlike both Farage and Trump) the simulacrum of a 'man of the people'. The blowsy style – and a casual relationship to truth – had characterised his career prior to his election as Conservative Party leader (and Prime Minister) in 2019 (see, for example, Yates, 2019). But increasingly, opponents and commentators observed that 'the joke is no longer funny'. His absence from, and avoidance of, key decisions had become recurring issues (see Calvert and Arbuthnott, 2021), inducing commentators to pose the question: 'Where's Boris?' (for example, Balls, 2020; Tomkins, 2020). More importantly the political-cultural centre of gravity of the Conservative Party appeared increasingly out of sync with wider public sentiments on a range of issues (from public spending to pandemic policies). The decline of Johnson's political-cultural persona coincided with worsening material conditions to unsettle the coherence of the bloc and made the relationships between the bloc and its forms of political leadership (Johnson and the Conservatives in general) increasingly unstable. In July 2022, as ministers resigned and Johnson's reputation was shredded, he stood down as Prime Minister and leader of the party.

As a result, the UK found itself confronting a world of deepening crises at a point when government was largely suspended while the Conservative

Party took the time to find a new leader. Troubles mounted – from the war in Ukraine, through rising fuel prices to a more generalised cost of living crisis that drove a revival of trades union action. Beginning with rail workers (the RMT union), strikes and strike ballots multiplied quickly: from dockers to criminal law barristers; from postal workers to nurses... most of whom had seen wages and salaries stall or decline even before inflation surged to 10 per cent. In this context, government calls for 'restraint' sounded hollow at best and, despite attempts to represent strikes as 'disruption', public opinion tended to split more or less evenly as strikes began, with younger people particularly sympathetic to strikers (Beckett, 2022).

The resulting period of transition – with a largely absentee government (Johnson refused to step down but spent much of the interim period on holiday) – ended with the election of Liz Truss as party leader. Almost immediately politics was again effectively suspended following the death of the Queen on 8 September, two days after receiving Truss to formally invite her to form a government.

## Choices, choices: the (lurching) entry of zombie Thatcherism

Liz Truss arrived as party leader after a long drawn out election process within the Conservative Party. First, MPs narrowed down the contenders for the leadership through a series of votes until only two remained: Truss and Rishi Sunak (previously Chancellor of the Exchequer). This winnowing process caused considerable anxiety within the Party and among conservative commentators because of the amount of vitriol and anger in exchanges between and about the candidates. More broadly, this was a strange exercise in 'democracy', involving an estimated 0.8 per cent of the UK population and a strikingly unrepresentative sample at that, being noticeably more white, old, property owning and living in the South of England than the average. The rest of us were able to watch in fascinated horror as the two candidates both claimed to be the true descendants of Thatcher, even as they invoked different versions of that inheritance. Sunak emphasised a Conservative history of fiscal probity while Truss went for the imagery of wealth creation via tax cuts and subsidies for the rich. An article by Eleni Courea quoted the historian Robert Saunders:

> 'Sunak wants to invoke the early Thatcher, who prioritized taming inflation over quick economic fixes; who raised taxes during a recession and spoke of "balancing the books,"' Saunders said. 'Truss, by contrast, invokes the triumphant, swashbuckling Thatcher of the later years: a Thatcher who cut taxes, "won the Cold War" and towered over British politics. Neither version is wholly false, but both

cherry-pick aspects of the Thatcher myth, to suit their own political purposes.' (Courea, 2022)

Courea wryly noted that Truss had started with an advantage thanks to a combination of sartorial choices and a PR strategy featuring photo ops that echoed Thatcheresque imagery (sitting in a tank, and so on). Truss triumphed in the membership vote and appointed a team of zealots and enthusiasts who saw themselves as part of that Thatcherite genealogy. They included Kwasi Kwarteng as Chancellor (who had been a co-author of the (in)famous *Britannia Unchained* with Truss), Suella Braverman as Home Secretary (whose first commitment was to insist that 'zero' small boats would cross the Channel carrying migrants), Jacob Rees Mogg as Business Secretary, Kemi Badenoch as Secretary for International Trade and, not least, Steve Baker as Minister for Northern Ireland.

Truss's full entry to government was delayed by the prolonged period of national mourning for Elizabeth Regina. This enabled the articulation of other visions of Britain as the nation was invited, and indeed, instructed to celebrate her lengthy reign. Many of these visions evoked conceptions of national unity and solidarity, embodied – more or less magically – in the frame of the monarch. Doubting voices were marginalised, or even criminalised as the recent Police Act was enforced. This celebration of the Monarch was a 'public mood' in Ahmed's terms (2014), elaborated in part through contrasts with the divisions and disunity of contemporary politics. The rather surreal suspension of hostilities lasted for ten days, culminating in the state funeral. At that point, the new government began to announce its plans, articulated around the theme of wealth creation and the pursuit of 'growth, growth, growth'.

Most of the wealth to be created was, in the first instance, the result of transfers from public funds to private ownership: subsidies to businesses to help with fuel costs, the non-implementation of a planned National Insurance rise and a planned rise in Corporation Tax, and, not least, the announcement of the abolition of the top rate (45 per cent) of income tax. The general direction of flow was symbolised in the decision to remove the EU/Cameron-era cap on bankers' bonuses, announced as the first step towards a major 'deregulation' of the financial sector. Deregulation emerged as a recurring theme: plans for low tax and low regulation 'opportunity zones' across the UK; the reduction of regulations on farming and the reduction of planning 'burdens' would all, it was claimed, contribute to a dynamic of economic growth and wealth creation in the UK. At the same time, the pursuit of 'energy security' was to be driven by maximising the use of existing (carbon) fuels, assisted by removing the moratorium on fracking. Business Secretary Rees Mogg insisted that Britain must 'get every cubic inch of gas out of the North Sea' (Horton, 2022).

Kwarteng's September 'fiscal event' (rather than a budget, thus avoiding scrutiny by the Office for Budgetary Responsibility) had spectacular consequences, causing the pound to plummet against the dollar. One investor was quoted as saying that the price of trading in sterling now included a 'moron premium bonus' (Tooze, 2022b) while a key fraction of the bloc – hedge funds – augmented their anticipated tax benefits with profits made from 'shorting' the pound. The Bank of England stepped in to buy government bonds, not least to avert an emerging crisis among pension funds. The inflationary effects of the budget were augmented by the increasing cost of public borrowing resulting from the pound's loss of value. Meanwhile, Truss became the first Prime Minister not to experience a significant public polling bounce on taking office as Labour's poll lead widened – and Conservative MPs showed the first signs of alarm. Then Truss sacked the Chancellor, Kwasi Kwarteng, and appointed Jeremy Hunt who immediately reversed most of the plans of the mini-budget and forecast the imminent arrival of austerity (again) to absorb the costs of this magical thinking (Tooze, 2022b).

As studies of the austerity years have shown, the effects of such policies are written on both the body politic and the social body (for example, McKee et al, 2012; Stuckler and Basu, 2013; Cooper and Whyte, 2017). Their return and intensification will overshadow lives and politics for years to come, even as the Brexit and Boris blocs crumble in the face of deepening crises and deepening disaffection. As always, such disaffection takes many forms, from active mobilisations confronting capital, the state and their agents through demands for more responsible economic management and the reversal of policies that would exacerbate the climate crisis. Perhaps its most popular form was a sullen, head-shaking, arms-folding, fury on the part of people who felt themselves betrayed once again.

The fantasies of friction-free growth and trickle-down wealth – and the public nightmares that are their shadows – marked the exhaustion of the bloc's strategies for securing power and wealth in the face of growing inequality. Its routes to constructing and securing consent – from consumerist attachment to culture wars – look threadbare and expose an alarming dependence on intensified varieties of authoritarianism, nationalism and populism. This moment (October 2022) is full of dangers, exposed by what might best be described as 'zombie Thatcherism'. Here I borrow and bend Jamie Peck's 2010 description of the persistence of neoliberalism in which he concluded '[t]he living dead of the free-market revolution continue to walk the earth, though with each resurrection their decidedly uncoordinated gait becomes even more erratic' (2010a: 109). Erratic now seems an understatement and, indeed, Truss then lurched off, resigning her position to be replaced by Rishi Sunak as Prime Minister.

These dynamics also point towards a wider 'crisis of the state', as legitimacy declines and the state has increasing trouble in performing like a state. The endlessly 'modernised' and 'reformed' version of the British state has found it difficult to contain the conjuncture's condensation of crises. There are important questions for how we think about states, which are taken up in the following chapter.

# Unstable Equilibria: The Life of the State

In this chapter, I explore a different focus of the turbulence and troubles of this conjuncture – the state. Many of the crises discussed earlier in the book have been threaded through the apparatuses and agencies of the state, not least as a result of the ways that the UK state has been – and continues to be – occupied and remade by the dominant bloc. From the policing of dissent and disorder to the management of migration; from pandemic governance to the regulation of public utilities; from the cost of living to the environmental crisis, the array of emerging crises and dominant efforts to manage them are intimately interwoven with the state. If, as Gramsci suggested, the 'life of the state can be conceived as a series of unstable equilibria', then this is a profoundly unsettled moment in the life of the UK state. These crises have different trajectories and temporalities (as I argued in Chapter 2). They have also involved different social forces and mobilisations. But they have consistently coalesced in and around the state, such that we might talk of a crisis *of* the state itself.

I will suggest that the current crisis of the British state has three distinctive, although interconnected, aspects. First, there is a *crisis of capacity* involving the state's ability to manage social, political, environmental and economic disorders. Second, there is a *crisis of legitimacy* that condenses varieties of anti-state scepticism alongside a deepening popular mistrust of politics, politicians or what is sometimes called 'the political class'. Third, this crisis of legitimacy is linked to a *crisis of authority*, in which the dominant bloc has found it harder to command popular support for its projects, policies and promises. As a result, I suggest, the state is 'not what it used to be' and needs to be considered in more carefully conjunctural terms (rather than assuming that there is a persistent and coherent entity called the state or even The State). In this chapter I consider each in turn, and end by asking what it means to 'perform like a state'.

# A crisis of capacity?

The contemporary crisis of *capacity* is intimately related to the changing form of the state, although that should not be taken to imply that states were previously coherent, effective and competent (they certainly were not). But the drive to transform the state into a 'lean and mean' form, to construct what Cerny (1997) called a 'competition state', and to roll back or shrink the machinery of the state in order to liberate enterprise from its 'shackles' has been a continuing theme since 1979. This new form was driven by the rhetoric of neoliberal anti-statism, legitimated by public choice theories of bureaucratic waste and ineffectiveness, and narrated as the liberation of people and corporations from 'red tape', 'interference' and 'excessive' taxation. But these ambitions were articulated with a complex social and economic and cultural programme, that sought to reform people through the imposition of 'workfare' and the cultivation of 'enterprising' and 'responsible' individuals, families and communities and the disciplining of those who 'failed'.

This long-running project of state reform was delivered through a range of processes – the privatisation of public goods, the contracting out of public services, the creation of 'quasi-markets' within public service (creating internal contracting) and the managerialisation of those services that remained in the public realm (Clarke and Newman, 1997). Programmes of cost-reductions (often badged as 'efficiency savings') were mandated by the Treasury, resulting in a 'hollowed-out' state, while promoting opportunities for capital accumulation (from the purchase of public utilities to winning service contracts). It was, as Harden (1992) argued, a *contracting state*, in both senses of the word: the state shrank and the contract became the favoured device for organising its relationships. This was a competition state of sorts, promoting competition in the field of public service contracts while simultaneously fostering the growth of monopolistic and oligopolistic market tendencies that consolidated the distinctive dynamics of rentier capitalism (Christophers, 2020).

State policy and practice were also reshaped by the multiple commitments to 'security', from New Labour's efforts to control 'bad neighbours' through anti-social behaviour orders to combatting the growing threat of international terrorism (and its domestic variants) after 9/11 and George Bush's declaration of the 'war on terror'. The expansion and intensification of criminalisation and the widening nets of 'suspicion' enlarged the reach of states, including the UK's, while incurring new economic costs and problems of public trust, especially among those communities who found themselves the targets of suspicion. Outsourcing was a growth business in this domain too, from the rise of private security business to the subcontracting of war-making.

These developments were connected in the emergence of what we (Clarke and Newman, 1997) called a 'dispersed' state form in which state powers, capacities and responsibilities were devolved through the medium of principal-agent relations to a range of private and non-profit organisations (and some powers were differentially devolved to the other nations in the tendentially dis-uniting kingdom). State business was put out to tender and the contractors were monitored (more or less effectively) for their performance in fulfilment of the contract, driving the growth of what Power (1994) called 'the audit explosion'. The dynamics and directions of change had important consequences for public imaginaries of statehood – in particular for questions of authority and accountability. It also weakened the state's capacity to do its business. In particular, the combination of reductions in public service spending and the dispersed relationships involved in subcontracting tended to disrupt the delivery of policy goals, even before the added costs of contracting and monitoring were taken into account. Policy makers found themselves lacking 'levers to pull' to deliver on promises (there is a different question about whether such levers ever existed or provided an effective means of governing). Both 'principals' and 'agents' found the business of contracting troublesome and difficult to manage. Meanwhile, the public had been invited to think of itself as a series of 'consumers' of public services – education, health, and so on (see Clarke et al, 2007). But people became increasingly sceptical about their new 'consumer' status and increasingly restive in the face of state failures – from problems of school choice to the inability of privatised water companies to provide an effective service or the growing waits for NHS appointments (and, later, ambulances). All contributed to a deepening cynicism about promised improvements and empty rhetorical gestures to 'progress'.

The crisis of capacity undermined public confidence in *both* government and the state. In relation to government, failures to deliver services or resources deepened popular scepticism about politics, politicians and politicians' promises. As public expectations of the state – especially around access to reliable public services – diminished, people made increasing use of private alternatives (in health care, schooling, and so on) – at least among those who could afford to make the choice. Here, the imaginary and practices of 'wealth' (its accumulation and preservation) played an increasingly significant articulating role: choice was justified as the 'right' of people to spend their own money; while declining services prompted more people to make such choices.

## A crisis of legitimacy?

This crisis of capacity deepened in the 'austerity years' of Conservative rule after 2010 and it bore heavily on questions of *legitimacy*. Despite the steady stream of innovation and reform projects, there were arguments about who was being served by this new model state. For example, the deepening housing crisis that followed from the Thatcher-era assault on council housing (and council house building) was shadowed by the deepening crisis of care (in both institutional and domestic forms). Meanwhile, failures of public transport policy and practice culminated in the crisis of a privatised rail system in which Conservative governments found themselves taking services back into public control after the contracted companies found they could not deliver the service (or make the anticipated profits).

Even in the coercive apparatuses of the state, problems were deepening. The courts were grinding to a standstill, as criminal cases took longer and longer to come to trial. The police responded to a declining proportion of reported crimes, often not recording a growing range of offences. A Police Inspectorate report on Greater Manchester Police found that the force was not recording one in five crimes reported to it, rising to one in four for violent offences (Williams, 2020). At the same time, police forces were being charged with policing in homophobic, racist and misogynist ways and faced a decline in public confidence (especially, but not only, the Metropolitan Police). Past cases had an unsettling tendency to reappear in the public gaze, revealing varieties of collusion and miscarriages of justice: examples included the Hillsborough football disaster that killed 97 Liverpool football fans, the policing of the miners' strike (by the same South Yorkshire Police Force); and the failures of the West Midlands Police to find those responsible for the Birmingham pub bombings (having arrested and prosecuted the wrong people in the 1970s). The Home Office's pursuit of hostile environments to deter 'illegal migrants' proved a disastrous failure in many respects. Its view of who might be illegal managed to target well-established British citizens, including many of the 'Windrush generation'. Even after a series of investigations, apologies and critical reports, it failed to pay compensation to most of those whom it illegally pursued. Despite many promises, it proved unable to manage cross-Channel migration, resulting, in 2022, in the almost certainly illegal plan to outsource the processing of migrants to Rwanda. Most strikingly, its lack of organisational capacity and competence was revealed in the mounting delays, costs and misjudgements in the treatment of asylum seekers, even allowing for its generally punitive orientation (Trilling, 2021).

So, who is served by a diminished and dispersed state? Undoubtedly, those with wealth (whether in the form of capital or property) have found this a relatively agreeable form of state. Reduced levels of individual and corporate taxation, combined with the protection of inherited wealth against increased taxation, have combined with a dramatically reduced state capacity for investigating fraud and tax evasion. In keeping with the spirit of Peter Mandelson's boast about New Labour, the British state had also become 'intensely relaxed about people getting filthy rich' (Rentoul, 2013). The rise of housing as a form of wealth (and income, through buy-to-rent practices) was enabled and encouraged by government policies and subsidies, following on from the Thatcher government's Right to Buy scheme, introduced in 1980. Overlapping to some extent with the expansion of home ownership, older and retired middle-class people were financially cushioned by the combination of state and private or occupational pensions.

In comparison, most other segments of the population experienced falling standards of living as wages stalled or even declined, while employment became more contingent for many groups. Deindustrialisation combined with desocialisation and decollectivisation proliferated experiences of marginalisation, dispossession and abandonment. This is the landscape popularly characterised as 'left behind' people and places (Chapter 3), signalling the experience of being forgotten or ignored. Koch drew out a potent ethnographic comparison between declining attachments to official or formal politics and a more rooted sense of everyday politics, arguing:

> On a council estate in England, politicians – as officials who are associated with the government – are not considered to be trusted as caring and trustworthy people. On the contrary, residents routinely contrast them to the locally valued person who is someone who invests in the local neighbourhood and the people who live there. (2017b: 116)

Koch insists that it is important to attend to the lived meanings and practices of 'politics' as well as the affective distances between everyday and formal politics. However, the questions of who 'belongs' where and what 'belongs' to whom have also remained contested political-cultural issues.

The sense of being ignored or abandoned often crystallised around a feeling of a lost 'social' in which public institutions, civic provision and a sense of mutuality bound lives together (see, for example, David Lammy's view that "People want the social back. They are clear that you cannot contract everything out" (Adams, 2017)). There are strong *residual* (in Raymond Williams' sense) attachments to the idea of the state providing forms of infrastructure, protection and security (in a social as much as an anti-violence sense). There have, of course, been *emergent* initiatives that have attempted to fill these gaps. But such initiatives have often been fractured, fragmentary and subject to co-option. In this respect, they reflect the strains and tensions captured in Andrea Muehlebach's analysis of volunteering in Italy as 'moral neoliberalism' (2012).

In sum, this crisis of *legitimacy* has been fuelled by twin dynamics. First, there is scepticism about state capacity and competence (can it deliver what we need?) and its motives and desires (what does it want to do to us?). Second, there is a deepening mistrust of politics and politicians. Studies of how the public rank occupations in terms of trust have regularly found politicians to be held in low regard, a dynamic that was deepened by the

MPs expenses scandal of 2009 (Pickard, 2013). The more recent revelations of cronyism, sleaze, rule-breaking and corruption have deepened public mistrust even further.

## A crisis of authority?

Both the crisis of capacity and the crisis of legitimacy have contributed to the emerging crisis of *authority*. Subaltern groups aligned in the dominant bloc began having doubts, while those groups already outside the bloc had their sense of distance and disaffection intensified. The dominant bloc – as articulated through Johnson's Conservative Party – was never a hegemonic project, being bedevilled by old and new problems of belief and commitment. Rather, it reflected what Jessop described, in the context of Thatcherism, as a 'two nation' strategy which was 'concerned to mobilise the support of strategically significant sectors of the population and to pass the costs of the project to other sectors' (1982: 244). In political-cultural terms, the bloc dominated a fractured country, in which popular support was limited to just over half of those who voted for Brexit and to the 43.6 per cent who voted Conservative (plus the 2 per cent who voted for the Brexit Party and UKIP, perhaps) from a 67.5 per cent voter turnout in 2019. The size of the Conservative majority (80 seats) owed much to the distribution of votes in the UK's first past the post electoral system. But that popular base had been eroded by the sense of failed promises: the travails of Brexit, the failure of 'levelling up' to materialise and the rapidly deepening economic crises of 2022. Of course, there were many who had never believed such promises or who had only believed them contingently or in a quasi-contractual sort of way (forms of what Jeremy Gilbert (2015) has called 'disaffected consent').

But the electoral sphere only catches part of the political-cultural shifts that point to an emerging crisis of authority. Beyond the sphere of formal politics, other realignments had been taking place. One was the deepening detachment from formal politics – increasingly viewed with mixtures of disgust, disappointment and disaffection. The view of politics as corrupt and ineffectual (for those who view themselves as 'ordinary people') represents a serious challenge for those who look for *political* solutions to the present troubles. This retreat from formal politics blurred into a condition of sullen and resentful distrust – a cynicism about the possibilities that politics could make a difference combined with an anger that there was no alternative. Others became active in the landscapes of voluntary action, mutual aid and local transformations (across issues that range from supporting refugees through food security to environmental initiatives). At the same time, many have sought out the emerging possibilities of 'angry politics' (Maskovsky and Bjork-James, 2020). In the UK (and elsewhere) many of these centred on the politics of resentment – demanding the restoration of lost privileges, powers and glories (real or imagined) in the form of white supremacy, patriarchal power, heteronormative order – and, not least, in the restoration of British/English nationalism. Despite their national and nationalist forms, such politics flowed through increasingly significant transnational connections (Worth, 2019).

Other forms of angry politics centred on political failures in the face of the environmental catastrophe: Extinction Rebellion, Insulate Britain, Just Stop Oil and other activist groups tried to disrupt the pursuit of 'business as usual' in performative ways. Such mobilisations had transnational reach as part of a widening planetary consciousness and emerging planetary movements (Isin, 2021). At the same time, others neglected or abused by the state challenged its failures in a series of counter movements, including campaigns against sexual violence (Reclaim These Streets and others), against patriarchal norms in policing and the courts, and against homophobic and anti-trans violence. Those who had been the focus of too much of the wrong sort of state attention challenged racist institutions and practices of policing – stop and search powers, the racialised enactment of justice and imprisonment, and the penetration of policing into schools – in ways that connected potently with the rise of Black Lives Matter movements internationally. The list of such counter movements was substantial and indicates just how extensively contested the authority of the bloc had become as it failed to manage the accumulating crises, contradictions and antagonisms of the current moment.

## Performing like a state?

There is an important distinction to be made between abstract conceptualisations of an entity called The State and less abstract, more conjunctural, attention to the dynamics of *state formation*: the forms taken by particular states as they attempt to govern specific social formations in all their complexity. This distinction remains important even in relation to the naming of types of state – the epochal conceptualisations of capitalist states, colonial (or post-colonial or neocolonial) states, or patriarchal states, for example. Such namings focus on the structuring principles that organise and orient states to the reproduction of particular forms of social relations and draw attention to the forms of structural violence needed to maintain them. They point to the tendential alignment of states and types of social relations but they do not explain the concrete forms in which those relations – or the condensed combinations of social relations – are managed in specific circumstances.

Knowing that the UK has a capitalist state, rather than just a state, illuminates some things – the maintenance of the preconditions of private property, the rule of market freedoms, the fostering of capital accumulation, the management of 'social peace' to enable capital accumulation to go on, and the like. But it does not tell us which fractions of capital are part of the dominant bloc (nor how the state interprets and tries to coordinate the 'general interest' of capital). Nor does it tell us what the prevailing balance of forces in the class struggle might be, or what means of incorporating and subordinating subaltern groups are in play. More particularly, it cannot tell us how the state is organised – how the apparatuses of governing are structured and coordinated or, indeed, the character of the prevailing 'teeth gritting harmony' between them (my favourite phrase from Althusser, 1971: 24). The same applies to the other abstractions – patriarchal, colonial and more – that identify the organising principle but not the concrete forms taken by the system of dominance (nor the state of the struggles around it, including the use of state power to mitigate and manage its disruptive effects). And, not least, such abstractions tell us nothing about how multiple forms of social relations are combined, condensed – and contested – in and through state forms.

In contrast, thinking more conjuncturally illuminates the dynamics of changing state forms and the reorganisation of state power. At the heart of these changes was the emerging relationships between what were nation-states and new forms of transnational relationships. Gupta (1998) has pointed to the 'destabilisation' of the peculiar hyphen that linked nation and state, arguing that the emergence of post-colonial development was at the core of this unsettling, affecting both the nation-form and the state-form (and the hyphen that signalled their articulated relationship). Beginning here – with the transition from the colonial to the post-colonial and the neocolonial – avoids one of the stranger conceptions of state change: the move from a 'closed' national system to an 'open' one in the face of globalisation. The colonial framing reminds us that many nation-states were never 'closed' but were formed by an earlier set of transnational relations, flows and dynamics (whether at the metropolitan centres or in their peripheral places). That history (and the complex transitions that followed from it) has typically been occluded in simplifying accounts that contrast the Old and the New, in which globalisation poses new challenges to the coherence and viability of the nation-state and in which the 'nation' has emerged as a new site of turbulent politics (as discussed in Chapter 1).

Alongside these changes, it is important to attend to the efforts of neoliberal-inflected governments as they sought to reform and instrumentalise the state. Many of the characteristic dynamics – privatisation of public resources, contracting out of services, selective reductions of public spending – combined ideological and material dimensions, aiming to demonstrate the proclaimed superiority of the market over the state while transferring public assets to private hands, and diminishing the capacities of the state to be effective (in social provision or regulation, for example). Even within those apparatuses and agencies that remained public, the logics of market rule became organisational norms, through the introduction of quasi-markets or purchaser–provider distinctions with public services such as social work or health care. And across the public sector there was a tidal wave of managerialisation, as dynamic and innovative management replaced old-fashioned and ossified bureaucracy (Clarke and Newman, 1997). Managerialisation, in its turn, brought new costs and inefficiencies, as well as new habits of organisational power.

The changing form of the state was accompanied by shifts in the organisation of state power and capacity which were dispersed through new relationships within civil society and the corporate world, rather than being diminished or surrendered (Clarke and Newman, 1997). In the process, new social agents were sutured into positions of power, effectivity, responsibility and dependency. In the UK, the complex realignments of the state have included forms of devolution and decentralisation as part of the dynamics of dispersal, allocating responsibilities and capacities to different scales and sites of governing. At the same time, crucial powers and capacities for direction, control and surveillance have been centralised into the departments of the UK government (the Westminster model). Audit, data collection and use, have been combined with direct control by secretaries of state (for example, in schooling, partly through the erosion of local government as an intermediary institution). The other dynamic of centralisation was the intensification of fiscal control from the centre, such that the dispersed state *devolves* fiscal stress onto local government and 'third sector' bodies contracted into governmental work. This has been critical to the implementation and management of Austerity policies (see Peck, 2012, on 'austerity urbanism').

At the same time, the challenges of managing a heterogeneous and contested social have driven varieties of co-option, compromise and coercion, with multiple projects of 'inclusion' and sponsored 'diversity' seeking to set the terms of engagement along non-antagonistic and individualised framings, typically obscuring structured inequalities (and the campaigns to contest them). Some versions of co-option attempted to set access to the national community for some groups against the denial and demonisation of others. For example, Lamble (2013) has explored the contradictions of 'hate crime' as a site for the organisation of state power, noting how it enrols those it defends (gay, lesbian and trans people) into the uncomfortable space of 'neoliberal citizenship'. In particular, she points to the punitive penality of such criminalising processes, often directed against other subordinated groups. Challenges to the normative ordering of the social across multiple fronts have been met with more coercive responses, notably around the policing of some communities and most forms of protest (with more coercive possibilities on the way).

The current state form, then, is an uncomfortable assemblage of elements, relationships, policies, practices and promises – not all of which can be fulfilled. An austerity-driven state has capacity problems which have been overlaid on the previous decades of 'reform' projects that sought to roll back the state and externalise its activities and powers – to private companies, voluntary organisations and to 'responsible' individuals, families and communities. This new state form continually sought to intensify its role in capital accumulation, through privatisations, outsourcing and reduced taxation. Indeed, from the pandemic through to Truss's 'wealth creation' politics, the one element of this state assemblage that functioned effectively was its ability to act as a cash machine for needy capitalists. Elsewhere, this hollowed-out, dispersed and increasingly coercive state had deepening problems of performing like a state.

These changing forms of the state highlight two sorts of problems: one set is practical (where do you find the state when you want it?) and the other set is conceptual (what is a state?). Practically, those seeking assistance or support from the state now have to work harder to find it – from obtaining Universal Credit to calling an ambulance. Once, the state tended to be located in identifiable bureaucratic agencies, often in relatively visible public buildings – easily discoverable (if not necessarily accessible). But dispersal means 'the state' – or its current frontline proxies (see Humphris, 2019) – may have to be searched for and may well be found in a temporary structure such as a Portakabin. Although some public institutions such as schools and hospitals have often spent much on architectural additions (frontages and entrances in a late modern or postmodern style), more often, the fiscal crisis means both sub-sub-contracted provision and temporary or rented sites. States, of course, still find it easier to locate you than the other way around, having extensive resources for ensuring that 'we know where you live'. And some groups receive considerably more attention from state agencies than they might want (most notably, black and Asian people's vulnerability to excess policing).

This increasing elusiveness of states (in some of their aspects) is paralleled by a conceptual puzzle: what exactly is a state? There is a growing literature that explores this question, through several different routes. Here, I will only briefly summarise three central themes: the problem of the spatiality of states; the idea of the 'state effect' and the question of how states perform state-ness. For the first, James Ferguson and Akhil Gupta have argued that '[t]wo images come together in popular and academic discourses on the state: those of verticality and encompassment … These two metaphors work together to produce a taken-for-granted spatial and scalar image of a state that both sits above and contains its localities, regions, and communities' (Ferguson and Gupta, 2002: 982). These metaphors (the state overlooking society; and the state framing the territorial system of its nation) are potent ones in both popular and more academic conceptions of state-ness, seeping into how states are imagined, discussed and, indeed, contested.

The discussion of spatial and scalar imaginaries is closely linked to the rediscovery of Philip Abrams' (1988) critique of the state as anything other than an idea, fantasy or ideological representation:

> In sum: the state is not the reality which stands behind the mask of political practice. It is itself the mask which prevents our seeing political practice as it is. ... There is a state-system ... a palpable nexus of practice and institutional structure centred in government and more or less extensive, unified and dominant in any given society. And its sources, structure and variations can be examined in fairly straight-forward empirical ways. There is, too, a state-idea, projected, purveyed and variously believed in in different societies at different times. And its modes, effects and variations are also susceptible to research. The relationship of the state-system and the state-idea to other forms of power should and can be central concerns of political analysis. (1988: 82)

Abrams challenged both political sociology and Marxist theories of the state to grasp the *representation* of the state as a unified and coherent entity, rather than taking this imagined entity as their object of study. How this illusion – the state idea – is produced and maintained needed to be addressed because of its profound consequences for politics and social life. Mitchell (1999) developed these insights to argue that the state is only present as an *effect* – produced by multiple practices by dispersed agents and agencies which congeal in the image or appearance of a state as a singular and over-arching entity. He focused particularly on the fictive character of the distinctions drawn to mark the boundaries between the state and its others: state and society, state and economy. Instead, he suggests that such distinctions are the 'product of political work' (or, in my terms, political-cultural work) and act as 'a mechanism that generates resources of power' (Mitchell, 1999: 83; see also Painter, 2006 on 'prosaic geographies of stateness'). These moves do not make the challenges of analysing the state any easier, since they present a double object in place of the one, apparently coherent, starting point. So, both the state idea and the state system are now in play, but this change of focus invites us to think about the shifting apparatuses, agencies, practices, sites and relationships of the state system as an assemblage or an articulated 'unity in difference'.

These arguments suggest a reframing of what it now means to speak of a 'crisis of the state'. It might point to a crisis arising in the 'state system' as the legitimacy, coherence and effectiveness of the dispersed agencies and apparatuses face growing problems in managing the crises, contradictions and conflicts that confront them. Yet it might also be a crisis of the 'state idea', as the assemblage of the British state fails to *perform like a state* for critical audiences, affecting the legitimacy of the image or illusion of a coherent and integrated state. William Davies has written suggestively of the failure of this dispersed and hollowed-out state to sustain the 'state effect', arguing that

> [w]hat we're witnessing in Britain today is the disintegration of 'the state' as we previously imagined it (not least, in a geographic sense, as policies splinter region by region) and a crumbling of the conditions of any possible hegemony. For better or worse (and many of us fear the latter), this will alter how power works. (Davies, 2020)

The question of legitimacy is doubly significant here. The legitimacy of the state (idea) is one condition for the maintenance of social-political legitimacy or the possibility of hegemony. But the state effect also requires different audiences to grant legitimacy to the state system's performance of state-ness. Davies focuses on the domestic audiences for these performances, but there are important regional-national variations as publics in Northern Ireland, the Republic of Ireland, Scotland and Wales experience and evaluate the performances of the 'British' state differently. There are also significant international audiences (including transnational capital, the 'markets', the EU and other governments, international organisations such as the IMF) and other forms of transnational publics, such as displaced people seeking refuge in the UK and transnational counter movements – all of whom may have good reason to take an interest in, or become concerned about the reliability, competence and trustworthiness of the British state.

## Desires and doubts: imagining the state

In the previous section, I quoted from William Davies talking about the state not performing as 'as we imagined it'. The question of how we imagine the state is an important one in many ways, not least for the practices by which the rule of dominant blocs has been secured and challenged. I think it is worthwhile to consider some of the current varieties of disillusionment, doubt and desire that swirl around ideas of the state. Larry Grossberg (2018: 145) has suggested that such orientations can be roughly, but productively, framed in Raymond Williams' categories of dominant, residual and emergent structures of feeling – a view that I share and think makes sense in the UK context. Here, the *dominant* view remains organised around the logics of neoliberal anti-statism, with a continuing commitment to withdrawing the state from its excessive 'interference' in the worlds of the economy and individual/familial choice. Whether talking about subsidies and transfers that distort the natural workings of the market (and the labour market especially) or pandemic period restrictions on both individual and corporate liberty, the state continues to be figured as an intrusive and expensive burden, even as (in practice) it has proved a vital tool for installing and recurrently rescuing the neoliberal project as well as subsidising capital. It is, however, a view that is always under strain: the state has never been rolled back far enough to satisfy neoliberal enthusiasts (and, as Peck (2010b) suggests, never could be). But this dominant structure of feeling rests on a deep desire for an 'effective' state: economically efficient, wealth-preserving, property-protecting: in short, a 'strong state'.

*Residual* imaginings of the state have proved powerfully persistent, and for good reason. Williams argued that the residual persisted 'as an effective element of the present' because 'certain experiences, meanings, and values which cannot be expressed or substantially verified in terms of the dominant culture, are nevertheless lived and practised on the basis of the residue – cultural as well as social – of some previous social and cultural institution or formation' (1977: 122). One of the strongest residual features is a view of the state as a necessary support for welfare and security: that people should not be 'abandoned' to the mercy of either fate or the market. In the UK, attachments to the NHS and other public institutions demonstrate the long hold that this conception of the state has exerted on the popular imagination. The residual is, of course, a complex and contradictory formation, mobilising different expectations and claims-making practices. In the UK, it often rests on an Us/Them distinction, invoking a moral economy understanding of the obligations of the powerful ('*They* should do something …'). It also evokes older notions of citizenship against the contemporary individualisation and familialisation of 'responsibility'. Such views of citizenship are constrained and contradictory, and always susceptible to nationalist closures in conflicts over who *belongs* to the Nation. Finally, the deeply held desires for the state as the source of collective provision co-exist with a deeply embedded suspicion of the state as intrusive and coercive in relation to 'people like us'.

Finally, *emergent* conceptions of the state have been driven by new desires and new demands, particularly in the face of (a) the deepening climate crisis), (b) the COVID-19 pandemic, and (c) the deepening troubles of inequalities, violence and domination. These have sometimes crystallised around racialised vulnerabilities to the virus, sometimes around the growing level of violence against women, and sometimes around the profound deepening of poverty (dramatised in the choice to 'eat or heat'). Such desires reflect the magnetic pull of the state as an institutionalisation of collective capacity that promises the possibility of changing things (whether it is the control of male violence or the control of corporate greed and its environmental effects). But these desires also imply something other than the current state form – internationalising it, localising it, cleansing it of its ties to capital, and more. For some, however, the sheer contradictoriness of the state revives anarchist conceptions of collective action, highlighting the state's history of incorporation and suppression of popular movements.

Each of these imaginaries points to the remarkable persistence of the state idea despite the many failings of actually existing states. They carry with them multiple and often contradictory conceptions and demands that make 'the state' such a peculiar object of desire. At the same time, they point to the multiplying sense of frustration with those actually existing states whose agents and practices fail to deliver what is desired – frustrations that have contributed substantially to the deepening 'crisis of the state'.

## The unsettled state and the unfinished conjuncture

Reading across the last few chapters, the growing sense of multiplying crises, the troubles of the governing party, the fissures in the dominant bloc and the flawed performances of the state (in all its complexity) reveal much about the trajectory of this conjuncture. The dominant project that gave shape and direction to this conjuncture is in difficulty on multiple fronts, despite the many attempts to renew and revive it across the intervening 40-plus years. In the ensuing turbulence, different possible projects have offered ways forward – from the reversal of planetary collapse to yet another version of restorationist politics (accompanied by the increasingly strained projection of 'business as usual'). The UK is, of course, not alone in experiencing such multiple and condensed crises, including crises of legitimacy, authority and the state. The causes and conditions are not purely national, even as they continue to take distinctive national forms and follow national trajectories. This is a key element of the challenge of thinking conjuncturally and why I have focused here on the distinctive forms that the crises of legitimacy, authority and the state have taken in the UK. In the final chapter, I turn to the problem of making sense of the trajectory of this conjuncture – and its focus in the Battle for Britain.

# 10

# The Battle for
# Britain – and Beyond

There is a strange paradox about trying to write a concluding chapter while the deepening crisis and conflicts of this conjuncture are still playing out in dramatic ways. The Battle for Britain has taken ever stranger turns as the Conservative Party flails around, trying on Prime Ministers as though in a hat shop. So this is certainly not an ending; rather, it is a chance to take stock of the issues and arguments developed in the book and consider some of the possible routes through the present troubles. In the first part I reflect on what I see as the main lines of argument in the book. I then turn to questions of where we are in the conjuncture, before asking whether we are lodged in what Gramsci called an 'interregnum' – a point at which 'the old is dying and the new cannot be born' (Gramsci, 1971: 276). The puzzle of the interregnum leads me into a slight detour through the strangeness of metaphors, conceptual and political. After that, I consider what ways forward are being imagined and offered, before exploring how the possibilities for thinking and acting otherwise might be mapped. I end by suggesting that the political-cultural struggles for the future might be viewed through three linked sets of practices – reimagining, repairing and rearticulating.

## Battling for Britain

Over the course of this book, I have tried to draw out the ways in which 'Britain' – this complex social and spatial imaginary – has been the focus of multiple conflicts over its past, present and future. From claims about 'our history' to the fracturing unity of the 'United Kingdom', from the discovery of the 'left behind' to the intensification of borders and bordering; from deepening coercion to deepening inequalities, Britain appears in multiple guises and is *always* contested. These battles for Britain have taken place around different focal points, on many different terrains and have involved different and complexly interwoven temporalities. These sites have included:

- The moment of Brexit (and the ensuing struggles to 'make it happen') which exacerbated fractures in the unitedness of the United Kingdom, particularly in the increasingly fraught relationships between the Westminster-London-English system of governing and the other nations, challenging both the constitutional formation and political-cultural imaginary of the nation-state.
- The environmental crisis – and the distinctive combination of its planetary form and national failures. This has called into question the direction and desires of the dominant bloc and its incessant search for 'growth'.
- The different (and interwoven) forms of inequality, exclusion, subordination and marginalisation which have both deepened and become more antagonistic during the conjuncture. They have animated multiplying forms of dissent, grievance, refusal and resistance. The increasingly authoritarian responses to them – not least in the policing of protest – point to deepening legitimation troubles.
- The failure of the UK state to manage the social, economic and political contradictions of implementing neoliberalism. The ensuing crises, fractures and frustrations have driven dissent from different social fractions: from neglected sections of capital to the 'left behind'; from organised labour to those entangled in the crises of social reproduction.
- Deepening crises of legitimacy and authority, increasingly centred on the state itself. Accumulating crises – from the pandemic to the return of inflation – have made a hollowed-out state vulnerable to doubt and disillusionment, and deepening crises of legitimacy and authority, increasingly centred on the state itself. The arrival in 2022 of what I have called 'zombie Thatcherism' accelerated all of these crises – and added new ones (a currency crisis; a fiscal crisis; a cost of living crisis).
- All of these are intimately interwoven with the battle of ideas: the political-cultural struggle to tell compelling stories about the state of Britain – and the world – in popular, political and even academic forms. As we saw with the social and spatial imaginary of the 'left behind' or claims about 'our history', these are not exclusive and separate domains.

Of course, this book is not innocent: it attempts to play a small part in the battle of ideas. It aims to demonstrate the political-cultural work that such stories perform as they are deployed to mobilise – or de-mobilise – different groups in the constant struggles to construct or contest a dominant bloc. A closely linked objective has been to argue for conjunctural analysis as an approach to thinking about the present – and how we got to be here. In the process, I have argued for the importance of escaping from the strangleholds of single, simplifying and reductive accounts – whether they are about globalisation or the 'left behind'. Instead, I have tried to show

how the conjuncture is formed in the fraught intersection and condensation of multiple dynamics.

The effort to think through this multiplicity forms the core of what Stuart Hall (1987/2017) called 'the discipline of the conjuncture', underscoring the work that needs to be done to map the conjuncture and to know our place within it. For me, it also points to the dynamic relationship between overdetermination and underdetermination: on the one hand, the conjuncture is itself *overdetermined* by the multiplicity of forces, dynamics, contradictions and conflicts that are condensed together. On the other hand, the politics of resolving the conjuncture's challenges – of finding an exit trajectory – are *underdetermined* precisely because they are the continuing focus of political–cultural struggles whose resolutions cannot be prescribed in advance.

It is this commitment to grasping the complex and condensed character of the conjuncture that has organised this book. It drove the engagement with the 'space-time' of the conjuncture in Chapters 1 and 2, opening up the shifting relational formation of the nation itself, and the diverse forms of nationalism that have been in play. Equally significant are the multiple temporalities whose compressed and intersecting trajectories give the conjuncture a distinctive trajectory – and make time itself the focus of political–cultural struggles, not least in the conflicts over 'our history' and the grim prospects for 'our future'. Chapter 2's attention to multiple temporalities has been underscored as the collective psychodrama of the Conservative Party has played out at an increasing tempo.

My insistence on *complexity* underpinned the examination of different ways of accounting for Brexit in Chapter 3. Attributing the vote to leave the EU – and the political forces involved – to a singular dynamic associated with any of neoliberalism, populism or the anger and frustrations of the 'left behind' collapses the complexity of the conjuncture into a single process. I pursued a parallel argument in Chapter 4 against the claim that Brexit was a working-class victory as a way of opening up the complexities of class formation (and the political–cultural significance of the middle classes). A relational understanding of class necessarily brings into view the shifting alignments of class and other social relations, including those of race/ethnicity, gender, sexuality, disability and more. Reductive conceptions of class have little value in conjunctural analysis, given that people do not inhabit a mode of production but live in shifting and heterogeneous social formations.

That relational view of social forces underpinned the exploration of processes and practices of political–cultural mobilisation in Chapter 5. I argued for a view of politics as the site of articulatory practices that aimed to speak to – and for – segments of the public in order to compose political alliances and blocs. This provided a conceptual base from which to think about the forging of a 'Brexit bloc' and its subsequent conversion into support for the Johnson-led Conservative Party around its promises to 'get Brexit done', 'unleash Britain's potential' and engage in 'levelling up' across some of the inequalities that traversed the UK. This view of articulation was developed in contrast to simplifying conceptions of politics as structured by binary divisions (for example, between identity liberals and conservatives), centring instead on a conception of plural subjects formed in heteroglossic dynamics. That orientation points to the political-cultural possibilities of mobile and contestable political subjectivities – rather than fixed formations.

The following four chapters traced different aspects of the accumulating crises and conflicts of this period of the conjuncture. Chapter 6 examined that accumulation across multiple sites and social fractures, giving attention to the ways in which both crises and conflicts tend to intersect and interact as they are condensed within the conjuncture. Chapter 7 highlighted the racialised effects of the pandemic and their intersection with other anti-colonial and anti-racist politics. One recurring strategy for trying to contain and deflect these issues involved the political-cultural work of treating them as sites of 'culture wars' that sought to construct – and solidify – the 'identity politics' divisions between liberals/cosmopolitans and conservative traditionalists. In Chapter 8, I explored some of the other strategies that the Conservative government deployed alongside – and entwined with – 'culture wars', centred on expanding coercive capacities of the state and centralising power and authority. I traced the limitations of these strategies in stabilising both the party and the bloc in the face of emerging crises of authority and legitimacy. Finally, in Chapter 9, I explored how these accumulating crises and conflicts were becoming condensed into a crisis of the state itself. The current (October 2022) condensation of these crises, as the UK economy collapsed and the Conservative Party sought to find yet another Prime Minister, has returned some familiar forces to the Battle for Britain.

## The return of the 'grown-ups': fiscal realism rules

The convulsions of the Conservative Party in 2022, as Johnson was replaced first by Truss and then Sunak, dramatised the political-cultural significance of 'the economy'. Truss devoted herself (briefly) to challenging the 'anti-growth coalition' in a bid to deliver 'growth, growth, growth' through tax cuts and bankers' bonuses. Living out the contradictions in person, this champion of the free market was consumed by the markets as they seized on the 'mini-budget' (put together by her, her Chancellor, Kwasi Kwarteng, and various assistants garnered from free market think tanks) and trashed it in an assault on the value of the pound. Kwarteng went first, followed by most of his budget, and then Truss herself. The Conservatives' sixth Prime Minister in six years – Rishi Sunak – was anointed by the Conservative

MPs to take his chance on governing what was being described by many commentators and some MPs as an 'ungovernable' party.

Sunak's elevation was greeted in many quarters as part of the return of the 'grown-ups': those who could be relied upon to understand how economies – and the markets – worked and take sensible, if 'painful', steps to put the public finances in order. For those with slightly longer memories, the desire for 'grown-ups' echoed the demand of Christine Lagarde, then head of the IMF, for 'adults in the room' when intervening in the Greek debt crisis of 2015 (Varoufakis, 2017). In both settings, 'grown-ups/adults' denote those who have a proper understanding of, and respect for, the 'real world' and how economies work. As Nesrine Malik observed, even before Sunak's arrival:

> 'The grownups are back,' declared Liam Fox after Jeremy Hunt and Penny Mordaunt's performance at the dispatch box last week. 'If Truss cannot quickly sort herself out,' the Sun (of all papers) told us, 'the grownups need to get in a room' and 'agree a peaceful transition to a sensible figure'. This trope exemplifies the detachment of both Westminster and Westminster watchers. As the country enters into the winter crisis proper, those at the top are looking for a leader with unspecified technocratic skills who, like a contracted management consultant, will be able to 'stabilise' UK plc. It's not the mouths of children that need feeding, but the markets.
>
> If this new leader must have an ideology, it should be one that aligns with the aim of 'fiscal responsibility', itself a byword for reduced state spending. They must 'look like a leader', and enact whatever callous cuts they have to, preferably while exhibiting suitable regret at having to make 'difficult decisions'. (Malik, 2022b)

Bundled together in this celebration of the 'grown-ups' are several important framings. First, the judgements of this strange collective entity – 'the markets' – rule. This is despite their errors, destructive judgements and lamentable tendencies to emotional instability: the markets are recurrently nervous, excited, or even prone to having 'breakdowns'. This means that what Mark Fisher (2007) called 'capitalist realism' has a governmental shadow which we might call 'fiscal realism' that requires the public books 'to be balanced' in an acceptable way. The 'grown-ups', notably Sunak (who had warned against the Truss approach during the first leadership contest) and Jeremy Hunt (who replaced Kwarteng as Chancellor), identified the key task as making 'painful decisions' about public finances in order to restore confidence (in the markets).

Second, the choices were framed by a distinctive Conservative history (and mind set): public spending remained the main focus of attention despite extensive warnings about the dire condition of public services. So fiscal realism was recoupled with its 2010 twin – austerity. Even faced with a stalling economy, a profound cost of living crisis, and public services collapsing in full public view – the 'grown-ups' returned to what they knew best: cutting public spending. On this occasion, however, it proved harder to make the TINA ('There Is No Alternative') claim stick as even mainstream voices – from the CBI to a former governor of the Bank of England (Mervyn King) – argued against a return to austerity and in favour of tax and investment policies.

Third, the current crisis reinforced the dominant ways of imagining economics, the economic and the economy. News – and TV news especially – foregrounded the markets, charted the rise and fall of the pound and government bonds, with mentions of the FTSE and other share indexes. Comments were sought from experts, usually economists employed by finance houses or banks (whose involvement in 2008 has been forgotten and forgiven). Secondary attention might be given to 'businesses' – exporters or the hospitality sector, for example – to give examples of economic distress. Sometime later, visits might be paid to struggling food banks or exemplary instances of people struggling to feed, clothe or warm themselves (the elderly) or their children (if parents). Such items were not led by 'our economics expert', but our 'social affairs correspondent' – marking the conceptual and institutional separation between the economic and the rest. Although such forms of popular representations know there are connections between these different domains, their separation, reification and hierarchisation are persistent and close off possibilities of imagining economies differently.

## Thinking conjuncturally: where are we now?

Taking stock, I think that what can be gained from conjunctural analysis (even an incomplete one such as this) is an understanding of why the Battle for Britain is, in practice, composed of *multiple* battles. They overlap and intersect, to be sure, but they are still multiple. This exemplifies Gramsci's idea of a *war of position* as opposed to the revolutionary seizure of power in a frontal assault – what Gramsci called a *war of manoeuvre* (see, for example, Boggs, 1976; Egan, 2015). The war of manoeuvre was the framing favoured by the dominant bloc as it attempted to project 'two nations', counterposing the people/the sensible majority and their enemies – the dangerous liberal/ cosmopolitan Others. By representing such divisions as foundational, the bloc (and its political representatives) tried to consolidate and solidify differences in the face of more mobile and contestable political subjectivities. In contrast, a war of position, Gramsci suggested, is the process of building a popular counter-hegemonic consciousness or culture, articulating different stories. It is this understanding that connects conjunctural analysis, Hall's vision of cultural studies and the engagement with popular culture as a site of contestation. It is where the shifting alignments of politics, culture and power are vital. It is also the focus of arguments about where and when within the conjuncture we now find ourselves. Are we, as some suggest, currently in an *interregnum* – a moment in which 'the old is dying and the new cannot be born'?

Gramsci's notion of an 'interregnum' has proved to be a compelling device for describing the present moment. As Gilbert Achcar has noted:

> Over the last few years there has been a huge increase in references to Gramsci's famous sentence on 'morbid symptoms' ('fenomeni morbosi' – literally 'morbid phenomena'): 'The crisis consists precisely in the fact that the old is dying and the new cannot be born; in this interregnum a great variety of morbid symptoms appear' (Gramsci, 1971: 276). (Achcar, 2021: 379)

These usages include Achcar's own work on the response to the Arab Spring (2016), Owen Worth's (2019) study of the global Far Right and, perhaps most morbidly of all, the lecture by Michael Gove, MP, on the need for a new approach to public services (Gove, 2020). The interregnum and its accompanying morbid symptoms is a compelling image and one that can be clearly bent to a variety of purposes. It evokes distinctive features of the present moment, particularly in the aftermath of the global financial crisis in which the promise (or the glimpse of the promise) of global transformation was overwhelmed by the restoration of 'business as usual'. The range of 'morbid symptoms' has multiplied domestically and internationally as the crises persist, deepen and are joined by new troubles (from the pandemic to Russia's war in Ukraine). Morbid symptoms have been particularly associated with the rise of distinct nationalist-populist-authoritarian political formations, including ones that took power in Brazil, India, Italy, Hungary, the Philippines and the US – as well as the UK.

The image of an interregnum has been much used while paradoxically remaining relatively unexplored. What, exactly, constitutes such an interregnum? Rune Møller Stahl (2019) has attempted to clarify the conditions and significance of the term and treats it as a distinctive period that follows on the collapse of a period of hegemonic rule. He offers a historical sketch of the oscillations between periods of hegemonic rule and the subsequent descent into periods of nonhegemonic conflict and confusion – interregnums. He suggests that an interregnum should be understood as the 'political form of an organic crisis' – the accumulation of insuperable contradictions and conditions that the dominant bloc cannot resolve, while striving to contain them and preserve the existing order. The resulting 'crisis of authority', he argues, combines two interconnected elements. First, there is a loss of consensus *within* the fracturing dominant bloc, with different projects beginning to contend for leadership. Second, the subaltern groups lose faith in, or withdraw consent from, the dominant bloc's project and legitimating strategies. In this unstable period, ideological and political competition increases. This, Møller Stahl argues, characterises the period since the 2008 financial crisis.

This brief summary does not do full justice to his arguments, nor to his sketch of the historic alternations of hegemonic rule and interregnums in the global North. Nor can I fully explore the problems of relying on a narrowly political-economic framing of the issues or the reduction of history to a binary distinction between periods of hegemony and interregnums. This distinction results in rather less attention to *how* crises of authority take place, such that any conjunctural focus is effectively displaced by attention to the 'organic' crises. Meanwhile, his view of hegemony is both frustratingly undialectical and narrowly imagined as 'ideological hegemony'. He pays little attention to the ways in which hegemonic rule involves – requires, indeed – shifting balances of consent and coercion and necessitates continuing political-cultural work to sustain domination.

Perhaps the best feature of Møller Stahl's view of interregnums is his refusal to attribute any *necessary* process or politics of closure to these unsettled and chaotic periods. Indeed, he gives due attention to the dangerous possibilities of reactionary forces gathering to secure existing concentrations of economic and political power. He reminds us of Gramsci's own analyses of Fascism and Caesarism and his interest in the dynamics of 'passive revolution' or 'transformation from above' [*trasformismo*] in which popular dissent may be co-opted into reactionary restorations of power (Morton, 2010). In the current situation, we have seen the rise of political projects that combine economic nationalism and authoritarian populism in promises to restore 'greatness' of different kinds – embodied, for example, in the figures of Trump and Johnson. Such developments, particularly combined with intensified political-cultural nationalism and varieties of political autocracy, remain potent reminders of the dangers of restorationist projects co-opting some forms of popular discontent while repressing others.

## A metaphorical interlude

I have had a difficult relationship with metaphors for a long time, especially ones that do conceptual work. Writing this book has reminded me about why – and its drafts have evoked similar troubled reactions from some readers. As a result, I think it is worth taking a little time out for some reflections on some of these troubling metaphors, beginning with the *interregnum*. In its usual monarchical frame of reference, an interregnum designates the gap between two rulers. This may, in constitutional terms, be as brief as the space between 'The Queen is dead' and 'Long live the King'. The uncertainty is merely about who gets to be named King. Sometimes, however, that transition may be long drawn out – an interruption of the normal process, as in Cromwell's Protectorate disrupting (violently) the transition between Charles I (executed in 1649) and his son Charles II, restored to the throne in 1660. As Gil Rodman commented to me, this was

> 'a moment that can only be properly understood as an interregnum (1) after it ends and (2) with a return to something very close to whatever was in place beforehand. If The Restoration had never happened, then the thing Cromwell started would never have been called an interregnum at all.'

He went on to argue that Gramsci was describing something other than just an interruption of normal service – and that 'interregnum' may not be the best word for us to use to think dialectically about such periods. Following this interlude, I will return to this puzzle, but need to deal with some more metaphorical troubles first.

The second one is also a monarchical metaphor. Gramsci's writings about politics and the possibilities of organising counter-hegemonic movements made creative use of his reading of Machiavelli's *The Prince*. Indeed, he coined the phrase the *Modern Prince* which, Thomas argues, is Gramsci's way of denoting 'the type of political party that would be capable of inheriting a Jacobin emphasis on both moral and intellectual reform, and, as an integral element of this, of the necessity of a concrete programme of economic reform' (Thomas, 2017: 17). The intervening changes in sites and forms of political struggle (and the decline of European communist parties) drove a search for other conceptions of counter-hegemonic organisational forms, including Gill's conception of the *Postmodern Prince* (following the rise of the alter-globalisation movements). He argued that the emerging movements 'are beginning to form what Gramsci called "an organism, a complex element of society" that is beginning to point towards the realisation of a "collective will" [Gramsci, 1971: 129]' (2000: 138).

While recognising the line of descent from Machiavelli through Gramsci to Gill, I find this persistent figure of 'the prince' deeply disturbing. Historically, it seems to neglect the varieties of republican thinking (and action: heads did actually roll) that have displaced princes at least in part from their roles as either embodiments of divine sovereignty or the personification of the state. From tsars (and government appointed tsars) to princes (including the current political-cultural troubles of the UK's Royal Family), the imagery is, at best, unfortunate. Politically and culturally, it is also a figure that also seems oddly undisturbed by the rise – and return – of varieties of feminism. Persisting with this image of a male action figure seems an odd framework for thinking about the possibilities of collective mobilisation.

Elsewhere, two of my readers (Morag McDermont and Janet Newman) have raised problems about the military metaphors – wars and battles – that have played significant roles in organising the book. I think they are right about the negative connotations of thinking about political-cultural struggles in violent, military and masculinist framings. They are also right about what is obscured in such framings – the labours of political-cultural articulation, the cultivation of the connections, attachments and affiliations that are involved in mobilising people, and the care that is needed to sustain energy, desire and commitment. As Janet Newman commented: 'the emergent not only comprises new movements struggling for change but also new affective practices of repair/care/support – not just identifying/voicing.'

As you will have noticed, this means the book is caught in a state of metaphorical flux: it both uses and challenges these metaphors. That is why this is merely an interlude.

## The trouble with normal (again)

Mike Davis raised a different puzzle about treating the current period as an interregnum: 'Everyone is quoting Gramsci on the interregnum, but that assumes that something new will be or could be born. I doubt it' (2022). Indeed, it is not just that the 'old will not die' but it feels as though this period has been dominated by recurring efforts to keep the 'the old' on a variety of life support systems, each of which saps the life out of everything else. Consequently, on most days I share Davis's 'pessimism of the intellect', feeling overwhelmed by the national, global, planetary scale of the current crises and the forces driving them – not to mention the massive concentrations of wealth, power, violence and destruction that accompany them. It can feel as though no escape is possible, and yet every day also brings glimpses of how to be (and act) 'otherwise'. They are, all too often, only glimpses – and even glimpses of *fragments* of possibility: from environmental struggles to mobilisations challenging misogynist or racist forms of state power; from newly organising workers (even in Amazon – the very 'belly of the beast') to mutual aid networks that combat exclusion, impoverishment and starvation.

The conjuncture – nationally and globally – is contested by very different projects that offer ways of 'moving forward', even if some of them are profoundly backward looking. These have been broadly summarised by Stephen McBride in a recent book as (i) 'back to normal', (ii) 'liberal reformism' and (iii) 'radical transformation' (2022: 209–211). 'Back to normal' promises the restoration of neoliberal imaginaries (growth, choice, consumption, and so on) despite the recurrent and deepening failures of such projects. It is the fantasy that inspired (if that is the right word) the

Truss/Kwarteng Conservative strategy of autumn 2022, with its disastrous consequences. In my view, 'liberal reformism' also promises a version of 'getting back to normal', just a gentler and kinder 'normal' based on a version of lightly managed capitalism with some added public spending and some 'green growth'.

This points to a serious problem with the imagery of the 'normal' – it is a potent 'floating signifier', capable of being filled with very different meanings, and of being deployed for very different political-cultural purposes. It spans a range of popular imaginaries, from everyday conviviality to 'business as usual' or patriarchal and colonial orderings of things and people. It speaks to desires to escape from crises and conflicts – and was a frequent trope during the most intense times of pandemic lockdowns (Clarke, forthcoming c). The sheer emptiness of the 'normal' enables it to act as the site of what Evelina Dagnino (2005) has called a 'perverse confluence', in which popular sentiments may be colonised by dominant political framings. This dynamic of elision and colonisation of meanings evokes what the Canadian singer-songwriter Bruce Cockburn brilliantly named as *The Trouble with Normal*. One verse of the song of the same name observes that:

Politician on the screen says,
  'We'll all get back to normal if we put our nation first'
  The trouble with normal is that it always gets worse. (Cockburn, 1981)

The idea of the normal is a persistent site of such dangers, offering points of articulation to dominant projects. But McBride also argues that one of the dangers is that versions of liberal reformist projects constantly reappear as the *alternative* to destructive versions of neoliberal rule. Hart (2020) suggests that this conjuncture has seen an alternation between authoritarian populist and liberal technocratic variants of managing the instabilities of neoliberal orders – the first trying to mobilise popular antagonisms; the latter trying to contain them. There is a further twist to this apparent choice: the liberal variants tend to inherit the crises of the conjuncture at their worst. Davies (2022) has pointed to the prospects facing the Labour Party should it succeed the Conservatives in the next UK general election, part of a dynamic in which 'the party of the centre-left takes on the role of cleaning up the economic messes left by the party of the right'. Certainly, another financial crisis, combined with the Labour Party's commitment to 'fiscal realism', will at least severely impede any progressive programmes the party might develop. This would be the case even before they arrive at the challenges of rebuilding infrastructures, resolving the interconnected crises of health and social care, addressing proliferating inequalities and averting a climate crisis.

This brings us to McBride's third possibility – *radical transformation*. There is no shortage of ideas, proposals and programmes for a world transformed.

McBride proposes revitalising democratic institutions and practices, valuing public over private interests, challenging inequalities of many kinds, and rolling back the power of international organisations – whether corporations or agencies like the IMF and WTO. He argues that there are constituencies who have an interest in such transformations – ranging from the discontented working class, through environmentalists to those groups – 'racialized communities, women, youth, migrants and others [who] experience the failures of the neoliberal strategy more harshly' (2022: 211). However, it is less clear how different groups can be connected, can come to recognise one another and develop an alternative way out of the conjuncture.

## Topographies and topologies: spaces of politics otherwise?

The question of emergent possibilities immediately encounters the problem of the political or the field of politics and a variety of critical approaches have explored the contemporary impoverishment of the political sphere. Wendy Brown (2015, 2019) has traced the ways in which neoliberal rationality has radically diminished the capacities and scope of the political sphere through the systematic pursuit of anti-democratic reforms. In a different register, Eva Cherniavsky (2009, 2017) has argued that a distinctive combination of neoliberal governmentality and the vast extension of surveillance capacities has created a mode of 'neocitizenship', displacing the political and the prospect of popular sovereignty with what she terms 'serial culture' which

> releases its subjects into a minutely regulated environment—regulated not because their positions are prescripted, but rather because their movements and affiliations are tracked (as so much social data), archived, mined, risk-assessed, and so (variably) policed, overlooked, or supported. The neocitizen who acts in and on this environment is visible to the state, even as the out-sourced state is rendered increasingly opaque and elusive to her. (2017: 37)

Meanwhile, Lauren Berlant (2011) explored the 'desire for the political' and the ways in which such desires have been frustrated, disappointed and defeated. This she described as a

> relation of cruel optimism, when, despite an awareness that the normative political sphere appears as a shrunken, broken, or distant place of activity among elites, members of the body politic return periodically to its recommitment ceremonies and scenes. Voting is one thing; collective caring, listening, and scanning the airwaves, are others. (2011: 227)

The result, she argued, has been the emergence of a 'politically depressive position' (2011: 230). This captures the contradictory simultaneity of desire and doubt in relation to the political: the wish to bring about change in tension with sceptical or even cynical distancing from politics as the means for doing so.

Each of these arguments reveals ways in which politics/the political is not transparently available to us to engage in or act upon (even if it ever was). Indeed, the accumulating arguments about the structural, infrastructural, institutional, affective and practical conditions for doing political-cultural work might just appear overwhelming, if not immobilising. Nevertheless, the question persists: are there spaces of possibility, ways of becoming, conditions for acting that elude these overwhelming alignments? Berlant ended by exploring the *possibilities* (never guaranteed) of the 'DIY practices' animating what she calls 'lateral politics' (2011: 261), linking her own consideration of emergent practices to wider arguments about forms of activism from David Graeber and J.K. Gibson-Graham. For me, Berlant's view of lateral politics has important echoes of the dynamics developed in Cindi Katz's thinking about 'countertopographies' (2001b).

Katz's conception of constructing countertopographies of globalisation draws attention to the relations that connect dispersed places and people – like the contour lines of topographical mapping – as the basis for revealing and creating connections, commonalities and solidarities. The topographies of connection mandated by the dynamics of globalisation create the possibilities for countertopographies of refusal and renewal. Tracing and pursuing such lines offers one way of mapping and enacting a 'war of position', seeking to connect the multiple sites, forms and collective actors in conflict with the dominant blocs and their rule. For Katz, such an approach avoids either excessive abstraction (a false universalism) or excessive concreteness (locked into localised responses):

> This is different from a 'place-based' politics. It is not merely about one locale or another, nor is it a matter of just building coalitions between such diverse places, vital as that is. Precisely because globalization is such an abstraction, albeit with varying forms, struggles against global capital have to mobilize equivalent, alternative abstractions. Built on the critical triangulation of local topographies, countertopographies provide exactly these kinds of abstractions interwoven with local specificities and the impulse for insurgent change. (2001b: 1232)

Although Katz talks about these possibilities in a topographical framing, her arguments offer potential links to other work by geographers that has taken a *topological* framing, concerned with how space is complexly stretched, bent and folded. In the process, what are treated as linear distances (in topographical terms) are revealed as having differently ordered relationships of proximity and distance (see, inter alia, Allen and Cochrane, 2010; Allen, 2011, 2016). For John Allen, the value of thinking topologically is 'to show how the ability to draw distant others within close reach or construct the close at hand at-a-distance are indicative of the cross-cutting mix of distanciated and proximate actions that is increasingly central to the workings of power today' (2011: 284). He has explored a variety of cases from forms of government through supranational bodies and corporations to NGOs to examine how power works through such arrangements: what he calls 'power-geometries'. Power, then, may be 'far-reaching' in ways that have potential political effects 'in so far as the mediated powers of reach practised by both institutions and social movements also change what can be demanded politically and how it may be brokered, contested and countered when presence and proximity are no longer simply a question of physical distance' (2011: 295).

Taken together, Katz's countertopographies and Allen's concern with topological reach create the conditions for rethinking the spaces of power and possibility. These intersect with Berlant's approach to thinking about politics, activism and the ambiguous spaces of possibility. Capturing this unsettling sense of possibility, MacLeavy, Fannin and Larner argue that Katz's view of reworking 'implies imagining and enacting alternative forms of politicisation (of "being-political") and indeed alternative political forms, which are neither modes of resistance wholly outside structures of power or wholly inside and therefore "co-opted" into structures not of our own making' (2021: 1570). Some of these arguments are also visible in Janet Newman's arguments about the 'political labour' which is 'fundamental to not only generating, but also sustaining progressive actions in the face of processes of erasure, colonisation and appropriation' (2019: 29; see also, Newman, 2012). Such *political-cultural* labour, she insists, necessarily outruns the images of party building, bargaining and negotiation by being performative, relational, symbolic and embodied (2019: 29–30). The question is how do such possibilities become articulated (in both senses) in the face of the concern to 'just get back to normal'?

Exploring 'spaces of possibility' is one way of reframing the problem of the political, unsettling the taken-for-granted orderings of power and politics. This starting point opens up other issues including the importance of thinking beyond pre-given 'constituencies' to find the links that enable mutual recognition, connection and solidarity across differences. In such conditions, we may also need to think about the complicated political-cultural and affective work that can imagine, construct and sustain progressive and, in the end, counter-hegemonic possibilities. In the final sections of this chapter, I explore 'three R's' – *reimagining*, *repairing* and *rearticulating* – as ways of engaging with these issues – without intending to write a manifesto. Indeed, who would want one?

## Reimagining

Having once been part of a collaborative project developed by Davina Cooper around the theme of 'reimagining the state' (Cooper, Dhawan and Newman, 2019), I find her pursuit of new ways of approaching, thinking about and engaging with states (and the wider political-cultural dynamics that they condense) productive. They have interesting echoes of Gramsci's concern with the varieties of common sense that will be in play in a given historical moment, including its fragments of 'good sense'. Across a range of work, Cooper has explored new angles for talking about states and stateliness – from everyday utopias, through the tactile dynamics of 'touching like a state', to work on legal forms of identification (such as gender). The work of reimagining, she argues, 'is simultaneously about what does and does not yet exist as it explores, but also at times troubles and explodes, the border between the two' (Cooper, 2019: 2). Reimagining both works with and unsettles dominant conceptions and imaginaries to trace lines of possibility that may be pursued and practised. The state is, of course, a difficult target for reimagining – in several ways. It is the focus of an accumulated body of investigations, analyses, commentaries and programmes, stretching back over many centuries. States are also plural (there are many different instances) and, as I argued in Chapter 9, they are not simple or singular entities. Indeed, Cooper herself argued that 'The capacity of states to simultaneously be progressive and regressive, authoritarian and enabling, remains whether the state is understood as an assemblage, terrain, idea or institutional effect' (2019: 7–8). But reimagining is by no means restricted to states and their possibilities.

One critical site of reimagining practices and politics has been the environmental crisis and the struggles to generate different ways of living together with the planet. In a recent article, Bjork-James, Checker and Edelman have explored transnational social movements (environmentalist, indigenous and agrarian) and their 'visions for planetary futures' (2022). The authors seek to 'emphasize the ways that social movements produce knowledge and meanings ... and envision, experiment with, propagate, and institutionalize alternative ways of organizing societies. In the case of the environmental, Indigenous, agrarian, and food justice movements highlighted here, these visions extend to human societies' relations with the nonhuman environment" (2022: 584). They go on to examine how such knowledges have been articulated in movements, coalitions and institutionalised forms.

Reimagining works across the full range of human possibilities – from how we care for one another and the planet, to how we organise economic activity (in commoning, for example). It can invoke questions of scale – reanimating the local or crafting translocal networks of connection. It can generate alternative approaches to doing politics, including ways of embedding politics in apparently non-political activities (such as workplaces). Most potently, reimagining acts in cultural registers, creating new ways of seeing, making new connections visible and unsettling or reworking notions of identity. Here the idea of reimagining intersects with many of Berlant's instances of DIY politics. Reimagining is both a banal practice – it operates in and across the everyday – and a resource for political-cultural reinvention. It is a practice that has the potential to undercut the dominant orderings of how we think about the world and our place in it while bringing into view the doubts and desires that swirl around them.

## Repairing

The second of the three R's is *repairing* which I use to point to a wide range of practices, concerns and commitments. They include the most banal – the commitments to repair, reuse and recycle that have become a means of resisting the drive to endless consumption (for example, Godfrey et al, 2022). Repair in this sense is both a matter of technique (notably the craft or technical skills necessary to keep things going) and an affective disposition, implying a relationship of care towards objects and the wider environment. Repairing also evokes responsibilities – whether to rebuilding relationships or mending tears in the material of life (in many different forms). The renewed interest in mutualism as a focus of self-organisation and activism exemplifies one aspect of this centred on finding ways of acting together in the pursuit of common purposes (for example, Bradley and Malki, 2022; Jupp, 2022).

It intrigues me that one of the most successful non-fiction programmes on BBC television in recent years has been *The Repair Shop* (10 seasons so far, 2017–22). It is described by the BBC as follows: 'Enter a workshop filled with expert craftspeople, bringing loved pieces of family history and the memories they hold back to life. A heartwarming antidote to throwaway culture' (BBC One: The Repair Shop). It contrasts sharply with other object-oriented TV programming (*The Antiques Road Show*; *Cash in the Attic*) in mobilising a different vocabulary of value. Where others centre on monetary valuation (what is this worth?), The Repair Shop works with valuation through affective attachments and memories and treats objects as articulating families or friends. It certainly goes out of its way to be 'heart warming', summoning emotional testimony about the significance of an object and its restoration – but it works through a vocabulary of repair and a set of embodied technical and social skills, not least those of its presenter, Jay Blades (Adams, 2022).

A different register of repair is to be found in the growing arguments around *reparation*. Although a long-standing focus of law (de Greiff, 2008) and particularly visible in the arguments surrounding reparative or restorative justice (Braithwaite, 2002), reparation has moved to a much more visible – and highly contested – position in public debates around issues of slavery, colonialism and exploitation. Martin and Yaquinto (2007) tease out the complex overlaps and intersections between a cluster of related ideas – repair, redress, reparation, reconciliation, restitution and restoration – in their collection on US slavery and its legacies. The US has become a central focus for such arguments (for example, Darity and Mullen, 2020) while others have examined more transnational dynamics involving the Americas, Europe and Africa (Araujo, 2017). Reparations have become a focus for argument in examinations of Europe's relationship to Africa (Howard-Hassman with Lombardo, 2018) and the UK's relationships with its former colonies – an argument that re-emerged during 2022, triggered by yet another Royal visit (Mohammed, 2022; see also Khalili, 2022). This same reparative framing is also visible in the concept of 'ecological debt' which, as Bjork-James, Checker and Edelman observe, 'refers to the Global North industrialized countries' responsibility to the Global South for the looting and usufruct of its natural assets (oil, minerals, forests, biodiversity, marine and fluvial resources), the exploitation of its peoples, and the destruction, devastation, and contamination of their natural heritage and sources of livelihood' (Bjork-James et al, 2022: 588).

Repairing, in these many meanings, embodies and expresses a disposition towards care and caring – for people, places and the planet. It involves trying to restore or rebalance that which is damaged or at risk and is attentive to the labour that is necessary to put things right. It reminds me of participating in a workshop (about the Charity Economy in Bielefeld in 2016) at which Brigitte Aulenbacher gave a presentation ('It's care, again'). She argued that care was best understood as the basis (*das Fundament*) of both individual and societal life. She contrasted the vital necessity of care to the 'structural carelessness' of capitalism in relation to all forms of life (Aulenbacher, 2016; see also Aulenbacher and Riegraf, 2018). I think it worth highlighting the ways in which repairing combines the disposition towards, and the practices of, caring for things – and people.

At the same time, I am reminded of how MacLeavy, Fannin and Larner (2021) engage with feminist scholarship and activism through concepts that they take from the work of Cindi Katz: resistance, resilience and reworking (forming a different 'three R's'). Indeed, 'reworking' seems to share some conceptual and political DNA with repairing. Both break the binary imaginary of time as split between old and new, or past and future, and involve a sense of work/labour that both rescues and creates worth. Macleavy, Fannin and Larner argue that Katz invests these three concepts with some distinctive orientations: they are always *emergent* (in the process of becoming); they are always *situated* (spatially, socially); and they are always *engaged* in struggles with formations of power – and therefore need thinking about in ways that transcend the reductive binary of things being either oppositional or incorporated. Instead, they foreground 'agentic subjects'

> who operate across multiple politicised domains. Recognising that individuals and groups may not act in any definitive way – as practices emerge through a 'tangled array of forces' (Allen and Cochrane, 2010: 1073) and are not necessarily coherent – necessarily changes the way in which resistance is conceived. (MacLeavy et al, 2021: 1567)

This returns me to the arguments in Chapters 4 and 5 about people who are always potentially multiple and mobile – embedded in multiple social relations and traversing heteroglossic political-cultural landscapes. Their actions are not given or guaranteed in advance but are the outcome of possibilities that are realised – or blocked – by practices of articulation.

## Rearticulating

These arguments bring me back to Gillian Hart's attention to Gramsci's concern with politics-as-translation (Kipfer and Hart, 2015). In a 2019 essay, she concluded – in terms that speak directly to the issues being explored here – for the importance of 'illuminating spatiohistorical specificities as well as relations and interconnections' as a means of revealing and opening up 'possibilities for translating and forging new connections and rearticulations' (Hart, 2019: 321). Despite the disappointments and failures of 'modern princes', Gramsci's emphasis on the challenge of 'intellectual and moral reform' in constructing a *popular* counter hegemony has persisted as a focal concern. So too has his concern with practices of translation and articulation as essential to that task (Kipfer and Hart, 2015). He envisaged this work of translation and articulation building on the footholds provided by the elements of 'good sense' that formed part of popular 'common sense'. The *dialogic* work of translation was at the heart of the commitment to 'intellectual and moral reform'. Crehan points to the vital connections between Gramsci's interest in subaltern cultures and the challenge of building a counter-hegemonic politics:

> Any effective, progressive political movement must speak a language and have a message that is recognized by the mass of those it seeks to reach. And this is certainly one reason why Gramsci saw the mapping of subaltern understandings of the world as so important. There is, however, another fundamental reason why he pays so much attention to collective subaltern common sense. Subaltern knowledge emerges in fragmented, often chaotic form, but the good sense embedded within it represents the embryonic beginnings of a genuine alternative to the

existing hegemony; an alternative that is an indispensable element of a new economic and political order. (2016: 186–187)

In its widest sense, the concern with translation and articulation as vital political-cultural practices centres on the challenge of imagining and enacting new collectivities: new forms of political subjectivity in which we might find ourselves spoken for and summoned. For Grossberg, 'It is at heart a question of bringing new political collectivities into existence, new forms and formations of the "we"' (2018: 154). Stuart Hall treated this as the central issue for reframing – and indeed, reimagining – the politics of identity:

> How can we organise these huge, randomly varied, and diverse things we call human subjects into positions where they can recognise one another for long enough to act together, and thus to take up a position that one of these days might live out and act through as an identity? Identity is at the end, not the beginning, of the paradigm. Identity is what is at stake in political organisation. It isn't that subjects are there and we just can't get to them. It is that they don't know yet that they are subjects of a possible discourse. And that always in every political struggle, since every political struggle is always open, is possible either to win their identification or lose it. (2010: 291)

This view of crafting new collective identities is a crucial issue for the field of political-cultural struggle. Hall's insistence that this field of action cannot be a matter of aggregating existing identities but requires transformative work in which a new 'we' can find ourselves is both a massive demand and a necessary one. It reimagines politics (political-cultural work) as creating the conditions in which people can recognise one another across differences, distances and divisions as having interests and identities in common.

# References

Abrams, P. (1988) Notes on the difficulty of studying the state (1977). *Journal of Historical Sociology*, 1(1): 58–89.

Achcar, G. (2021) Morbid symptoms: what did Gramsci really mean? *Notebooks: The Journal for Studies on Power*, 1: 379–387.

Adams, T. (2017) David Lammy Interview. *The Guardian*, 2 July: https://www.theguardian.com/politics/2017/jul/02/david-lammy-mp-grenfell-towerinterview-blair-brown-black.

Adams, T. (2022) Interview: Jay Blades: 'I talk a lot about black history, but I also love black future'. *The Guardian*, 18 September: https://www.theguardian.com/food/2022/sep/18/jay-blades-i-talk-a-lot-about-black-history-but-i-also-love-black-future

Adi, H. (2019) *Black British History: New Perspectives*. London: Zed Books.

Ahmed, S. (2010) 'Happy objects.' In G.J. Seigworth and M. Gregg (eds) *The Affect Theory Reader*. Durham, NC: Duke University Press, 29–51.

Ahmed, S. (2014) Not in the mood. *New Formations*, 82: 13–28. doi: 10.3898/NeWF.82.01.2014.

Alexander, B. (2022) How do we think of our present time, looking to the future? The 2022 polycrisis and what comes next. https://bryanalexander.org/futures/how-do-we-think-of-our-present-time-looking-to-the-future-polycrisis-and-what-comes-next/

Allen, J. (2011) Topological twists: power's shifting geographies. *Dialogues in Human Geography*, 1(3): 283–298. doi: 10.1177/2043820611421546.

Allen, J. (2016) *Topologies of Power: Beyond Territory and Networks*. London: Routledge.

Allen, J. and Cochrane, A. (2010) Assemblages of state power: topological shifts in the organization of government and politics. *Antipode*, 42(5): 1071–1089.

Allen, J. and Pryke, M. (2013) Financialising household water: Thames Water, MEIF, and 'ring-fenced' politics. *Cambridge Journal of Regions, Economy and Society*, 6(3):419–439. doi: 10.1093/cjres/rst010.

Althusser, L. (1971) 'Ideology and ideological state apparatuses (notes towards an investigation).' In *Lenin and Philosophy and Other Essays* (translated by Ben Brewster). London: Verso, 127–186.

Althusser, L. and Balibar, E. (1970) *Reading Capital* (translated by Ben Brewster). London: New Left Books.

Anderson, Ben (2009) Affective atmospheres. *Emotion, Space and Society*, 2: 77–81.

Anderson, Bridget (2013) *Us and Them? The Dangerous Politics of Immigration Control*. Oxford: Oxford University Press.

Anderson, P. (2021a) Ever closer union? *London Review of Books*, 43(1): 25–27. https://www.lrb.co.uk/the-paper/v43/n01/perry-anderson/ever-closer-union

Anderson, P. (2021b) The breakaway. *London Review of Books*, 43(2): https://www.lrb.co.uk/the-paper/v43/n02/perry-anderson/the-breakaway

Ang, I. (2021) Beyond the crisis: transitioning to a better world? *Cultural Studies*, 35(2–3): 598–615.

Araujo, A. (2017) *Reparations for Slavery and the Slave Trade: A Transnational and Comparative History*. London: Bloomsbury.

Aspinall, P. (2002) Collective terminology to describe the minority ethnic population: the persistence of confusion and ambiguity in usage. *Sociology*, 36(4): 803–816.

Aughey, A. (2010) Anxiety and injustice: the anatomy of contemporary English nationalism. *Nations and Nationalism*, 16(3): 506–524.

Aulenbacher, B. (2016) '"It's Care Again." Care Regimes between Marketization and Charity Economy.' Presentation to ZIF Workshop on *Charity Economy: International Dimensions and Political Perspectives*, Bielefeld, 21–23 September.

Aulenbacher, B. and Riegraf, B. (2018) Between dystopias and alternative ideas of caring. *Equality, Diversity and Inclusion: An International Journal*, 37(4): 314–317.

Back, L. and Ware, V. (2002) *Out of Whiteness: Color, Politics and Culture*. Chicago and London: University of Chicago Press.

Bagehot (2021) Boris Johnson's Conservatives plan to create a bigger, busier state. *The Economist*, 6 November: https://www.economist.com/britain/2021/11/06/boris-johnsons-conservatives-plan-to-create-a-bigger-busier-state

Baillie, S., Cates, M., Fletcher, N., Gideon, J., Gullis, J., Howell, P., et al (2021) *Trusting the People: The Case for Community-powered Conservatism*. London: New Local and the New Social Covenant Unit: https://www.newlocal.org.uk/wp-content/uploads/2021/09/Trusting-the-People.pdf

Balibar, E. (1991) 'The nation form: history and ideology.' In G. Eley and R. Suny (eds) *Becoming National: A Reader*. Oxford: Oxford University Press, 132–149.

Balibar, E. (2003) *We, the People of Europe: Reflections on Transnational Citizenship* (translated by James Swenson). Princeton and Oxford: Princeton University Press.

Balibar, E. (2021) Living, learning, imagining in the middle of the crisis. *Crisis and Critique* (Special Issue; 2020 The Year of the Virus. Sars 2/Covid-19), 7(3): 10–24.

Balls, K. (2020) Why has Boris Johnson disappeared from view? He's betting you don't care. *The Guardian*, 27 February: www.theguardian.com/commentisfree/2020/feb/27/boris-johnson-mop-no-10-media-public.

Barrington, R. (2021) What does the Owen Paterson case reveal about corruption in UK politics? *UK in a Changing Europe*, 5 November: https://ukandeu.ac.uk/what-does-the-owen-paterson-case-reveal-about-corruption-in-uk-politics/

Barua, M. (2021) Feral ecologies: the making of postcolonial nature in London. *Journal of the Royal Anthropological Institute*: https://doi.org/10.1111/1467-9655.13653

Baston, L. (2019) The myth of the red wall. *The Critic*, 18 December: https://thecritic.co.uk/the-myth-of-the-red-wall/

BBC (2021a) Dalian Atkinson: PC Benjamin Monk jailed for ex-footballer's death. BBC News, 29 June: https://www.bbc.co.uk/news/uk-england-shropshire-57603091.

BBC (2021b) Nadine Dorries: new culture secretary says BBC needs real change. BBC News, 4 October: https://www.bbc.co.uk/news/entertainment-arts-58792515

BBC (2021c) Lord Frost resigns as Brexit minister. *BBC News*, 19 December: https://www.bbc.co.uk/news/uk-politics-59714241

BBC (2021d) Conservative conference: Dominic Raab criticised for misogyny comments. *BBC News*, 6 October: https://www.bbc.co.uk/news/uk-politics-58814271

BBC Reality Check (2019) Theresa May: did she solve her seven burning injustices? BBC News website: https://www.bbc.co.uk/news/uk-politics-48380610

Beckett, A. (2022) Striking workers are providing the opposition that Britain desperately needs. *The Guardian*, 1 July: https://www.theguardian.com/commentisfree/2022/jul/01/striking-workers-opposition-britain-strikes-public-opinion

Beebeejaun, Y. (2021) 'Race, ethnicity and the politics of memorialisation.' Paper presented to the *Debating Urban Ethics as Research Agenda* conference, 26–28 April.

Bell, E. (2019) Brexit: towards a neoliberal real utopia? *Observatoire de la société britannique*, 24: http://journals.openedition.org/osb/3196

Berlant, L. (2011) *Cruel Optimism*. Durham, NC: Duke University Press.

Bhambra, G. (2017) Brexit, Trump, and 'methodological whiteness': on the misrecognition of race and class. *British Journal of Sociology*, 68(S1): S214–S232.

Bhambra, G. (2022) Relations of extraction, relations of redistribution: empire, nation, and the construction of the British welfare state. *British Journal of Sociology*, 73(1): 4–15.

Bhambra, G., Gebrial, D. and Nişancıoğlu, K. (eds) (2018) *Decolonising the University*. London: Pluto Press.

Bialasiewicz, L. (2012) Off-shoring and outsourcing the borders of Europe: Libya and EU borderwork in the Mediterranean. *Geopolitics*, 17(4): 843–866.

Birch, K. and Mykhnenko, V. (2008) *Varieties of Neoliberalism? Restructuring in large industrially-dependent regions across Western and Eastern Europe*. Centre for Public Policy for Regions, University of Glasgow, Working Paper No. 14.

Bjork-James, C., Checker, M. and Edelman, M. (2022) Transnational social movements: environmentalist, indigenous, and agrarian visions for planetary futures. *Annual Review of Environment and Resources*, 47: 583–608.

Bjork-James, S. (2020) 'Americanism, Trump, and uniting the white right.' In J. Maskovsky and S. Bjork-James (eds) *Beyond Populism: Angry Politics and the Twilight of Neoliberalism*. Morgantown, VA: West Virginia University Press, 42–60.

Bjork-James, S. (2021) *The Divine Institution: White Evangelicalism's Politics of the Family*. New Brunswick and London: Rutgers University Press.

Blackburn, P. (2020) Outsourced and undermined: the COVID-19 windfall for private providers. *BMA News and Opinion*: https://www.bma.org.uk/news-and-opinion/outsourced-and-undermined-the-covid-19-windfall-for-private-providers

Blagojević, M. (2009) *Knowledge Production at the Semi-Periphery: A Gender Perspective*. Belgrade: Institute for Criminological and Sociological Research.

Blick, A. and Hennessy, P. (2019) *Good Chaps No More? Safeguarding the Constitution in Stressful Times*. London: The Constitution Society: https://consoc.org.uk/wp-content/uploads/2019/11/FINAL-Blick-Hennessy-Good-Chaps-No-More.pdf

Bloomfield, J. (2020) John Gray: the nationalist philosopher stoking 'culture wars' fires. *Open Democracy*, 19 October: https://www.opendemocracy.net/en/can-europe-make-it/john-gray-the-nationalist-philosophe-stoking-culture-wars-fires/

Blyth, M. (2013) *Austerity: The History of a Dangerous Idea*. Oxford: Oxford University Press.

Boggs, C. (1976) *Gramsci's Marxism*. London: Pluto Press.

Boletsi, M., Mika, K., Robbe, K. and Dekker, L.M. (2021) 'Introduction.' In M. Boletsi, L.M. Dekker, K. Mika and K. Robbe (eds) *(Un)Timely Crises: Chronotopes and Critique*. Cham, Switzerland: Palgrave Macmillan/Springer Nature.

Bonnett, A. (1998) How the working class became white: the symbolic (re)formation of racialised capitalism. *Journal of Historical Sociology*, 11(3): 316–340.

Bonneuil, C. and Fressoz, J.-B. (2016) *The Shock of the Anthropocene* (translated by David Fernbach). London: Verso.

Booth, W. (1890) *In Darkest England and the Way Out*. London: The Salvation Army & The Carlyle Press.

Bourdieu, P. (1998) L'essence du néolibéralisme. *Le monde diplomatique*, March.

Bourdieu, P. (1999) *Acts of Resistance*. New York: New Press.

Bracke, S. and Aguilar, L. (2020) 'They love death as we love life': the 'Muslim Question' and the biopolitics of replacement. *British Journal of Sociology*, 71(4): 680–701.

Bradley, T. and Malki, I. (2022) 'Localism, mutualism and the significant impact of anarchist movement – inspired groups during the pandemic: a theoretical and empirical analysis of British data on greening markets and COVID-19 mutual aid groups': https://ssrn.com/abstract=4019319 or http://dx.doi.org/10.2139/ssrn.4019319

Braithwaite, J. (2002) *Restorative Justice and Responsive Regulation*. Oxford: Oxford University Press.

Braudel, F. (1958) Histoire et sciences sociales: la longue durée. *Annales. Histoire, Sciences Sociales* 13(4): 725–753.

Braudel, F. and Wallerstein, I. (2009) History and the social sciences: the long durée. *Review Fernand Braudel Center*, 32(2): 171–203: www.jstor.org/stable/40647704

Breach, A. (2019) Did home-owners cause Brexit? Centre for Cities: https://www.centreforcities.org/blog/did-homeowners-cause-brexit/

Breeze, R. (2018) Positioning 'the people' and its enemies: populism and nationalism in AfD and UKIP. *Javnost – The Public: Journal of the European Institute for Communication and Culture*, 26: 89–104.

Brenner, N. (2004) *New State Spaces: Urban Governance and the Rescaling of Statehood*. Oxford: Oxford University Press.

Bresser-Pereira, L.C. (2012) Five models of capitalism. *Revista Economia Politica* [online], 32(1): 21–32. http://dx.doi.org/10.1590/S0101-31572012000100002

Brewis, H. (2020) UK is 'one of the best countries in the world to be a black person,' says Tory MP. *Evening Standard*, 4 June: https://www.standard.co.uk/news/uk/uk-best-countries-black-person-kemi-badenoch-a4459751.html

Bromley, R. (2018) The politics of displacement: the Far Right narrative of Europe and its 'others'. *From the European South*, 3: 13–26. http://europeansouth.postcolonialitalia.it

Brown, W. (2005) 'Untimeliness and punctuality: critical theory in dark times.' In W. Brown *Edgework: Critical Essays on Knowledge and Politics*. Princeton and Oxford: Princeton University Press, 1–16.

Brown, W. (2015) *Undoing the Demos: Neoliberalism's Stealth Revolution*. New York: Zone Books.

Brown, W. (2019) *In the Ruins of Neoliberalism: The Rise of Anti-Democratic Politics in the West*. New York: Columbia University Press.

Brownlow, R. and Wood, M. (2017) Not about white workers: the perils of popular ethnographic narrative in the time of Trump. *Lateral: Journal of the Cultural Studies Association*, 6(2). https://csalateral.org/issue/6-2/not-about-white-workers-ethnographic-narrative-trump-brownlow-wood/

Bullough, O. (2022) *Butler to the World: How Britain Became the Servant of Tycoons, Tax Dodgers, Kleptocrats and Criminals*. London: Profile Books.

Burney, E. (2005) *Making People Behave: Anti-social Behaviour, Politics and Policy*. Cullompton, Devon: Willan Publishing.

Butler, J. (1999) Merely cultural. *New Left Review*, 227: 33–44.

Butler, P. and Siddique, H. (2021) Politicians and media getting more hostile towards charities, poll finds. *The Guardian*, 15 January: https://www.theg uardian.com/society/2021/jan/15/politicians-and-media-getting-more-hostile-towards-charities-poll-finds

Buxton, X. (2017) Lexit: looking forwards, not backwards. *Open Democracy*, 21 September: https://www.opendemocracy.net/en/lexit-looking-forwards-not-backwards/

Cairney, P. (2021) The UK government's COVID-19 policy: what does 'guided by the science' mean in practice? *Frontiers in Political Science*, 15 March: https://www.frontiersin.org/articles/10.3389/fpos.2021.624 068/full

Calvert, J. and Arbuthnott, G. (2021) *Failures of State: The Inside Story of Britain's Battle with Coronavirus*. London: Mudlark.

Cameron, D. (2013) EU speech at Bloomberg: https://www.gov.uk/ government/speeches/eu-speech-at-bloomberg

Cameron, D. (2019) *For the Record*. London: William Collins.

Canovan, M. (1999) Trust the people! Populism and the two faces of democracy. *Political Studies*, 47: 2–16. doi: 10.1111/1467-9248.00184.

Cantat, C. and Rajaram, P.K. (2018) 'The politics of refugee crisis in Hungary: b/ordering the nation and its others.' In C. Menjivar, M. Ruiz and I. Ness (eds) *The Oxford Handbook of Migration Crises*. Oxford: Oxford University Press, 180–196.

Carchedi, G. (1986) Review article: two models of class analysis. *Capital and Class*, 29: 195–215.

Carrington, D. (2021) How to spot the difference between a real climate policy and greenwashing guff. *The Guardian*, 5 May: https://www.theg uardian.com/commentisfree/2021/may/06/difference-real-climate-policy-greenwashing-emissions

Casey, Baroness L. (2022) Letter to Commissioner Sir Mark Rowley. London: Metropolitan Police: https://www.met.police.uk/police-forces/ metropolitan-police/areas/about-us/about-the-met/bcr/baroness-casey-letter-to-commissioner/

Centre for Contemporary Cultural Studies (1982) *The Empire Strikes Back: Race and Racism in 70s Britain*. London: Hutchinson/CCCS (reprinted by Routledge, 1992).

Centre for Evidence Based Medicine (2020) BAME COVID-19 deaths – what do we know? Rapid data & evidence review. https://www.cebm.net/covid-19/bame-covid-19-deaths-what-do-we-know-rapid-data-evidence-review/

Cerny, P. (1997) Paradoxes of the competition state: the dynamics of political globalization. *Government and Opposition*, 32(2): 251–274.

Charlesworth, A., Tallack, C. and Alderwick, H. (2021) If not now, when? The long overdue promise of social care reform. The Health Foundation, 10 May: https://www.health.org.uk/news-and-comment/blogs/if-not-now-when-the-long-overdue-promise-of-social-care-reform

Cherniavsky, E. (2009) Neocitizenship and critique. *Social Text*, 27(2): 1–23.

Cherniavsky, E. (2017) *Neocitizenship: Political Culture after Democracy*. New York: New York University Press.

Chesney, M. (2018) *Permanent Crisis: The Financial Oligarchy's Seizing of Power and the Failure of Democracy*. Cham, Switzerland: Palgrave Macmillan.

Christophers, B. (2020) *Rentier Capitalism*. London: Verso.

Cinelli, M., Quattrociocchi, W., Galeazzi, A., Valensise, C.M., Brugnoli, E., Schmidt, A.L., et al (2020) The COVID-19 social media infodemic. *Scientific Reports* 10: 16598. https://doi.org/10.1038/s41598-020-73510-5

Clarke, J. (2004) *Changing Welfare, Changing States*. London: Sage Publications.

Clarke, J. (2008) Living with/in and without neo-liberalism. *Focaal*, 51: 135–147.

Clarke, J. (2011) Alla ricerca di una Big Society? Conservatorismo, coalizioni e controversie. *La Rivista Delle Politiche Sociali*, 2: 183–198.

Clarke, J. (2014) Imagined economies: austerity and the moral economy of 'fairness'. *Topia: Canadian Journal of Cultural Studies*, 30–31: 17–30.

Clarke, J. (2017) 'Doing the dirty work: the challenges of conjunctural analysis.' In J. Henriques, D. Morley and V. Goblot (eds) *Stuart Hall: Conversations, Projects and Legacies*. London: Goldsmiths Press, 79–86.

Clarke, J. (2019) A sense of loss? Unsettled attachments in the current conjuncture. *New Formations*, 96–97: 132–146.

Clarke, J. (2020a) Building the 'Boris' bloc: angry politics in turbulent times. *Soundings: A Journal of Politics and Culture*, 74: 118–135.

Clarke, J. (2020b) 'Re-imagining scale, space and sovereignty: The United Kingdom and "Brexit".' In D. Nonini and I. Susser (eds) *Unsettled States, Movements in Flux, Migrants out of Place: The Tumultuous Politics of Scale*. London and New York: Routledge, 138–150.

Clarke, J. (2020c) 'A sovereign people? Political fantasy and governmental time in the pursuit of Brexit.' In M. Gunderjan, H. Mackay and G. Steadman (eds) *Contested Britain: Brexit, Austerity, Agency*. Bristol: Policy Press, 117–130.

Clarke, J. (2020d) 'Looking for the conjuncture: condensations of time and space.' In E. Maigret and L. Martin (eds) *Cultural Studies/Etudes Culturelles: Au-delà des Politiques des Identités*. Lormont: Les Editions Le Bord de l'Eau, 75–86.

Clarke, J. (2020e) 'Frustrations, failures and fractures: Brexit and "politics as usual" in the UK.' In J. Maskovsky and S. Bjork-James (eds) *Beyond Populism: Angry Politics and the Twilight of Neoliberalism*. Morgantown, VA: West Virginia University Press, 99–116.

Clarke, J. (2021a) 'Which nation is this? Brexit and the not so United Kingdom'. In I. Corut and J. Jongerden (eds) *Beyond Nationalism and the Nation-State: Radical Approaches to Nation*. London: Routledge, 98–116.

Clarke, J. (2021b) Following the science? Covid-19, 'race' and the politics of knowing. *Cultural Studies*, 35(2–3): 248–256.

Clarke, J. (forthcoming a) 'Anti-elitism, populism and the question of the conjuncture.' In M. Ege and J. Springer (eds) *Against the Elites*. Routledge.

Clarke, J. (forthcoming b) 'Turbulent times? Towards a conjunctural analysis of neoliberalism and the politics of the present.' In L. Harder, C. Kellogg and S. Patten (eds) *Neoliberal Contentions: Diagnosing the Present*. University of Toronto Press.

Clarke, J. (forthcoming c) 'Traversing troubled waters: emergent ethics and pandemic politics.' In M. Ege et al (eds) *Urban Ethics as Research Agenda*. London: Routledge.

Clarke, J. and Newman, J. (1993) The right to manage: a second managerial revolution? *Cultural Studies*, 7(3): 427–441.

Clarke, J. and Newman, J. (1997) *The Managerial State: Power, Politics and Ideology in the Remaking of Social Welfare*. London: Sage Publications.

Clarke, J. and Newman, J. (2004) 'Governing in the modern world?' In D. Steinberg and R. Johnson (eds) *Blairism and the War of Persuasion: New Labour's Passive Revolution*. London: Lawrence & Wishart, 53–65.

Clarke, J. and Newman, J. (2012) The alchemy of austerity. *Critical Social Policy*, 32(3): 299–319.

Clarke, J. and Newman, J. (2017) 'People in this country have had enough of experts': Brexit and the paradoxes of populism. *Critical Policy Studies*, 11(1): 101–116. http://dx.doi.org/10.1080/19460171.2017.1282376

Clarke, J. and Newman, J. (2019) What's the subject? Brexit and politics as articulation. *Journal of Community and Applied Social Psychology*, 29: 67–77.

Clarke, J. and Newman, J. (2022) What's at stake in the culture wars? *Soundings: A Journal of Politics and Culture*, 18: 13–22.

Clarke, J., Bainton, D., Lendvai, N. and Stubbs, P. (2015) *Making Policy Move: Towards a Politics of Translation and Assemblage*. Bristol: The Policy Press.

Clarke, J., Newman, J., Smith, N., Vidler, E. and Westmarland, L. (2007) *Creating Citizen-Consumers: Changing Publics and Changing Public Services*. London: Sage Publications.

Closs Stephens, A. (2019) Feeling 'Brexit': nationalism and the affective politics of movement. *GeoHumanities*, 5(2): 405–423.

Cochrane, A. (2007) *Understanding Urban Policy: A Critical Approach.* Oxford: Blackwell.

Cochrane, A. (2020) 'From Brexit to the break-up of … England? Thinking in and beyond the nation.' In M. Guderjan, H. Mackay and G. Stedman (eds) *Contested Britain: Brexit, Austerity, Agency.* Bristol: Policy Press, 161–174.

Cockburn, B. (1981) *The Trouble with Normal.* Lyrics at http://cockburn project.net/songs&music/ttwn.html. It appears on the album of the same name, released by True North Records in 1983.

Coleman, R., Sim, J., Tombs, S. and Whyte, D. (eds) (2009) *State, Power, Crime.* London: Sage Publications.

Collins, M. (2004) *The Likes of Us.* Cambridge: Granta.

Commission on Race and Ethnic Disparities (CRED) (2021) *The Report.* London: https://assets.publishing.service.gov.uk/government/uploads/system/uploads/attachment_data/file/974507/20210331_-_CRED_Report_-_FINAL_-_Web_Accessible.pdf

Cooney, R. (2021) Fundraiser to buy RNLI hovercraft named after Nigel Farage passes £100,000 goal. Third Sector, 11 August: https://www.third sector.co.uk/fundraiser-buy-rnli-hovercraft-named-nigel-farage-passes-100000-goal/fundraising/article/1724467

Cooper, D. (2013) *Everyday Utopias: The Conceptual Life of Promising Spaces.* Durham, NC: Duke University Press.

Cooper, D. (2019) 'Introduction.' In D. Cooper, N. Dhawan and J. Newman (eds) *Reimagining the State: Theoretical Challenges and Transformative Possibilities.* London: Routledge, 1–15.

Cooper, D., Dhawan, N. and Newman, J. (eds) (2019) *Reimagining the State: Theoretical Challenges and Transformative Possibilities.* London: Routledge.

Cooper, V. and Whyte, D. (eds) (2017) *The Violence of Austerity.* London: Pluto Press.

Courea, E. (2022) Margaret Thatcher's ghost looms over Liz Truss and Rishi Sunak. *Politico*, 4 August: https://www.politico.eu/article/uk-pm-boris-johnson-rishi-sunak-liz-truss-tory-party-chasing-the-ghost-of-margaret-thatcher/

Crace, J. (2021) Party pooper George Freeman pours cold water on Boris Johnson's Christmas. *The Guardian*, 2 December: https://www.theguard ian.com/politics/2021/dec/02/party-pooper-george-freeman-pours-cold-water-on-boris-johnsons-christmas

Crehan, K. (2016) *Gramsci's Common Sense.* Durham, NC: Duke University Press.

Crenshaw, K. (1989) Demarginalizing the intersection of race and sex: a black feminist critique of antidiscrimination doctrine, feminist theory and antiracist politics. *University of Chicago Legal Forum*, 1989: 139–167.

Dagnino, E. (2005) ' "We all have rights but …": contesting conceptions of citizenship in Brazil.' In N. Kabeer (ed.) *Inclusive Citizenship: Meanings and Expressions of Citizenship*. London: Zed Books, 147–163.

Darity, W. and Mullen, K. (2020) *From Here to Equality: Reparations for Black Americans in the Twenty First Century*. Chapel Hill, NC: University of North Carolina Press.

Davies, W. (2019) England's new rentier alliance. Political Economy Research Centre blog, 1 August: https://www.perc.org.uk/project_posts/englands-rentier-alliance/

Davies, W. (2020) The decline of the 'state effect'. Political Economy Research Centre blog, 21 December: https://www.perc.org.uk/project_posts/the-decline-of-the-state-effect/

Davies, W. (2021) New-found tribes. *London Review of Books*, 43(3). https://www.lrb.co.uk/the-paper/v43/n03/william-davies/new-found-tribes.

Davies, W. (2022) Madman economics. *London Review of Books*, 44(20). https://www.lrb.co.uk/the-paper/v44/n20/william-davies/madman-economics

Davis, J., Moulton, A., Van Sant, L. and Williams, B. (2019) Anthropocene, Capitalocene, … Plantationocene? A manifesto for ecological justice in an age of global crises. *Geography Compass*, 13(5): doi: 10.1111/gec3.12438

Davis, M. (2022) Thanatos triumphant. *New Left Review Sidecar*, 7 March: https://newleftreview.org/sidecar/posts/thanatos-triumphant

de Greiff, P. (ed.) (2008) *The Handbook of Reparations*. Oxford: Oxford University Press.

de Sousa Santos, B. (2017) *Decolonising the University: The Challenge of Deep Cognitive Justice*. Cambridge: Cambridge Scholars Publishing.

Deacon, M. (2016) Michael Gove's guide to Britain's greatest enemy … the experts. *The Telegraph*, 10 June: https://www.telegraph.co.uk/news/2016/06/10/michael-goves-guide-to-britains-greatest-enemy-the-experts/

Delanty, G. (2019) What does self-determination mean today? The resurgence of nationalism and European integration in question. *Global Discourse*, 9(1): 93–107.

Dench, G., Gavron, K. and Young, M. (2006) *The New East End: Kinship, Race and Conflict*. London: Profile Books.

Devine, T.M. (2006) The break-up of Britain? Scotland and the end of empire: The Prothero Lecture. *Transactions of the Royal Historical Society*, 16: 163–180. www.jstor.org/stable/25593865.

Dianotto, R. (2007) *Europe (in Theory)*. Durham, NC: Duke University Press.

Dickey, S. (2012) The pleasures and anxieties of being in the middle: emerging middle class identities in urban South India. *Modern Asian Studies*, 46(3): 559–599.

Docx, E. (2021) All hail the clown king: how Boris Johnson made it by playing the fool. *The Guardian*: https://www.theguardian.com/news/2021/mar/18/all-hail-the-clown-king-how-boris-johnson-made-it-by-playing-the-fool

Dodd, V. (2022) Met police placed in special measures due to litany of new 'systemic' failings. *The Guardian*, 28 June: https://www.theguardian.com/uk-news/2022/jun/28/met-police-placed-special-measures-series-scandals

Donaldson, M. (2008) 'Gramsci, class and post-Marxism.' University of Wollongong, Arts Papers: https://ro.uow.edu.au/artspapers/182

Donzelot, J. (1984) *L'invention du social: Essai sur le déclin des passions politiques*, Paris: Fayard.

Dorling, D. (2016) Brexit: the decision of a divided country. http://www.dannydorling.org/?p=5568 10.1136/bmj.i3697

Dorling, D. and Tomlinson, S. (2019) *Rule Britannia: Brexit and the End of Empire*. London: Biteback Publishing.

Dowling, E. (2021) *The Care Crisis: What Caused It and How Can We End It?* London: Verso.

Duffy, B. (2021) *Who Cares about Climate Change? Attitudes across the Generations*. London: The Policy Institute, King's College, London. https://www.kcl.ac.uk/policy-institute/assets/who-cares-about-climate-change.pdf

Duggan, L. (2003) *The Twilight of Equality? Neoliberalism, Cultural Politics, and the Attack on Democracy*. Boston: Beacon Press.

Dunn, J. (2016) Nigel Farage calls for a new bank holiday to mark UK's 'Independence Day' as his life's work comes to fruition as the country votes for Brexit. *Mail Online*, 24 June: http://www.dailymail.co.uk/news/article-3657627/What-Nigel-Farage-s-lifes-work-comes-fruition-stunning-Brexit-vote-lauds-new-dawn-Britain-outside-EU.html#ixzz4Cngl7Zj9

Dyke, J., Watson, R. and Knorr, W. (2021) Climate scientists: concept of net zero is a dangerous trap. *The Conversation*, 22 April: https://theconversation.com/climate-scientists-concept-of-net-zero-is-a-dangerous-trap-157368

*Economist, The* (2019) A new index finds neglect in Britain's banlieues. *The Economist*: https://www.economist.com/britain/2019/09/05/a-new-index-finds-neglect-in-britains-banlieues

Edgerton, D. (2019) *The Rise and Fall of the British Nation: A Twentieth Century History*. London: Penguin.

Edgerton, D. (2021) Labour didn't lose its 'red wall' – it never had one. *The Guardian*, 9 July: https://www.theguardian.com/commentisfree/2021/jul/09/labour-red-wall-working-class-brexit-conservatives

Edmiston, D. with Begum, S. and Kataria, M. (2022) *Falling Faster amidst a Cost-of-Living Crisis: Poverty, Inequality and Ethnicity in the UK*. London: The Runnymede Trust.

Edwards, J. (2019) 'Brexit and "left behind places".' *Douglas Distinguished Lecture*, American Anthropological Association Conference, Vancouver.

Egan, D. (2015) Insurrection and Gramsci's 'War of Position'. *Socialism and Democracy*, 29(1): 102–124. http://dx.doi.org/10.1080/08854 300.2014.1001559

Electoral Commission (2016) *Results and turnout at the EU referendum*. https://www.electoralcommission.org.uk/who-we-are-and-what-we-do/electi ons-and-referendums/past-elections-and-referendums/eu-referendum/ results-and-turnout-eu-referendum

Evans, G. (2019) Gavin Williamson roasted after saying children shouldn't 'bunk off school' for climate protests. *The Independent*, 21 September: https://www.indy100.com/news/global-climate-strike-tory-gavin-williamson-protest-children-school-9114556

Featherstone, S. (2008) *Englishness: Twentieth-Century Popular Culture and the Forming of English Identity*. Edinburgh: Edinburgh University Press.

Felski, R. (2000) *Doing Time: Feminist Theory and Postmodern Culture*. New York: New York University Press.

Ferguson, J. and Gupta, A. (2002) Spatializing states: towards an ethnography of neoliberal governmentality. *American Ethnologist*, 29(4): 981–1002.

Ferguson, J. and Li, T. (2018) *Beyond the 'Proper Job': Political-economic Analysis after the Century of Labouring Man*. Working Paper 51, PLAAS, UWC, Cape Town.

*Financial Times, The* (2018) Time to clean up the London Laundromat. *Financial Times*, 27 September: https://www.ft.com/content/6c9cfd92-c188-11e8-95b1-d36dfef1b89a

Fisher, M. (2007) *Capitalist Realism: There Is No Alternative*. London: Zero Books.

*Fishing Daily, The* (2020) Appalling physical assault on volunteers at St Ives RNLI Lifeboat Station. *The Fishing Daily*, 25 July: https://thefishingdaily.com/uk-fishing-industry-news-blog/appalling-physical-assault-on-volunteers-at-st-ives-rnli-lifeboat-station/

Fitzgerald, D., Hinterberger, A., Narayan, J. and Williams, R. (2020) Brexit as heredity redux: imperialism, biomedicine and the NHS in Britain. *Sociological Review*, 68(6): 1161–1178.

Flemmen, M. and Savage, M. (2017) The politics of nationalism and white racism in the UK. *British Journal of Sociology*, 68(S1): S234–S264.

Fletcher, M. (2020) Munira Mirza: the former radical leftist advising Boris Johnson. *New Statesman*, 30 September: https://www.newstatesman.com/ uncategorized/2020/09/munira-mirza-adviser-boris-johnson-aide-for mer-radical-leftist

Ford, R. (2016) Older 'left-behind' voters turned against a political class with values opposed to theirs. *The Guardian*, 25 June: https://www.theguardian.com/politics/2016/jun/25/left-behind-eu-referendum-vote-ukip-revolt-brexit

Ford, R. and Goodwin, M. (2014) Understanding UKIP: identity, social change and the left behind. *Political Quarterly*, 85(3): 277–284.

Forkert, K. (2017) *Austerity as Public Mood*. London: Rowman and Littlefield International.

Fortier, A.-M. (2021) *Uncertain Citizens: Life in the Waiting Room*. Manchester: University of Manchester Press.

Francois, M. (2021) *Spartan Victory: The Inside Story of the Battle for Brexit*. Great Britain/EU: Kindle Direct Publishing.

Frank, T. (2016) Millions of ordinary Americans support Donald Trump. Here's why. *The Guardian*, 7 March: https://www.theguardian.com/commentisfree/2016/mar/07/donald-trump-why-americans-support

Fraser, N. (1997) *Justice Interruptus: Critical Reflections on the 'Post-Socialist' Condition*. London: Routledge.

Fraser, N. (2017) The end of progressive neoliberalism. *Dissent*, 2 January: https://www.dissentmagazine.org/online_articles/progressive-neoliberalism-reactionary-populism-nancy-fraser

Freeman, C. (2001) Is local: global as feminine: masculine? Rethinking the gender of globalization. *Signs*, 26(4): 1007–1037.

Freeman, C., Heiman, R. and Liechty, M. (eds) (2012) *Charting an Anthropology of the Middle Classes*. Santa Fe: SAR Press.

Friedman, G. (2014) Workers without employers: shadow corporations and the rise of the gig economy. *Review of Keynesian Economics*, 2(2): 171–188.

Galbraith, J.K. (1958) *The Affluent Society*. Cambridge, MA: The Riverside Press (Houghton Mifflin).

Gamble, A. (2017) 'The resistible rise of Theresa May.' In M. Perryman (ed.) *The Corbyn Effect*. London, Lawrence & Wishart, 54–67.

Gamlin, J., Gibbon, S. and Calestani, M. (2021) 'The biopolitics of COVID-19 in the UK: racism, nationalism and the afterlife of colonialism.' In L. Manderson, N. Burke and A. Wahlberg (eds) (2021) *Viral Loads: Anthropologies of Urgency in the Time of Covid-19*. London: UCL Press, 108–127.

Gentleman, A. (2019) *The Windrush Betrayal: Exposing the Hostile Environment*. London: Guardian Faber Publishing.

Geoghegan, P. (2020) Cronyism and clientelism. *London Review of Books*, 42(21): https://www.lrb.co.uk/the-paper/v42/n21/peter-geoghegan/cronyism-and-clientelism

Gerbaudo, P. (2021) *The Great Recoil: Politics after Populism and Pandemic*. London: Verso.

Gibson-Graham, J.K., Resnick, S. and Wolff, R. (eds) (2000) *Class and Its Others*. Minneapolis, MN: University of Minnesota Press.

Gilbert, J. (2015) Disaffected consent: that post-democratic feeling. *Soundings: A Journal of Politics and Culture*, 60: 29–41.

Gilbert, J. and Williams, A. (2022) *Hegemony Now*. London: Verso Books.

Gill, R. and Pratt, A. (2008) In the social factory: immaterial labour, precariousness and cultural work. *Theory, Culture and Society*, 25(7–8): 1–30. doi: 10.1177/0263276408097794.

Gill, S. (2000) Toward a postmodern prince? The battle in Seattle as a moment in the new politics of globalisation. *Millennium*, 29(1): 131–140. https://doi.org/10.1177/03058298000290010101

Gill, S. (2002) *Power and Resistance in the New World Order*. Basingstoke: Palgrave Macmillan.

Gilroy, P. (2005) *Postcolonial Melancholia*. New York: Columbia University Press.

Gimson, A. (2021) Profile: Steve Baker, Christian Conservative, ERG organiser, small stater – and thorn in Johnson's side. *Conservative Home*, 22 December: https://www.conservativehome.com/highlights/2021/12/profile-steve-baker-christian-conservative-erg-organiser-controversial-backbencher-and-thorn-in-johnsons-side.html

Godfrey, D.M., Price, L. and Lusch, R. (2022) Repair, consumption, and sustainability: fixing fragile objects and maintaining consumer practices. *Journal of Consumer Research*, 49(2): 229–251. https://doi.org/10.1093/jcr/ucab067

Goodfellow, M. (2019) *Hostile Environment: How Immigrants Became Scapegoats*. London: Verso.

Gordon, M. (2016) The UK's sovereignty situation: Brexit, bewilderment and beyond... . *King's Law Journal*, 27(3): 333–343.

Goswami, M. (2020) The political economy of the nation form. *Geografiska Annaler: Series B, Human Geography*, 102(3): 267–272. doi: 10.1080/04353684.2020.1782093

Gove, M. (2020) The privilege of public service: The Gilbert Ditchley Lecture. *New Statesman*: https://www.newstatesman.com/politics/uk/2020/06/privilege-public-service-michael-gove-s-ditchley-lecture-full-text

Graham, S. (2010) *Cities Under Siege: The New Military Urbanism*. London: Verso.

Gramsci, A. (1971) *Selections from the Prison Notebooks*, edited by Geoffrey Nowell Smith and Quintin Hoare. London: Lawrence & Wishart.

Grayson, D. (2022) Charity, politics and the culture wars. *Soundings: A Journal of Politics and Culture*, 81: 65–84.

Green, M. and Lawson, V. (2011) Recentring care: interrogating the commodification of care. *Social and Cultural Geography*, 11(6): 639–654.

Grossberg, L. (2010) Standing on a bridge: rescuing economies from economists. *Journal of Communication Inquiry*, 34(4): 316–336.

Grossberg, L. (2018) *Under the Cover of Chaos: Trump and the Battle for the American Right*. London: Pluto Press.

Guajardo, J., Leigh, D. and Pescatori, A. (2011) *Expansionary Austerity: New International Evidence*. International Monetary Fund: IMF Working Papers.

*Guardian, The* (nd) The Cambridge Analytica files: https://www.theguardian.com/news/series/cambridge-analytica-files

Guinan, J. and Hanna, T. (2017) Lexit: The EU is a neoliberal project, so let's do something different when we leave it. *New Statesman*, 20 July: https://www.newstatesman.com/politics/brexit/2017/07/lexit-eu-neoliberal-project-so-lets-do-something-different-when-we-leave-it

Gupta, A. (1998) *Postcolonial Developments*. Durham, NC: Duke University Press.

Hall, C. (2002) *Civilising Subjects: Metropole and Colony in the English Imagination 1830–1867*. Chicago, IL: University of Chicago Press.

Hall, C. (2020) The slavery business and making of 'race' in Britain and the Caribbean. *Current Anthropology*, 61(Suppl 22): S172–S182.

Hall, C., Draper, N., McLelland, K., Donington, K. and Lang, R. (2016) *Legacies of British Slave-Ownership: Colonial Slavery and the Formation of Victorian Britain*. Cambridge: Cambridge University Press.

Hall, R. (2021) Donations to RNLI rise 3,000% after Farage's migrant criticism. *The Guardian*, 29 July: https://www.theguardian.com/world/2021/jul/29/rnli-donations-soar-in-response-to-farages-migrant-criticism

Hall, S. (1979) The great moving right show. *Marxism Today*, January: 14–20.

Hall, S. (1985) Authoritarian populism: a reply. *New Left Review*, 1(151) (May–June): 115–124.

Hall, S. (1987) Gramsci and us. *Marxism Today*, June: 16–21. Republished as a Verso Books blog on 10 February 2017: https://www.versobooks.com/blogs/2448-stuart-hall-gramsci-and-us.

Hall, S. (1988) *The Hard Road to Renewal: Thatcherism and the Crisis of the Left*. London: Verso.

Hall, S. (2003) Marx's notes on method: a 'reading' of the '1857 Introduction'. *Cultural Studies*, 17(2): 113–149. https://doi.org/10.1080/0950238032000114868.

Hall, S. (2010) 'Subjects in history: making diasporic identities.' In W. Lubiano (ed.) *The House that Race Built: Original Essays by Toni Morrison, Angela Y. Davis, Cornell West and Others on Black Americans and Politics in America Today*. Vintage: New York. Reprinted in Paul Gilroy and Ruth Wilson Gilmore (eds) (2021) *Stuart Hall: Writings on Race and Difference*. Durham, NC: Duke University Press.

Hall, S. (2017) *The Fateful Triangle: Race, Ethnicity, Nation* (edited by Kobena Mercer). Cambridge, MA: Harvard University Press.

Hall, S. and Jefferson, T. (eds) (1976) *Resistance through Rituals: Youth Subcultures in Post-war Britain*. London: Hutchinson (second edition, 2006, Routledge).

Hall, S., Critcher, C., Jefferson, T., Clarke, J. and Roberts, B. (2013) *Policing the Crisis: Mugging, the State and Law and Order* (second edition). Basingstoke: Macmillan.

Hall, S.M. (2021) Waiting for Brexit: crisis, conjuncture, method. *Transactions of the Institute of British Geographers*, 47(1): 200–213. https://doi.org/10.1111/tran.12505

Hameleers, M. (2018) A typology of populism: toward a revised theoretical framework on the sender side and receiver side of communication. *International Journal of Communication*, 12: 2171–2190.

Hannah, S. (2020) *Can't Pay, Won't Pay: The Fight to Stop the Poll Tax*. London: Pluto Press.

Hansen, B.R. (2020) The interest of breathing: towards a theory of ecological interest formation. *Crisis & Critique*, 7(3): 109–137.

Hansen, R. (2000) *Citizenship and Immigration in Post-War Britain: The Institutional Origins of a Multicultural Nation*. Oxford: Oxford University Press.

Haraway, D. (2015) Anthropocene, Capitalocene, Plantationocene, Chthulucene: making kin. *Environmental Humanities*, 6: 159–165.

Harden, I. (1992) *The Contracting State*. Maidenhead: Open University Press.

Hargrave, R. (2021) The budget showed why charities can't trust government promises. *Civil Society*, 1 November: https://www.civilsociety.co.uk/voices/trust-me-i-m-the-chancellor.html

Harris, J. (2003) *The Social Work Business*. London: Routledge.

Harris, J. (2019) England can be better than the Brexit caricature. We have to make the case for it. *The Guardian*, 28 January: https://www.theguardian.com/commentisfree/2019/jan/28/england-brexit-caricature-modern-diverse

Hart, G. (2019) From authoritarian to left populism: reframing debates. *The South Atlantic Quarterly*, 118(2): 307–323.

Hart, G. (2020) Resurgent nationalisms & populist politics in the neoliberal age. *Geografiska Annaler: Series B, Human Geography*, 102(3): 233–238. doi: 10.1080/04353684.2020.1780792

Hartman, A. (2015) *A War for the Soul of America: A History of the Culture Wars*. Chicago, IL: University of Chicago Press.

Hay, C. (2020) Brexistential angst and the paradoxes of populism: on the contingency, predictability and intelligibility of seismic shifts. *Political Studies*, 68(1): 187–206.

Hayward, F. (2021) What do Jake Berry and the Tory Northern Research Group want? *New Statesman*, 1 March: https://www.newstatesman.com/politics/2021/03/what-do-jake-berry-and-tory-northern-research-group-want

Hechter, M. (1975) *Internal Colonialism: The Celtic Fringe in British National Development, 1536–1966*. Berkeley, CA: University of California Press.

Heifetz, R., Grashow, A. and Linsky, M. (2009) Leadership in a (permanent) crisis. *Harvard Business Review*, July–August: https://hbr.org/2009/07/leadership-in-a-permanent-crisis

Hennessy, P. (1994) 'Harvesting the cupboards': why Britain has produced no administrative theory or ideology in the twentieth century. *Transactions of the Royal Historical Society*, 4: 203–219.

Higgins, M. (2021) Empire shaped Ireland's past. A century after partition, it still shapes our present. *The Guardian*, 11 February: https://www.theg uardian.com/commentisfree/2021/feb/11/empire-ireland-century-partit ion-present-britain-history

Hindess, B. (2017) Working class racism. *Open Democracy*, 12 February: https://www.opendemocracy.net/en/working-class-racism/

Hindess, B. and Hirst, P. (1977) *Mode of Production and Social Formation: An Auto-Critique of Pre-Capitalist Modes of Production*. London: Palgrave Macmillan.

Hines, S. (2020) Sex wars and (trans) gender panics: identity and body politics in contemporary UK feminism. *The Sociological Review Monographs*, 68(4): 699–717.

Ho, K. (2009) *Liquidated: An Ethnography of Wall Street*. Durham, NC: Duke University Press.

Hochschild, A.R. (1983) *The Managed Heart: Commercialization of Human Feeling*. Berkeley, CA: University of California Press.

Holland, D. and Lave, J. (2001) 'Introduction.' In D. Holland and J. Lave (eds) *History in Person: Enduring Struggles, Contentious Practices, Intimate Identities*. Santa Fe: School of American Research. Oxford: James Currey Ltd.

Home Office (2019) *Life in the United Kingdom: A Guide for New Residents*. London: The Stationery Office.

Home Office (2021) *Police, Crime, Sentencing and Courts Bill 2021: Protest Powers Factsheet*. London: Home Office Policy Paper updated July 2021: https://www.gov.uk/government/publications/police-crime-sen tencing-and-courts-bill-2021-factsheets/police-crime-sentencing-and-cou rts-bill-2021-protest-powers-factsheet

Horton, H. (2022) Rees-Mogg: 'Britain must get every cubic inch of gas out of North Sea'. *The Guardian*, 23 September: https://www.theguardian.com/politics/2022/sep/23/rees-mogg-tells-staff-britain-must-get-every-cubic-inch-gas-out-of-north-sea

Hotten, R. (2021) HS2 rail extension to Leeds scrapped amid promise to transform rail. *BBC News*, 19 November: https://www.bbc.co.uk/news/business-59334043

Howard-Hassman, R. with Lombardo, A. (2018) *Reparations to Africa*. Philadelphia: University of Pennsylvania Press.

Howarth, D. (2021) Government's poisonous elections bill is designed to cement Tory rule. *Open Democracy*, 6 September: https://www.opende mocracy.net/en/opendemocracyuk/governments-poisonous-elections-bill-is-designed-to-cement-tory-rule/

Huber, E. and Stephens, J.D. (2001) *Development and Crisis of the Welfare State: Parties and Policies in Global Markets*. Chicago, IL: University of Chicago Press.

Huebener, P., O'Brien, S., Porter, T., Stockdale, L. and Zhou, R. (2016) Exploring the intersection of time and globalization. *Globalizations*, 13(3): 243–255. doi: 10.1080/14747731.2015.1057046

Humphris, R. (2019) *Home-Land: Romanian Roma, Domestic Spaces and the State*. Bristol: Bristol University Press.

Huysmans, J. (2006) *The Politics of Insecurity: Fear, Migration and Asylum in the EU*. London: Routledge.

Hyman, R. (2008) *Britain and the European Social Model: Capitalism against Capitalism?* IES Working Paper (19). Brighton, UK: Institute for Employment Studies.

Independent Sage (2021) The 'following the science' timeline: What SAGE and Independent SAGE advised as key behavioural mitigations versus what the Westminster Government did January 2020–July 2021. *Independent SAGE Report 46*: https://www.independentsage.org/wp-content/uploads/2021/08/IS-Timeline-Complete-1.pdf

Innes, D. (2021) *What has driven the rise of in-work poverty?* York: Joseph Rowntree Foundation: https://www.jrf.org.uk/report/what-has-driven-rise-work-poverty

Isin, E. (ed.) (2008) *Recasting the Social in Citizenship*. Toronto: University of Toronto Press.

Isin, E. (2021) 'Planetary Movements: Willing, Knowing, Acting.' University of London Institute in Paris: *Theory in Crisis* seminar, 10 December: https://london.ac.uk/institute-in-paris/events/engin-isin-planetary-movements-willing-knowing-acting

Jablonowski, K. (2020) There are cracks in the EU settlement scheme: who will fall through them? LSE blog, 6 June: https://blogs.lse.ac.uk/brexit/2020/05/06/there-are-cracks-in-the-eu-settlement-scheme-who-will-fall-through-them/

Jacotine, K. (2017) The split in neoliberalism on Brexit and the EU. http://speri.dept.shef.ac.uk/2017/06/21/the-split-in-neoliberalism-on-brexit-and-the-eu/

Jacques, M. (2016) The death of neoliberalism and the crisis in western politics. *The Observer*, 21 August: https://www.theguardian.com/commentisfree/2016/aug/21/death-of-neoliberalism-crisis-in-western-politics

James, M. (2016) 'Response to *A Working Class Brexit*.' https://workingclassstudies.wordpress.com/2016/06/27/a-working-class-brexit/

Jasanoff, S. and Kim, S.H. (eds) (2015) *Dreamscapes of Modernity: Sociotechnical Imaginaries and the Fabrication of Power*. Chicago, IL: The University of Chicago Press.

Jefferson, T. (2015) The 2011 English riots: a contextualised, dynamic, grounded explanation. *Contention: The Multidisciplinary Journal of Social Protest*, 2(2): 5–22.

Jefferson, T. (2017) 'Race, immigration and the present conjuncture.' In J. Henriques, D. Morley and V. Goblot (eds) *Stuart Hall: Conversations, Projects, Legacies*. London: Goldsmiths Press, 117–127.

Jefferson, T. (2021) *Stuart Hall, Conjunctural Analysis and Cultural Criminology: A Missed Moment*. London/Cham, Switzerland: Palgrave Macmillan.

Jessop, B. (1982) *The Capitalist State: Marxist Theories and Methods*. London: Blackwell.

Jessop, B. (1990) *State Theory: Putting the Capitalist State in Its Place*. Cambridge: Polity Press.

Jessop, B. (2000) The crisis of the national spatio-temporal fix and the ecological dominance of globalizing capitalism. *International Journal of Urban and Regional Studies*, 24(2): 323–360.

Jessop, B. (2014) What follows Fordism? On the periodisation of capitalism and its regulation. Available at: https://bobjessop.wordpress.com/2014/01/03/what-follows-fordism-on-the-periodisation-of-capitalism-and-its-regulation/

Jessop, B. and Knio, K. (eds) (2019) *The Pedagogy of Economic, Political and Social Crises: Dynamics, Construals and Lessons*. London and New York: Routledge.

Jessop, B., Bonnett, K., Bromley, S. and Ling, T. (1984) Authoritarian populism, two nations, and Thatcherism. *New Left Review*, 147: 32–60

Johnson, B. (2019) PM statement on priorities for the government. 25 July. https://www.gov.uk/government/speeches/pm-statement-on-priorities-for-the-government-25-july-2019

Johnson, T. (1972) *Professions and Power*. London: Palgrave Macmillan.

Jones, C. and Novak, T. (1999) *Poverty, Welfare and the Disciplinary State*. London: Routledge.

Jones, O. (2012) *Chavs: The Demonization of the Working Class*. London: Verso.

Judis, J.B. (2016) *The Populist Explosion: How the Great Recession transformed American and European Politics*. New York: Columbia Global Reports.

Judt, T. (2010) *Ill Fares the Land: A Treatise on Our Present Discontents*. London and New York: Penguin Books.

Juncker, J.C. (2016) *Speech by President Jean-Claude Juncker at the Annual General Meeting of the Hellenic Federation of Enterprises*. European Commission, 21 June: https://ec.europa.eu/commission/presscorner/detail/de/SPEECH_16_2293

Jupp, E. (2022) *Care, Crisis and Activism: The Politics of Everyday Life*. Bristol: Bristol University Press.

Jupp, E., Pykett, J. and Smith, F. (eds) (2017) *Emotional States: Sites and Spaces of Affective Governance*. London: Routledge.

Kagarlitsky, B. (2017) Brexit and the future of the left. *Globalizations*, 14(1): 110–117. doi: 10.1080/14747731.2016.1228800

Karadağ, S. (2019) Extraterritoriality of European borders to Turkey: an implementation perspective of counteractive strategies. *Comparative Migration Studies*, 7: 12. https://comparativemigrationstudies.springeropen.com/track/pdf/10.1186/s40878-019-0113-y.pdf

Katz, C. (2001a) Vagabond capitalism and the necessity of social reproduction. *Antipode*, 33(4): 709–728.

Katz, C. (2001b) On the grounds of globalization: a topography for feminist political engagement. *Signs: Journal of Women in Culture and Society*, 26(4): 1213–1234.

Katz, C. (2018) The Angel of Geography: Superman, Tiger Mother, aspiration management, and the child as waste. *Progress in Human Geography*, 42(5): 723–740.

Keith, M. (2008) Between being and becoming? Rights, responsibilities and the politics of multiculture in the new East End. *Social Research Online*, 13(5): 11. https://www.socresonline.org.uk/13/5/11.html

Kelly, M. (2021) Frosty the No Man is to Brexit diplomacy what King Herod was to childcare. *Irish News*, 16 October: https://www.irishnews.com/paywall/tsb/irishnews/irishnews/irishnews//opinion/columnists/2021/10/16/news/mary-kelly-frosty-the-no-man-is-to-brexit-diplomacy-what-king-herod-was-to-childcare-2478097/content.html

Kennedy, H. (2005) *Just Law*. London: Vintage.

Kenny, M. (2014) *The Politics of English Nationhood*. Oxford: Oxford University Press.

Khalili, L. (2022) How the empire degraded Britain. *New Statesman*, 22 June: https://www.newstatesman.com/culture/books/2022/06/reviews-tackys-revolt-white-debt-uncommon-wealth-british-empire

Khan, O. (ed.) (2015) How far have we come? Lessons from the 1965 Race Relations Act. London: Runnymede Trust. https://www.runnymedetrust.org/uploads/publications/pdfs/Race%20Relations%20Act%20Perspectives%20report.pdf

Kipfer, S. and Hart, G. (2015) 'Conclusion: translating Gramsci in the current conjuncture.' In M. Ekers, G. Hart, S. Kipfer and A. Loftus (eds) *Gramsci: Space, Nature, Politics*. New Malden, MA: Antipode Book Series, Wiley-Blackwell, 321–343.

Klein, N. (2008) *The Shock Doctrine*. New York: Penguin Books.

Koch, I. (2017a) What's in a vote? Brexit beyond culture wars. *American Ethnologist*: http://onlinelibrary.wiley.com/doi/10.1111/amet.12472/full

Koch, I. (2017b) When politicians fail: zombie democracy and the anthropology of actually existing politics. *The Sociological Review Monographs*, 65(1): 105–120.

Koivisto, J. and Lahtinen, M. (2012) Conjuncture, politico-historical. *Historical Materialism*, 20(1): 267–277.

Kolstø, P. (2016) 'Western Balkans' as the New Balkans: regional names as tools for stigmatisation and exclusion. *Europe-Asia Studies*, 68(7): 1245–1263. doi: 10.1080/09668136.2016.1219979

Laclau, E. (2005) *On Populist Reason*. London: Verso.

Lamble, S. (2013) Queer necropolitics and the expanding carceral state: interrogating sexual investments in punishment. *Law Critique*, 24: 229–253.

Lammy, D. (2020) Britain needs leadership on race inequality. Not just another review. *The Guardian*, 16 June: https://www.theguardian.com/commentisfree/2020/jun/16/race-inequality-review-boris-johnson-black-lives-matter-david-lammy

Langan, M. (2018) *Neo-colonialism and the Poverty of 'Development' in Africa*. London: Palgrave Macmillan.

Lapavitsas, C. (2013) The financialization of capitalism: 'profiting without producing'. *City: Analysis of Urban Change, Theory, Action*, 17(6): 792–805.

Lapavitsas, C. (2019) *The Left Case Against the EU*. Cambridge: Polity Press.

Larner, W. (2000) 'Neo-liberalism: policy, ideology, governmentality'. *Studies in Political Economy*, 63: 5–25.

Lawrence, Baroness (2020) *An Avoidable Crisis: The disproportionate impact of Covid-19 on Black, Asian and minority ethnic communities. A review by Baroness Doreen Lawrence*. London: The Labour Party. https://www.lawrencereview.co.uk

Lawrence, M., Janzwood, S. and Homer-Dixon, T. (2022) What is a global polycrisis? Cascade Institute, Technical Paper 2022-4: https://cascadeinstitute.org/technical-paper/what-is-a-global-polycrisis/

Lawson, N. (2021) *All You Need to Know about a Progressive Alliance*. London: Compass. https://www.compassonline.org.uk/publications/all-you-need-to-know-about-a-progressive-alliance/

Leach, B. and Winson, A. (2002) *Contingent Work, Disrupted Lives: Labour and Community in the New Rural Economy*. Toronto: University of Toronto Press.

Learmonth, A. (2021) Boris Johnson attacks 'woke' plans to rewrite British history. *Holyrood*, 6 October: https://www.holyrood.com/news/view,boris-johnson-attacks-woke-plans-to-rewrite-british-history

Lefebvre, H. (2013) *Rhythmanalysis: Space, Time and Everyday Life*. London: Bloomsbury.

Leitner, H. and Sheppard, E. (2020) Towards an epistemology for conjunctural inter-urban comparison. *Cambridge Journal of Regions, Economy and Society*, 13: 491–508.

Lester, A. (2021) The Common Sense Group's culture war, the 'woke' and British history. Brighton: University of Sussex blog: https://blogs.sussex.ac.uk/snapshotsofempire/2021/05/28/the-common-sense-groups-culture-war-the-woke-and-british-history/

Levidow, L. and Raman, S. (2020) Sociotechnical imaginaries of low-carbon waste-energy futures: UK techno-market fixes displacing public accountability. *Social Studies of Science*, 50(4): 609–641.

Lewis, G. (2000) *'Race', Gender, Social Welfare: Encounters in a Postcolonial Society*. Cambridge: Polity Press.

Lewis, G. (2003) 'Difference and social policy.' In N. Ellison and C. Pierson (eds) *Developments in British Social Policy 2*. Basingstoke: Palgrave, 90–106.

Lewis, G. (2013) Unsafe travel: experiencing intersectionality and feminist displacements. *Signs: Journal of Women in Culture and Society*, 38(4): 869–892.

Lewis, P. (2010) Birmingham stops camera surveillance in Muslim areas. *The Guardian*, 17 June: https://www.theguardian.com/uk/2010/jun/17/birmingham-stops-spy-cameras-project

Lindaman, K. and Haider-Markel, D. (2002) Issue evolution, political parties, and the culture wars. *Political Research Quarterly*, 55(1): 91–110.

Lister, R. (2018) From Windrush to Universal Credit – the art of 'institutional indifference'. *Open Democracy*, 10 October: https://www.opendemocracy.net/en/opendemocracyuk/from-windrush-to-universal-credit-art-of-institutional-indifference/

Lo, K.H. (2018) 'Selling techno-futurism: exploring Pepper's Images and discourses Taiwanese news media make.' In A. Cheok and D. Levy (eds) *Love and Sex with Robots*. LSR 2017. *Lecture Notes in Computer Science*, vol. 10715. Cham: Springer. https://doi.org/10.1007/978-3-319-76369-9_7

Loftsdóttir, K., Smith, A. and Hipfl, B. (eds) (2018) 'Introduction.' In K. Loftsdóttir, A. Smith and B. Hipfl (eds) *Messy Europe: Crisis, Race, and Nation-State in a Postcolonial World*. New York: Berghahn Books, 1–30.

London-Edinburgh Weekend Return Group (1979/2021) *In and Against the State*. London: Pluto (book version).

Lowe, C. (2001) The trouble with tribe. Center for African Studies, Howard University. https://cfas.howard.edu/sites/cfas.howard.edu/files/2020-07/ArticleTheTroublewithTribe.pdf

Lucey, H. and Reay, D. (2002) Carrying the beacon of excellence: social class differentiation and anxiety at a time of transition. *Journal of Education Policy*, 17(3): 321–336.

MacKenzie, J.M. and Devine, T.M. (eds) (2011) *Scotland and the British Empire*. Oxford: Oxford University Press.

MacLeavy, J., Fannin, M. and Larner, W. (2021) Feminism and futurity: geographies of resistance, resilience and reworking. *Progress in Human Geography*, 45(6): 1558–1579.

Macleod, G. and Jones, M. (2018) Explaining 'Brexit capital': uneven development and the austerity state. *Space and Polity*, 22(2): 111–136.

Maggs, J. (2019) Fightin Sus! then and now. London: Institute of Race Relations. https://irr.org.uk/article/fighting-sus-then-and-now/

Maisano, C. (2010) Tony Judt and the limits of social democracy. *Monthly Review*, 9 April: https://mronline.org/2010/04/09/tony-judt-and-the-limits-of-social-democracy/

Major, J. (1993) Speech to the Conservative Group on Europe. 22 April: https://johnmajorarchive.org.uk/1993/04/22/mr-majors-speech-to-conservative-group-for-europe-22-april-1993/

Malik, N. (2021a) Covid jingoism will not protect the west from the threat of Omicron. *The Guardian*, 6 December: https://www.theguardian.com/commentisfree/2021/dec/06/covid-jingoism-omicron-pandemic

Malik, N. (2021b) The culture war isn't harmless rhetoric, it's having a chilling effect on equality. *The Guardian*, 22 February: https://www.theguardian.com/commentisfree/2021/feb/22/culture-war-chilling-effect-equality-government-rightwing-press

Malik, N. (2021c) The right is winning the culture war because its opponents don't know the rules. *The Guardian*, 19 July: https://www.theguardian.com/commentisfree/2021/jul/19/right-winning-culture-war

Malik, N. (2022a) For the Tory party, Boris Johnson is a blip not a crisis. *The Guardian*, 17 January: https://www.theguardian.com/commentisfree/2022/jan/17/tory-party-boris-johnson-polls-britain

Malik, N. (2022b) The very last thing the UK needs is more 'grownup' politics. That's what got us into this mess. *The Guardian*, 24 October: https://www.theguardian.com/commentisfree/2022/oct/24/conservative-leadership-grownup-politics-poverty

Mallaby, S. (2016) The cult of the expert – and how it collapsed. *The Guardian*, 20 October: https://www.theguardian.com/business/2016/oct/20/alan-greenspan-cult-of-expert-and-how-it-collapsed

Mann, M.E. (2021) *The New Climate War: The Fight to Take Back Our Planet.* New York: Public Affairs.

Manyika, J., Lund, S., Bughin, J., Robinson, K., Mischke, J. and Mahajan, D. (2016) *Independent Work: Choice, Necessity, and the Gig Economy.* San Francisco:, CA: McKinsey Global Institute. https://www.mckinsey.com/featured-insights/employment-and-growth/independent-work-choice-necessity-and-the-gig-economy#

Martin, M. and Yaquinto, M. (2007) 'Preface.' In M. Martin and M. Yaquito (eds) *Redress for Historical Injustices in the United States: On Reparations for Slavery, Jim Crow and Their Legacies.* Durham, NC and London: Duke University Press, xii–xviii.

Marx, K. (1857/1973) 'Introduction to a Contribution to the Critique of Political Economy.' In M. Nicolaus (ed. and trans.) *Grundrisse: Foundations of the Critique of Political Economy.* Harmondsworth: Penguin, 81–114.

Maskovsky, J. and Bjork-James, S. (2020) 'Introduction.' In J. Maskovsky and S. Bjork-James (eds) *Beyond Populism: Angry Politics and the Twilight of Neoliberalism.* Morgantown, VA: West Virginia University Press, 1–19.

Maskovsky, J. and Ruben, M. (2008) The homeland archipelago: neoliberal urban governance after September 11. *Critique of Anthropology*, 28(2): 199–217.

Mason, R. (2021) Boris Johnson accepts responsibility for North Shropshire by-election mauling. *The Guardian*, 17 December: https://www.theguard ian.com/politics/2021/dec/17/boris-johnson-accepts-responsibility-for-north-shropshire-byelection-mauling

Massey, D. (1994) *Space, Place and Gender*. Cambridge: Polity Press.

Massey, D. (2005) *For Space*. London: SAGE Publications.

Massey, D. (2007) *World City*. Cambridge: Polity.

Massey, D. (nd) The future of landscape: Doreen Massey: an interview by Andrew Stevens. *3:AM Magazine*: http://www.3ammagazine.com/3am/the-future-of-landscape-doreen-massey/

Mattinson, D. (2020) *Beyond the Red Wall: Why Labour Lost, How the Conservatives Won and What Will Happen Next?* London: Biteback Publishing.

May, T. (2002) Speech to the Conservative Party Conference: Full text in *The Guardian*, 7 Oct: https://www.theguardian.com/politics/2002/oct/07/conservatives2002.conservatives1

Mayblin, L. (2021) The Nationality and Borders Bill 2021: From Empty Threats to Further Erosion of the Right to Seek Asylum. Available at: https://www.law.ox.ac.uk/research-subject-groups/centre-criminol ogy/centreborder-criminologies/blog/2021/07/nationality-and

Mayblin, L., Wake, M. and Kazemi, M. (2019) Necropolitics and the slow violence of the everyday: asylum seeker welfare in the postcolonial present. *Sociology*, 54(1): 107–123.

McBride, S. (2022) *Escaping Dystopia: Rebuilding a Public Domain*. Bristol: Bristol University Press.

McElwee, S. and McDaniel, J. (2017) Fear of diversity made people more likely to vote Trump. *The Nation*, 14 March: https://www.thenation.com/article/fear-of-diversity-made-people-more-likely-to-vote-trump/

McFarlane, P. (2020) Opinion: can actions of undercover police who had relationships with targets ever be justified? *University College London News*: https://www.ucl.ac.uk/news/2020/dec/opinion-can-actions-und ercover-police-who-had-relationships-targets-ever-be-justified

McIntyre, N., Mohdin, A. and Thomas, T. (2020) BAME workers disproportionately hit by UK Covid-19 downturn, data shows. *The Guardian*, 4 August: https://www.theguardian.com/society/2020/aug/04/bame-workers-disproportionately-hit-uk-economic-downturn-data-shows-coronavirus

McKee, M., Karanikolos, M., Belcher, P. and Stuckler, D. (2012) Austerity: a failed experiment on the people of Europe. *Clinical Medicine*, 12(4): 346–350.

McKenzie, L. (2016) Brexit: a two-fingered salute from the working class. *Red Pepper*, August–September: https://www.redpepper.org.uk/brexit-a-two-fingered-salute-from-the-working-class/

McKenzie, L. (2017) 'It's not ideal': reconsidering 'anger' and 'apathy' in the Brexit vote among an invisible working class. *Competition and Change*, 21(3): 199–210.

McNeil, K. and Harding, R. (2021) *Counter Culture*. London: The Fabian Society.

McQuarrie, M. (2017) The revolt of the Rust Belt: place and politics in the age of anger. *British Journal of Sociology*, 68(S1): S120–S152.

Mikelis, K. (2016) 'Neocolonial power Europe'? Postcolonial thought and the Eurozone crisis. *French Journal for Media Research*, 5. https://frenchjournalformediaresearch.com/lodel-1.0/main/index.php?id=753

Mishra, P. (2020) *Bland Fanatics: Liberals, Race and Empire*. London: Verso.

Mitchell, T. (1999) 'Society, economy and the state effect.' In G. Steinmetz (ed) *State/Culture: State-Formation after the Cultural Turn*. Ithaca, NY: Cornell University Press, 76–99.

Mohammed, K. (2022) Sorrow and regret are not enough. Britain must finally pay reparations for slavery. *The Guardian*, 29 March: https://www.theguardian.com/global-development/2022/mar/29/sorrow-and-regret-are-not-enough-britain-must-finally-pay-reparations-for-slavery

Møller Stahl, R. (2019) Ruling the interregnum: politics and ideology in nonhegemonic times. *Politics & Society*, 47(3): 333–360.

Monbiot, G. (2021a) Filthy business: who will stop Britain's illegal waste-dumping mafia? *The Guardian*, 21 November: https://www.theguardian.com/commentisfree/2021/nov/24/waste-dumping-uk-environment

Monbiot, G. (2021b) Jailed for 51 weeks for protesting? Britain is becoming a police state by stealth. *The Guardian*, 1 December: https://www.theguardian.com/commentisfree/2021/dec/01/imprisoned-51-weeks-protesting-britain-police-state

Mondon, A. (2017) Limiting democratic horizons to a nationalist reaction: populism, the radical right and the working class. *Javnost – The Public*, 24(4): 355–374. doi: 10.1080/13183222.2017.1330085

Mondon, A. and Winter, A. (2019) Whiteness, populism and the racialisation of the working class in the United Kingdom and the United States. *Identities*, 26(5): 510–528. doi: 10.1080/1070289X.2018.1552440

Moody, K. (2016) Was Brexit a working-class revolt? *Against the Current* (September/October), 184: https://againstthecurrent.org/atc184/p4771/

Moore, J. (ed.) (2016) *Anthropocene or Capitalocene? Nature, History and the Crisis of Capitalism*. San Francisco, CA: Kairos/PM Press.

Morton, A.D. (2010) The continuum of passive revolution. *Capital & Class*, 34(3): 315–342.

Mount, F. (2022) Shades of Peterloo. *London Review of Books*, 44(13). https://www.lrb.co.uk/the-paper/v44/n13/ferdinand-mount/shades-of-peterloo

Muehlebach, A. (2012) *The Moral Neoliberal: Welfare and Citizenship in Italy*. Chicago, IL: University of Chicago Press.

Muehlebach, A. and Shoshan, N. (2012) Post-Fordist affect: introduction. *Anthropological Quarterly*, 85(2): 317–343.

Müller, J.-W. (2016) *What is Populism?* Philadelphia, PA: University of Pennsylvania Press.

Murray, C. (1984) *Losing Ground: American Social Policy, 1950–1980*. New York: Basic Books.

Murray, C. (1990) *The Emerging British Underclass*. London: Institute of Economic Affairs.

Nairn, T. (1977) *The Break-Up of Britain: Crisis and Neo-Nationalism*. London: Verso.

National Audit Office (2021) *The bounce back loan scheme: an update*. London: National Audit Office. https://www.nao.org.uk/report/the-bounce-back-loan-scheme-an-update/

National Audit Office (2022) *Investigation into the management of PPE contracts*. London: National Audit Office. https://www.nao.org.uk/wp-content/uploads/2022/03/Investigation-into-the-management-of-PPE-contracts.pdf

National Centre for Social Research (2016) Understanding the Leave Vote. Available at: https://natcen.ac.uk/our-research/research/understanding-the-leave-vote/

Neal, S., Bennett, K., Cochrane, A. and Mohan, G. (2018) *The Lived Experiences of Multiculture: The New Spatial and Social Relations of Diversity*. London: Routledge.

New Social Covenant Unit (nd) *New Social Covenant Unit*. https://www.newsocialcovenant.co.uk

Newman, Janet (2012) *Working the Spaces of Power: Activism, Neoliberalism and Gendered Labour*. London: Bloomsbury Academic.

Newman, J. (2019) 'The political work of reimagination.' In D. Cooper, N. Dhawan and J. Newman (eds) *Reimagining the State: Theoretical Challenges and Transformative Possibilities*. London: Routledge, 19–36.

Newman, J. and Clarke, J. (2018) The instabilities of expertise: remaking knowledge, power and politics in unsettled times. *Innovation: The European Journal of Social Science Research*, 31(1): 40–54. doi: 10.1080/13511610.2017.1396887

Nicholson, K. (2021) Boris Johnson may like Peppa Pig World but no-one liked his shoutout for it. *Huffington Post*, 22 November: https://www.huffingtonpost.co.uk/entry/boris-johnson-peppa-pig-world-speech_uk_619bc086e4b0451e54fd3c89

Niebuhr, R. (1959) *The Structure of Nations and Empires*. New York: Scribner.

Norris, P. and Inglehart, R. (2019) *Cultural Backlash: Trump, Brexit and the Rise of Authoritarian Populism*. Cambridge: Cambridge University Press.

Nurse, A. and Sykes, O. (2019) It's more complicated than that! Unpacking 'Left Behind Britain' and some other spatial tropes following the UK's 2016 EU referendum. *Local Economy*, 34(6): 589–606.

Nutley, S. and Walter, I. (2007) *Using Evidence: How Research Can Inform Public Services*. Bristol: Policy Press.

O'Connor, R. (2020) Rule Britannia! What are the lyrics to the anthem and why are they controversial? *The Independent*, 13 September: https://www.independent.co.uk/arts-entertainment/music/news/rule-britannia-lyrics-meaning-bbc-last-night-at-the-proms-controversy-slavery-a9687166.html

O'Toole, F. (2018) *Heroic Failure: Brexit and the Politics of Pain*. London: Head of Zeus.

O'Toole, F. (2021) Facing chaos and needing a scapegoat, the Tories seek an endless fight with Europe. *The Guardian*, 17 October: https://www.theguardian.com/commentisfree/2021/oct/17/facing-chaos-and-needing-a-scapegoat-the-tories-seek-endless-fight-with-europe

OECD (2019) *Under Pressure: The Squeezed Middle Class*. Paris: OECD Publishing. https://doi.org/10.1787/689afed1-en

Okolosie, L., Harker, J., Green, L. and Dabiri, E. (2015) Is it time to ditch the term 'black, Asian and minority ethnic (BAME)'? *The Guardian*, 22 May: https://www.theguardian.com/commentisfree/2015/may/22/black-asian-minority-ethnic-bame-bme-trevor-phillips-racial-minorities

Okri, B. (2020) 'I can't breathe': why George Floyd's words reverberate around the world. *The Guardian*, 8 June: https://www.theguardian.com/commentisfree/2020/jun/08/i-cant-breathe-george-floyds-words-reverberate-oppression

Olson, G. and Worsham, L. (2000) Changing the subject: Judith Butler's politics of radical resignification. *JAC: A Journal of Composition Theory*, 20(4): 727–765.

Olusoga, D. (2016) *Black and British: A Forgotten History*. London: Macmillan.

Omi, M. and Winant, H. (1986) *Racial Formation in the United States*. New York: Routledge.

Painter, J. (2006) Prosaic geographies of stateness. *Political Geography*, 25(7): 752–774.

Parliament Science and Technology Committee (2021) The UK Response to COVID-19: Use of Scientific Advice. 8 January: https://publications.parliament.uk/pa/cm5801/cmselect/cmsctech/136/13608.htm

Peck, J. (2010a) Zombie neoliberalism and the ambidextrous state. *Theoretical Criminology*, 14(1): 104–110.

Peck, J. (2010b) *Constructions of Neoliberal Reason*. Oxford: Oxford University Press.

Peck, J. (2012) Austerity urbanism. *City: Analysis of Urban Trends, Culture, Theory, Policy, Action*, 16(6): 626-655.

Peck, J. (2017) Transatlantic city, part 1: conjunctural urbanism. *Urban Studies*, 54: 4–30.

Peck, J. (2020) 'Contextualizing neoliberalism: an interview with Jamie Peck.' In S. Dawes and M. Lenormand (eds) *Neoliberalism in Context: Governance, Subjectivity and Knowledge*. London: Palgrave Macmillan, 289–309.

Peck, J. and Tickell, A. (2002) Neoliberalizing space. *Antipode*, 34: 380–404.

Peck, J. and Whiteside, H. (2018) 'Neoliberalizing Detroit.' In S. Schram and M. Pavlovskaya (eds) *Rethinking Neoliberalism: Resisting the Disciplinary Regime*. New York and London: Routledge, 177–196.

Perryman, M. (ed.) (2017) *The Corbyn Effect*. London: Lawrence & Wishart.

Petersen, A., Barns, I., Dudley, J. and Harris, P. (1999) *Post-Structuralism, Citizenship and Social Policy*. London: Routledge.

Pickard, S. (2013) 'Sleaze, freebies and MPs. The British parliamentary expenses and allowances scandal.' In D. Fée, and J.-C. Sergeant (eds) *Éthique, politique et corruption au Royaume-Uni*. Aix-en-Provence: Presses universitaires de Provence, 117–141. http://books.openedition.org/pup/22934

Piketty, T. (2014) *Capital in the Twenty First Century*. Cambridge, MA: Belknap.

Pirie, M. (2016) *Rebooting Britain: Making the Most of Brexit*. London: Adam Smith Research Trust.

Plavšić, D. (2019) Neoliberalism and Brexit: why Brexit is about more than just Brexit. *Counterfire*: https://www.counterfire.org/articles/analysis/20249-neoliberalism-and-brexit-why-brexit-is-about-more-than-just-brexit

Plimmer, G. and Provan, S. (2021) Serco upgrades profit guidance as test-and-trace demand persists. *Financial Times*, 14 June: https://www.ft.com/content/9f3c353d-611a-4297-8007-1272b07d4a1d

Politics.co.uk (2021) Conservative MP announces plans for new campaign to push low-tax agenda. *Politics.co.uk*, 28 November: https://www.politics.co.uk/news-in-brief/conservative-mp-announces-plans-for-new-campaign-to-push-low-tax-agenda/

Powell, E. (1968) Enoch Powell's 'Rivers of Blood' speech. Reproduced at: https://anth1001.files.wordpress.com/2014/04/enoch-powell_speech.pdf

Powell, K. (2017) Brexit positions: neoliberalism, austerity and immigration – the (im)possibilities? of political revolution. *Dialectical Anthropology*, 41: 225–240.

Power, M. (1994) *The Audit Explosion*. London: Demos.

Prutsch, U. (2020) The Populist Twins: Donald Trump and Jair Bolsonaro. In N. Zadoff, S. Schüler-Springorum, M. Zadoff and H. Paul (eds) *Four Years After: Ethnonationalism, Antisemitism and Racism in Trump's America*. Heidelberg: Universitatsverlag Winter. Publications of the Bavarian American Academy, 24: 123–146.

Public Health England (2020a) *Disparities in the risk and outcomes of COVID-19*. London: UK Government (www.ukgov/phe).

Public Health England (2020b) *Beyond the data: understanding the impact of COVID-19 on BAME groups*. London: UK Government (www.ukgov/phe).

Quarmby, K. and Norris, S. (2021) The great social care gold rush: how hedge funds and private investors are distorting the 'market' of people in need. *Byline Times*, 8 September: https://bylinetimes.com/2021/09/08/the-great-social-care-gold-rush-how-hedge-funds-and-private-investors-are-distorting-the-market-of-people-in-need/

Quinn, B. (2011) David Starkey claims 'the whites have become black'. *The Guardian*, 13 August: https://www.theguardian.com/uk/2011/aug/13/david-starkey-claims-whites-black

Race Disparity Unit (2020) *Quarterly report on progress to address COVID-19 health inequalities*. London: HM Government. https://www.gov.uk/government/publications/quarterly-report-on-progress-to-address-covid-19-health-inequalities

Raghuram, P. (2012) Global care, local configurations – challenges to conceptualizations of care. *Global Networks*, 12(2): 155–174.

Rancière, J. (2016) Europe: the return of the people, or of populism? Interview with Guillaume Erner, reprinted at *The Verso Blog*: https://www.versobooks.com/blogs/2896-europe-the-return-of-the-people-or-of-populism

Rao, R. (2020) *Out of Time: The Queer Politics of Postcoloniality*. Oxford: Oxford University Press.

Rayson, S. (2020) *The Fall of the Red Wall: 'The Labour Party no longer represents people like us'*. Independently Published.

Reiner, R. (2010) *The Politics of the Police* (4th edition). Oxford: Oxford University Press.

Rentoul, J. (2013) Intensely relaxed about people getting filthy rich. *Eagle Eye*, 14 February: https://independentblogposts.wordpress.com/2018/01/21/intensely-relaxed-about-people-getting-filthy-rich/

Resolution Foundation, The (2022) *Stagnation Nation: Navigating a route to a fairer and more prosperous Britain* (The Economy 2030 Inquiry interim report). London: The Resolution Foundation. https://economy2030.resolutionfoundation.org/reports/stagnation-nation/

Reynolds, D. (2019) *Island Stories: Britain and its History in the Age of Brexit*. London: William Collins.

Rhodes, J., Ashe, S. and Valluvan, S. (2019) Reframing the 'Left Behind': Race and Class in Post-Brexit Oldham. Manchester Centre on the Dynamics of Ethnicity (CODE): http://hummedia.manchester.ac.uk/institutes/code/research/projects/left-behind/oldham-report-2-september-2019.pdf

Riley, D. (2011) Tony Judt: a cooler look. *New Left Review*, September–October: https://newleftreview.org/issues/ii71/articles/dylan-riley-tony-judt-a-cooler-look

Robinson, C.J. (1983) *Black Marxism: The Making of the Black Radical Tradition.* London: Zed Books.

Rodger, J. (2021) Woman arrested at Sarah Everard vigil abused by trolls after sharing Tinder messages from '50 cops'. *Birmingham Evening Mail,* 7 October: https://www.birminghammail.co.uk/news/midlands-news/woman-arrested-sarah-everard-vigil-21794894

Rosanvallon, P. (2011) A reflection on populism. *Books and Ideas,* 10 November: https://booksandideas.net/A-Reflection-on-Populism.html

Rose, N. (1999) *Powers of Freedom: Reframing Political Thought.* Cambridge: Cambridge University Press.

Ross, T. (2021) Boris Johnson's 'f★★★ business' approach to the supply chain crisis is a risk for Brexit Britain. *New Statesman,* 5 October: https://www.newstatesman.com/politics/conservatives/2021/10/boris-johnsons-f-business-approach-to-the-supply-chain-crisis-is-a-risk-for-brexit-britain

Roth, S. (2018) Introduction: contemporary counter-movements in the age of Brexit and Trump. *Sociological Research Online,* 23(2): 496–506.

Rowley, T. (2022) The UK's Russia sanctions are not enough, experts warn. *Open Democracy,* 22 February: https://www.opendemocracy.net/en/odr/uk-russia-sanctions-ukraine-not-enough-boris-johnson/

Rutter, J. (2020) 'World beating': the phrase of 2020? *UK in a Changing Europe:* https://ukandeu.ac.uk/world-beating-the-phrase-of-2020/

Sanghera, S. (2021) *Empireland: How Imperialism Has Shaped Modern Britain.* Dublin: Penguin Books.

Saunders, R. (2021) Has the 'good chaps' theory of government always been a myth? *Prospect,* 3 August: https://www.prospectmagazine.co.uk/politics/has-the-good-chaps-theory-of-government-always-been-a-myth-peter-hennessy-boris-johnson

Schwarz, B. (2019) Boris Johnson's Conservatism: an insurrection against political reason? *Soundings: A Journal of Politics and Culture,* 73(Winter): 12–23.

Scott, D. (2017) *Stuart Hall's Voice.* Durham, NC: Duke University Press.

Shakespeare, S. (2021) Farage's RNLI attack improves Britons' perceptions of charity. *Yougov:* https://yougov.co.uk/topics/politics/articles-reports/2021/08/12/farage-rnli-attack-improves-britons-perceptions-ch

Shaw, K. (2021) Red wall diary: how Covid-19 has newly exposed the north-south divide. *New Statesman,* 14 January: https://www.newstatesman.com/politics/uk-politics/2021/01/red-wall-diary-how-covid-19-has-newly-exposed-north-south-divide

Shenker, J. (2021) Meet the 'inactivists', tangling up the climate crisis in culture wars. *The Guardian,* 11 November: https://www.theguardian.com/environment/2021/nov/11/inactivists-tangling-up-the-climate-crisis-in-culture-wars-manston-airport-kent

Shilliam, R. (2018) *Race and the Undeserving Poor: From Abolition to Brexit*. Newcastle upon Tyne: Agenda Publishing Ltd.

Shilliam, R. (2020) Redeeming the 'ordinary working class'. *Current Sociology Monograph*, 68(2): 223–240.

Showstack Sassoon, A. (1987) *Gramsci's Politics*. Minneapolis: University of Minnesota Press.

Shrimsley, R. (2018) Boris Johnson's Brexit explosion ruins Tory business credentials. *Financial Times*, 25 June: https://www.ft.com/content/8075e 68c-7857-11e8-8e67-1e1a0846c475

Siddique, H. and Syal, R. (2021) Raab to claim overhaul of human rights law will counter 'political correctness'. *The Guardian*, 14 December: https:// www.theguardian.com/law/2021/dec/14/raab-to-claim-overhaul-human- rights-law-counter-political-correctness

Sim, J. and Tombs, S. (2022) Narrating the coronavirus crisis: state talk and state silence in the UK. *Justice, Power and Resistance*, 5(1–2): 67–90. doi: 10.1332/XFUQ5523

Sobolewska, M. and Ford, R. (2020a) *Brexitland: Identity, Diversity and the Reshaping of British Politics*. Cambridge: Cambridge University Press.

Sobolewska, M. and Ford, R. (2020b) Brexit and Britain's culture wars. *Political Insight*, March: 4–7. https://journals.sagepub.com/doi/pdf/ 10.1177/2041905820911738

Somerville, P. (2011) *Understanding Community: Politics, Policy and Practice*. Bristol: The Policy Press.

Spours, K. (2020) *Shapeshifters: The Evolving Politics of Modern Conservatism*. London: Compass.

Standing, G. (2011) *The Precariat: The New Dangerous Class*. London: Bloomsbury.

Statista (2016) Brexit votes in the United Kingdom by social class 2016. https://www.statista.com/statistics/518395/brexit-votes-by-social-class/

Steinberg, D.L. and Johnson, R. (eds) (2004) *Blairism and the War of Persuasion: Labour's Passive Revolution*. London: Lawrence & Wishart.

Stoler, A. (2006) *Haunted by Empire: Geographies of Intimacy in North American History*. Durham, NC: Duke University Press.

Stone, J. (2020) Boris Johnson appoints aide who said institutional racism was a myth and railed against multiculturalism. *The Independent*: https:// www.independent.co.uk/ news/uk/politics/boris-johnson-westminster- insider-institutional-racism-munira-mirza-a9568456.html

Stratton, J. (2019) The language of leaving: Brexit, the second world war and cultural trauma. *Journal for Cultural Research*, 23(3): 225–251. doi: 10.1080/ 14797585.2019.1633073

Stuckler, D. and Basu, S. (2013) *The Body Economic: Why Austerity Kills*. New York: Basic Books.

Sumner, C. (1981) Race, crime and hegemony: a review essay. *Contemporary Crises*, 5: 277–291.

Sumner, W.G. (2006[1906]) *Folkways: A Study of the Sociological Importance of Usages, Manners, Customs, Mores and Morals.* Hong Kong: Hesperides Press.

Sveinsson, K. (ed) (2009) *Who Cares about the White Working Class?* London: Runnymede Trust.

Swales, K. (2016) Understanding the Leave Vote. London: NatCen for Social Research. https://natcen.ac.uk/media/1319222/natcen_brex planations-report-final-web2.pdf

Sykes, O. (2018) Post-geography worlds, new dominions, left behind regions, and 'other' places: unpacking some spatial imaginaries of the UK's 'Brexit' debate. *Space and Polity*, 22(2): 137–161.

Telford, L. and Wistow, J. (2020) Brexit and the working class on Teesside: moving beyond reductionism. *Capital & Class*, 44(4): 553–572.

The Combahee River Collective (1977) The Combahee River Collective Statement. April: http://circuitous.org/scraps/combahee.html

Theocharis, Y., Cardenal, A., Jin, S., Aalberg, T., Hopmann, D.N., Strömbäck, J., et al (2021) Does the platform matter? Social media and COVID-19 conspiracy theory beliefs in 17 countries. *New Media & Society*, 1–26. doi: 10.1177/14614448211045666

Thomas, D. (2019) *Political Life in the Wake of the Plantation: Sovereignty, Witnessing, Repair.* Durham, NC: Duke University Press.

Thomas, P.D. (2017) 'The modern prince: Gramsci's reading of Machiavelli'. *History of Political Thought*, 38(3): 523–544.

Thomas, T., Wilson, A., Tonkin, E., Miller, E.R. and Ward, P.R. (2020) How the media places responsibility for the COVID-19 pandemic: an Australian media analysis. *Frontiers in Public Health*, 8(483): 1–14. doi: 10.3389/fpubh.2020.00483

Thompson, E.P. (1991) *The Making of the English Working Class.* London: Penguin.

Thrift, N. (2005) *Knowing Capitalism.* London: SAGE Publications.

Tollefson, J. (2020) Why deforestation and extinctions make pandemics more likely. *Nature*, 7 August: https://www.nature.com/articles/d41586-020-02341-1

Tomkins, L. (2020) Where is Boris Johnson? When and why it matters that leaders show up in a crisis. *Leadership*, 16(3): 331–342.

Tooze, A. (2022a) Chartbook # 130 Defining Polycrisis: From Crisis Pictures to the Crisis Matrix. Adam Tooze, blog, 24 June: https://adamtooze.com/2022/06/24/chartbook-130-defining-polycrisis-from-crisis-pictures-to-the-crisis-matrix/

Tooze, A. (2022b) What is Kwasi Kwarteng really up to? One answer: this is a reckless gamble to shrink the state. *The Guardian*, 27 September: https://www.theguardian.com/commentisfree/2022/sep/27/kwasi-kwarteng-cut-taxes-austerity

Topping, A. (2021) 'A crossroads': the impact of the Sarah Everard case on women's safety. *The Guardian*, 9 July: https://www.theguardian.com/uk-news/2021/jul/09/a-crossroads-the-impact-of-the-sarah-everard-case-on-womens-safety

Trentmann, F. (2020) Britain First: The official history of the United Kingdom according to the Home Office – a critical review. *History: The Official Journal of The Historical Association*: https://historyjournal.org.uk/2020/09/11/britain-first-the-official-history-of-the-united-kingdom-according-to-the-home-office-a-critical-review/

Trilling, D. (2021) Cruel, paranoid, failing: inside the Home Office. *The Guardian*, 13 May: https://www.theguardian.com/politics/2021/may/13/cruel-paranoid-failing-priti-patel-inside-the-home-office

Turner, J. (2018) Internal colonisation: the intimate circulations of empire, race and liberal government. *European Journal of International Relations*, 24(4): 765–790.

UK in a Changing Europe (2021) *Comfortable Leavers: The Expectations and Hopes of Overlooked Brexit Voters*. London: UK in a Changing Europe Briefing Paper. https://ukandeu.ac.uk/wp-content/uploads/2021/04/Comfortable-Leavers-1.pdf

Ungerson, C. (1997) Social politics and the commodification of care. *Social Politics*, 4(3): 362–381. doi:10.1093/sp/4.3.362

Valluvan, S. (2019) *The Clamour of Nationalism: Race and Nation in Twenty-First-Century Britain*. Manchester: Manchester University Press.

Varoufakis, Y. (2017) *Adults in the Room: My Battle with Europe's Deep Establishment*. London: Bodley Head.

Virdee, S. (2014) *Racism, Class and the Racialized Outsider*. Basingstoke: Palgrave.

Virdee, S. and McGeever, B. (2018) Racism, crisis, Brexit. *Ethnic and Racial Studies*, 41(10): 1802–1819.

Vittorio, M. (2017) Can populism be an ally of democracy? *Online International Journal of Philosophy*, November, Year XII N. 24. http://www.metabasis.it/articoli/24/24_Vittorio.pdf

Walker, P., Mohdin, A. and Topping, A. (2021) Downing Street suggests UK should be seen as model of racial equality. *The Guardian*, 31 March: https://www.theguardian.com/world/2021/mar/31/uk-an-exemplar-of-racial-equality-no-10s-race-commission-concludes

Walters, W. (2004) The frontiers of the European Union: a geostrategic perspective. *Geopolitics*, 9(8): 674–698.

Ware, V. (2008) Towards a sociology of resentment: a debate on class and whiteness. *Sociological Research Online*, 13(5). http://www.socresonline.org.uk/13/5/9.html

Ware, V. (2022) *Return of a Native*. London: Repeater Books.

Wayne, M. (2021) Roadmaps after Corbyn: parties, classes, political cultures. *New Left Review*, 131(September–October): 37–65.

Weiss, H. (2019) *We Have Never Been Middle Class: How Social Mobility Misleads Us*. London: Verso.

Wellings, B. (2010) Losing the Peace: Euroscepticism and the foundations of contemporary English nationalism. *Nations and Nationalism*, 16(3): 488–505.

Wellings, B. (2012) *English Nationalism and Euroscepticism: Losing the Peace (1)*. London: Peter Lang.

Wemyss, G. (2009) *The Invisible Empire: White Discourse, Tolerance and Belonging*. London: Ashgate.

Wetherell, M. (2013) Feeling rules, atmospheres and affective practices: some reflections on the analysis of emotional episodes. In C. Maxwell and P. Aggleton (eds) *Privilege, Agency and Affect: Understanding the Production and Effects of Action*. Basingstoke: Palgrave Macmillan, 221–239.

Wetherell, M. and Potter, J. (1992) *Mapping the Language of Racism: Discourse and the Legitimation of Exploitation*. London and New York: Harvester Wheatsheaf and Columbia University Press.

White, N. (2021) Sewell says commission did find evidence of 'persistent discrimination' despite controversial race report. *The Independent*, 28 May: https://www.independent.co.uk/news/uk/home-news/race-commission-racism-britain-sewell-b1855304.html

Whiteley, P., Poletti, M., Webb, P. and Bale, T. (2019) Oh Jeremy Corbyn! Why did Labour Party membership soar after the 2015 general election? *British Journal of Politics and International Relations*, 21(1): 80–98.

Williams, F. (1989) *Social Policy: A Critical Introduction*. Cambridge: Polity Press.

Williams, F. (1995) Race/ethnicity, gender and class in welfare states: A framework for comparative analysis. *Social Politics*, 2(2): 127–159.

Williams, F. (2010) Migration and care: themes, concepts and challenges. *Social Policy and Society*, 9(3): 385–396.

Williams, F. (2018) A global crisis in care? Compas, 24 October: https://www.compas.ox.ac.uk/2018/a-global-crisis-in-care/

Williams, F. (2021) *Social Policy: A Critical and Intersectional Analysis*. Cambridge: Polity.

Williams, F. (2022) Extraction, exploitation, expropriation and expulsion in the domestic colonial relations of the British welfare state in the twentieth and twenty first centuries. *British Journal of Sociology*, 73(1): 23–34.

Williams, J. (2020) GMP failed to record 80,000 crimes in 12-months and people are being 'denied justice', says blistering report. *Manchester Evening News*, 10 December: https://www.manchestereveningnews.co.uk/news/greater-manchester-news/greater-manchester-police-failing-record-19430359

Williams, R. (1977) *Marxism and Literature*. Oxford: Oxford University Press.

Williams, Z. (2022) Labour needs to own its policy on gender – and unequivocally back trans rights. *The Guardian*, 6 April: https://www.the guardian.com/commentisfree/2022/apr/06/labour-policy-gender-back-trans-rights-boris-johnson

Williamson, J. (1986) *Consuming Passions: The Dynamics of Popular Culture*. London: Marion Boyards.

Wilson, H. (2011) Passing propinquities in the multicultural city: the everyday encounters of bus passengering. *Environment and Planning. Part A*, 43(3): 634–649.

Wilson, J. and Swyngedouw, E. (eds) (2015) *The Post-Political and its Discontents*. Edinburgh: Edinburgh University Press.

Winlow, S., Hall, S. and Treadwell, J. (2017) *The Rise of the Right: English Nationalism and the Transformation of Working-Class Politics*. Bristol: Policy Press.

Wodak, R. (2016) *'We Have the Character of an Island Nation': A Discourse-historical Analysis of David Cameron's 'Bloomberg Speech' on the European Union*. Florence: European University Institute Robert Schuman Centre for Advanced Studies Working Paper 2016/36.

Women's Studies Group (1976) *Women Take Issue: Aspects of Women's Subordination*. London: Hutchinson/CCCS (reprinted in 2006 by Routledge).

Worrad-Andrews, A. (2015) Tony Blair was not cynical – a history lesson on Blair's socialism. Medium, 17 August: https://medium.com/@alexworrad andrews/tony-blair-was-not-cynical-a-history-lesson-on-blair-s-socialism-50079ab9253c

Worth, O. (2015) *Rethinking Hegemony*. London: Palgrave Macmillan.

Worth, O. (2019) *Morbid Symptoms: The Global Rise of the Far Right*. London: Bloomsbury.

Wren-Lewis, S. (2016) Brexit and neoliberalism. *Mainly Macro Blog*, 29 October: https://mainlymacro.blogspot.com/2016/10/brexit-and-neolib eralism.html

Wright, P. (1985) *On Living in an Old Country: The National Past in Contemporary Britain*. London: Verso.

Yates, C. (2019) The seductions of Boris Johnson: hot air as political strategy. *LSE Blog*, 24 July: https://blogs.lse.ac.uk/brexit/2019/07/24/the-seducti ons-of-boris-johnson-the-brotherly-teddy-bear-with-retro-appeal/

Young, T. (2019) All these striking kids want is a day off school. *Spectator*, 16 February: https://www.spectator.co.uk/article/all-these-striking-kids-want-is-a-day-off-school

Younge, G. (2016) Brexit: a disaster decades in the making. *The Guardian*, 30 June: http://www.theguardian.com/politics/2016/jun/30/brexit-disaster-decades-in-the-making

Younge, G. (2021) What Covid taught us about racism – and what we need to do now. *The Guardian*, 16 December: https://www.theguardian.com/society/2021/dec/16/systemic-racism-covid-gary-younge

Yuval-Davis, N., Wemyss, G. and Cassidy, K. (2019) *Bordering*. Cambridge: Polity Press.

Zappettini, F. (2021) The tabloidization of the Brexit campaign: power to the (British) people? *Journal of Language and Politics*, 20(2): 277–303.

Zeitlin, J., Nicoli, F. and Laffer, B. (2019) Introduction: the European Union beyond the polycrisis? Integration and politicization in an age of shifting cleavages. *Journal of European Public Policy*, 26(7): 963–976. doi: 10.1080/13501763.2019.1619803

Zuboff, S. (2019) *The Age of Surveillance Capitalism: The Fight for a Human Future at the New Frontier of Power*. London: Profile.

# Index